Policing and Community Partnerships

❖

DENNIS J. STEVENS

Editor

University of Massachusetts–Boston

M.L. DANTZKER

Series Editor

Upper Saddle River, New Jersey 07458

Library of Congress Catalog-in-Publication Data
Policing and community partnerships/Dennis J. Stevens, editor.
p.m.
Includes bibliographical references and index.
ISBN 0-13-028049-6
1. community policing—United States. 2. Police-community relations—States.
I. Stevens, Dennis J.

HV7936.C83 P654 2002
363.2'3—dc21   00-068203

Publisher: Jeff Johnston
Senior Acquisitions Editor: Kim Davies
Production Editor: Lori Dalberg, Carlisle Publishers Services
Production Liaison: Barbara Marttine Cappuccio
Director of Production & Manufacturing: Bruce Johnson
Managing Editor: Mary Carnis
Manufacturing Buyer: Cathleen Petersen
Art Director: Marianne Frasco
Cover Design Coordinator: Miguel Ortiz
Cover Designer: Wanda España
Cover Photo: © Tracey L. Williams/Courtesy of the Bernards Township (NJ) Police
Department, Basking Ridge, NJ; Chief of Police: Thomas Kelly
Marketing Manager: Ramona Sherman
Editorial Assistant: Sarah Holle
Composition: Carlisle Communications, Ltd.
Printing and Binding: R. R. Donnelley & Sons

Prentice-Hall International (UK) Limited, *London*
Prentice-Hall of Australia Pty. Limited, *Sydney*
Prentice-Hall of Canada Inc., *Toronto*
Prentice-Hall Hispanoamericana, S.A., *Mexico*
Prentice-Hall of India Private Limited, *New Delhi*
Prentice-Hall of Japan, Inc., *Tokyo*
Prentice-Hall Singapore Pte. Ltd.
Editora Prentice-Hall do Brasil, Ltda., *Rio de Janeiro*

10 9 8 7 6 5 4 3 2 1
ISBN 0-13-028049-6

Contents

❖

Preface

❖

Leaping from the earlier literature of policing and community partnership are stories, remedies, and models that are more different than alike. Often, most of that literature seems monopolized by specific yet admirable individuals who have now fulfilled their mission. One of the aims of the collection of articles in this book is to reveal the common thread that runs through contemporary policing and community partnerships from the professional and the personal experiences of individuals on the front lines of those issues. One consistent tread in this work is that change in policing and community partnerships is unchanging. It isn't constant, it's intensifying. Keeping abreast of those changes is a full time occupation. Yet, it is among those changes that efficient and productive measures can be harnessed to enhance quality-of-life issues—something all of us seek. One of the aims of this book is to bring to your doorstep some of those intense changes. Some of us will quickly identify with and even agree with them. On the other hand, some of us will seat in wonderment about and take issue with other descriptions and changes. Yet, if the authors of these articles know anything about quality-of-life issues, maybe they have more to offer than meets a first read. Perhaps, what Ralph Waldon Emerson said in Society and Solitude rings clear, "It's true that the only sin which we never forgive in each other is difference of opinion." I think an informed decision-making process can far outweigh an uninformed one. With that said, the flow of the work among these chapters can prepare us to better understand police and community partnerships and to comprehend the huge effort and challenge confronting an American population about law and public order.

The centerpiece of this book is the community component of community policing as evidenced by the chapters revealing the necessity of winning community participation including community input and community decision-making prerogatives. First, we hear from experienced community organizers on methods, myths, and merits of community recruitment, followed by the personal experiences of a police chief from an affluent city who offers his impressions of dealing with the obstacles outside a police organization in an attempt to further community policing initiatives. Those articles pave the way for Washington, D.C.'s chief of police who instructs us in the art of involving community members as partners leading to a professor who evaluates his hometown police department and their innovative arrangements through partnerships with the community in Columbia, South Carolina. Yet, a question arises about measuring police performance, who is better suited to make those evaluations, volunteers, consultants, academics, or police personnel, the next article asked? A revelation comes from writers who bring evidence to police measuring their own organizational performance as opposed to outsiders. It appears that police personnel are better suited to test the community than others for various reasons as expressed in this article.

A study of policing service and community prerogatives suggests that an enormous amount of energy and resources are utilized in fulfilling those aims, and yet the question of reality or rhetoric about community policing becomes a point of concern for some observers. Evaluating police service from the perspective of the community to see how closely it is meeting objectives might help bring evidence to the question of limited resources. Quality police service, however, seems to be a different thing to different people. Some police strategies linked to community demands are revealed in community outcomes of police saturation practices followed by an examination of another method of community policing that highlights a successful program in Miami to curb youth school violence. There's always talk about reorganizing line officers but little talk about investigators, which is the subject of the next article leading to an examination of managerial styles of the police executives who manage our police agencies. What follows is a summary of each chapter and a frank discussion about the community component in the community policing initiative.

In **Chapter 1,** Jill DuBois and Susan Harnett tell the story of Chicago's Alternative Policing Strategy (CAPS), giving special attention to the community component of community policing. After years of field observations in Chicago, the writers were able to answer some important questions that have not been addressed adequately in prior research. Because of their extensive experiences at the grass root levels of community policing, these authors offer clear and precise recommendations for future reform activity in other cities. They argue that community participation doesn't just happen. It's up to a professional police agency to encourage a community to "buy in."

In **Chapter Two,** Chief Francis D'Ambra at Manteo, North Carolina, believes that an important part of establishing a sound community-oriented policing philosophy within a police agency requires, first and foremost, a commitment to organizational change. His primary focus relates to how an affluent small community manages the community oriented policing concept. He examines some of the obstacles to a community policing effort and reveals the problems of his office through what he calls nine "phantom menaces." Being aware of those obstacles, the chief argues, will aid others toward establishing good police-community partnerships.

Chapter Three, Chief Charles Ramsey of the Metropolitan Police of Washington, D.C., examines the next level of community policing. His discussions include the additional organizational reforms required to move departments in a more sophisticated level of community policing. The chief articulates the changes that will need to take place in the community to ensure the continued development of community policing. Largely, Chapter Three's focus is on the future of community policing and the expanded role the community must play as this strategy continues to develop and mature. That is, community responsibility. The chief argues that the most significant hurdle in taking community policing to the next level lies outside the police organization. It involves fully preparing the community for its role in community policing and then providing the community with the tools it needs to fulfill that new role.

Professor Carroy U. Ferguson in **Chapter Four** examines community policing initiatives in Columbia, South Carolina as characterized by the concept of a "shared responsibility" by the department and the community. A systematic evaluation of Columbia's community policing initiatives, using network analysis and multidimensional scaling techniques, confirmed that Columbia seems to have established a common vision for community policing among police and community leaders, bureaucrats, and citizens.

Chapter Five argues that the Madison Police Department believes that social order can be accomplished when community members participate in police decisions. However, measuring police performance and gaining neighborhood input, Captain Michael Masterson and Professor Dennis Stevens argue, is best left to police personnel. Compelling evidence presented in this chapter demonstrated that the typical community member would be more open with an officer than others, and that police personnel would be more respective in spotting potential criminal activity during the data collection process.

Professor Kent Kerley examines in **Chapter Six** the idea that many police departments adopt the rhetoric of community policing, in part to avail themselves of federal grants, but make few changes in their organizational structures and the tactics of their officers. In this chapter, no pretense is made of providing a resolution to the debate over the potential efficacy of community policing. There is, however, a contribution to the discussion by investigating perceptions of key community policing issues. Using data from a survey of 3000 members of various groups, the writer investigated perceptions regarding familiarity with community policing, extent to which community policing is utilized, police training needs, police-minority relations, and the focus of community policing training.

Professor Thomas Priest and Professor Deborah Carter in **Chapter Seven** examined the outcomes of one component of community-oriented policing, a police saturation operation, conducted in Charlotte, North Carolina. When police increase enforcement of laws bearing on a specific community problem, do residents or business people perceive any decrease in quality-of-life problems or in crime following the saturation operation?

In **Chapter Eight,** Lt. Gerald Rudoff and Professor Ellen Cohn examine community partnerships in public schools to help curb school violence. Their perspective is that violence has jeopardized the safety and the security of our children in one of the few places that students believe they are safe. One answer, the authors offer to curb the threat of violence is a collaborative community-based response to juvenile crime through The Youth Crime Watch originally developed under the Citizen's Crime Watch supported by the Miami Dade Police Department. The Miami Dade Police Department and the public schools in Miami have partnered together to bring safety back to the classroom. The city has had so much success with this innovative partnership that Youth Crime Watch programs are now in use throughout the country.

In **Chapter Nine,** Captain Michael Masterson is concerned with how investigative units within a police agency must reorganize to their workplace in order to meet the challenges of partnerships with the community.

Professor Dennis J. Stevens in **Chapter Ten** wanted to better understand the capability of police leadership linked to community policing opportunities. He surveyed ninety-seven police supervisors from lieutenants to chiefs who had command duties from eighteen police agencies across the United States. Results showed that the participants largely held leadership characteristics which generally supported traditional police practices as opposed to contemporary managerial practices required of community policing practitioners. One implication of his study is that police supervisors should blend police managerial techniques with Total Quality Management (TQM) skills since those managerial skills appear to optimize community policing practices.

Finally, the text concludes with a summation chapter in which Professor M.L. Dantzker provides the initial literature basis for community policing that leads into a brief discussion of the outcomes for each previous chapter.

Overall, this text was developed to offer a closer look at a very important component of community policing, the community partnership. By no means has this book exhausted all that pertains to this vital aspect of community policing. However, it has provided a starting point for those who are interested in learning more about how to emphasize the community in community policing.

Dennis J. Stevens, Ph.D.
Editor

About the Authors

❖

Deborah Brown Carter is a professor and chair of the Psychology and Social Science department at Johnson C. Smith University in Charlotte, North Carolina. She performs many performance tests for the Charlotte Mecklenburg Police Department. She can be reached at deborah.carter@jcsu.edu.

Ellen G. Cohn is an associate professor of criminology in the School of Policy and Management at Florida International University and a member of the steering committee of the Miami-Dade Police Department's Citizens' Volunteer Program. She received her Ph.D. in criminology in 1991 from Cambridge University, England. Her research interests include the effect of the natural environment on crime and criminal behavior and various aspects of community policing. She is the lead author of *Evaluating Criminology and Criminal Justice,* published in 1998, and has published in many criminology and psychology journals, including *Criminology, Journal of Criminal Justice,* and *Journal of Personality and Social Psychology.* Dr. Cohn can be reached at cohne@fiu.edu.

Francis D'Ambra is the chief of police of Manteo, North Carolina. He has extensive training in law enforcement including workshops with the FBI. He is a police instructor at the local community college, and writes articles for various publications.

Jill DuBois is a project manager at the Institute for Policy Research, Center for Law and Justice Studies, at Northwestern University. She has been involved with the Chicago Alternative Policing Strategy (CAPS) evaluation project since its earliest days, interviewing police personnel ranging from patrol officers to high-ranking and civilian executives in the department. She also attends and documents meetings of many types within the Chicago Police Department. In addition to being a key evaluator of the implementation of the CAPS program citywide, she has authored a paper on the experiences of the prototype

District Advisory Committees, which is part of the consortium's project paper series. Along with her colleagues, she has written a recently released book on the CAPS problem-solving model entitled *On the Beat: Police and Community Problem Solving* (Westview Press, 1999). She serves as main compiler and editor for CAPS evaluation reports and papers and provided extensive editorial assistance for *Community Policing, Chicago Style,* by Wesley G. Skogan and Susan M. Hartnett (Oxford University Press, 1997). She has authored five books in a world cultures series for high school students as well. Jill DuBois can be reached at jdubois@nwu.edu.

Carroy U. Ferguson, Ph.D., is a professor at the College of Public and Community Service, University of Massachusetts/Boston and the director of the college's Peer Advising and Service Internship Program. He is also a practicing clinical psychologist and he co-founded two organizations, Interculture, Inc. and Associates in Human Understanding. He is on a number of boards, including the national board of the Association for Humanistic Psychology. He has years of experience as a consultant and workshop leader on a variety of topics involving personal growth, social change, and social justice. He is the co-author of the book *Innovative Approaches to Education and Community Service: Models and Strategies for Change and Empowerment* (1993) and the author of the book *A New Perspective on Race and Color* (1997). He has also authored a new book *Transitions in Consciousness from an African American Perspective* (in review) and a forthcoming book manuscript *Evolving the Race Game: A Transpersonal Perspective.* He also has publications in journals, as well as chapters in other books. His research and professional work involves looking at the phenomenon of consciousness and its relationship to the quality of societal life, self-healing, self-empowerment, and social justice. Dr. Ferguson can be reached at carroy.ferguson@umb.edu.

Susan M. Hartnett has been a research associate and administrator at Northwestern University for the last twelve years. Her background includes a decade of survey research and program evaluation in such areas as education, crime prevention, the media, juvenile delinquency, and community policing. She managed the Northwestern University Survey Laboratory for seven years. Subsequently, she has directed an evaluation of Chicago's Alternative Policing Strategy program. She co-authored (with Wesley G. Skogan) a book about the impact of Chicago's community policing program on residents and police, entitled *Community Policing, Chicago Style,* published by the Oxford University Press, 1997. More recently, she co-authored a book entitled *On The Beat: Police and Community Problem Solving in Chicago,* by Skogan, Hartnett, et al., published by Westview Press, 1999. Susan Hartnett can be reached at susanhartnet@aol.com.

Kent R. Kerley has recently received his Ph.D. and is currently an assistant professor in the Department of Sociology at the University of Tennessee. His main areas of research are community policing, crime and the life course, and white-collar crime. His most recent work appears in *Police Quarterly* and *Police Practice and Research: An International Journal.* Dr. Kerley can be reached at kkerley@utk.edu.

Captain Michael F. Masterson, Commanding Officer—Detective Team and Dane County Narcotics and Gang Task Force [1991–1995] and Personnel and Training Team [1996–1999]. Currently he is the Commander of the North Police District of Madison, Wisconsin. Captain Masterson can be reached at mmasterson@ci.madison.wi.us.

Thomas B. Priest is a professor of criminal justice and sociology at Johnson C. Smith University in Charlotte, North Carolina. He has evaluated police performance for the city of Charlotte, North Carolina, for some time. He has conducted many surveys in Charlotte and is a significant contributor to the sociological press. His expertise is in stratified societies with an emphasis on the Philadelphia elite. Professor Priest can be reached at tbpriest@jcsu.edu.

Chief Charles H. Ramsey was appointed chief of the Metropolitan Police Department on April 21, 1998. A nationally recognized innovator, educator, and practitioner of community policing, Chief Ramsey has refocused the MPDC on crime fighting and crime prevention through a more accountable organizational structure, new equipment and technology, and an enhanced strategy of community policing. A native of Chicago, Illinois, Chief Ramsey served the Chicago Police Department for nearly three decades in a variety of assignments. At the age of eighteen, he became a Chicago Police cadet. In 1994, he was named Deputy Superintendent of the Bureau of Staff Services, where he managed the department's education and training, research and development, labor affairs, crime prevention and professional counseling functions.

Chief Ramsey was instrumental in designing and implementing the Chicago Alternative Policing Strategy, the city's nationally acclaimed model of community policing. As co-manager of the CAPS project in Chicago, Chief Ramsey was one of the principal authors of the police department's strategic vision. He also designed and implemented the CAPS operational model and helped to develop new training curricula and communications efforts to support implementation. As head of the 4600-member Metropolitan Police Department, Chief Ramsey has worked to improve police services, enhance public confidence in the police and bring down the District of Columbia's crime rate.

Chief Ramsey holds both bachelor's and master's degrees in criminal justice from Lewis University in Romeoville, Illinois. A graduate of the FBI National Academy and the National Executive Institute, Chief Ramsey has lectured nationally on community policing as an adjunct faculty member of both the Northwestern University Traffic Institute's School of Police Staff and Command and Lewis University. For his national contributions to community policing, Chief Ramsey received the 1994 Gary P. Hayes Award from the Police Executive Research Forum, the group's highest honor for achievement in policing. The chief can be reached at mpdcchief_org@excite.com.

Gerald A. Rudoff is a lieutenant with the Miami-Dade Police Department, Community Affairs Bureau, one of the original founders of the Youth Crime Watch concept, and the current president-elect of Youth Crime Watch of America. He is a graduate of the Southern Police Institute, University of Louisville, Louisville, KY, where he studied the concepts and philosophies of community oriented policing in depth, and of the National Crime Prevention Institute, also in Louisville, KY. Lt. Rudoff is a certified practitioner of Kingian Nonviolence Conflict Reconciliation. Lt. Rudoff can be reached at gar_mia@yahoo.com.

About the Editor

❖

Dennis J. Stevens, Ph.D. (Loyola University of Chicago) is an Associate Professor of Criminal Justice, College of Public & Community Service at the University of Massachusetts at Boston. In addition to teaching traditional and nontraditional students, he has taught, counseled, and lectured law enforcement officers at police academies and police stations such as the North Carolina Justice Academy. He has also taught and led group encounters among felons at maximum-custody penitentiaries such as Attica in New York, Eastern and Women's Institute in North Carolina, Stateville and Joliet near Chicago, and Carolina Correctional Institute in Columbia, South Carolina. Currently, contracted through Boston University, Dr. Stevens instructs male and female felons at high-custody prisons in Massachusetts and has conducted extensive profile assessments among sexual offenders, most recently child molesters. With over sixty articles (many refereed) published in the international and the U.S. academic and popular press on criminology, corrections, and police, his current book, a case study of community policing strategies among nine agencies in the United States (Prentice Hall, 2001), will help establish Dr. Stevens as a strong contributor to the study of criminal justice in both the university and the academy classroom. Previous books include *Inside the Mind of the Serial Rapist* (Austin Winfield 1998) and a corrections reader for Coursewise. Lastly, he is a group facilitator for a national organization that specializes in court-ordered sexual abuse counseling for parents and has devoted countless hours guiding physically and sexually abused children. Dr. Stevens can be reached at dennis.stevens@umb.edu.

1

Making the Community Side of Community Policing Work

What Needs to be Done

Jill DuBois and Susan M. Hartnett

❖

All too often community-policing initiatives focus either on changes inside the police organization or on community-oriented programs that have little effect on the basic structure or function of routine police activity. A notable exception is the sizable and dramatic reform efforts in Chicago where both police and citizens were expected to change the way they do business and work together to solve neighborhood problems. This chapter tells the story of Chicago's Alternative Policing Strategy (CAPS), giving special attention to the community component of community policing. After years of field observations in Chicago, we were able to answer some important questions that we believe have not been addressed adequately in prior research, as well as offer some clear recommendations for future reform activity in other cities.

To help us understand the optimal relationship between the police and the community, we draw upon the conceptual framework established by Skogan and Hartnett (1997), in their first book about the Chicago project. They offer four defining principles of community policing. First, community policing "relies upon organizational decentralization and a reorientation of patrol in order to facilitate the two-way communication between police and the public" (p. 5). With the large-scale infusion of money from the federal Office of Community Oriented Policing (COPS), many police departments have initiated plans for decentralization and, more frequently, retooling patrol officers. Observational case studies have described the struggle to introduce changes in police bureaucracies (e.g., Greene, Bergman, & McLaughlin, 1994; Wilkinson & Rosenbaum, 1994). Despite some success stories, researchers frequently report widespread resistance to change from the police culture, numerous organizational barriers, and a desire by recalcitrant personnel to "weather the storm" (i.e., outlast the current administration). In Chicago, we have reported some real changes in organizational structure and training programs (Skogan, Hartnett, DuBois, Comey, Kaiser, & Lovig, 1999), and there were some corresponding positive changes in police attitudes and behaviors (Skogan & Lurigio, 1994), although the causal link remains uncertain. Most important though, our field observations indicate that some police officers and community residents are exhibiting a new set of behaviors with respect to their relationship with each other and the types of strategies they employ for solving neighborhood problems. This chapter describes some of these new behaviors, how they were achieved, and the problems associated with this type of social engineering.

The second principle of community policing, according to Skogan and Hartnett (1997), is a commitment to broadly focused, problem-oriented policing. Goldstein (1979, 1990) provided the theoretical foundation for this type of approach, and the SARA model (Eck & Spelman, 1987) promoted by the Police Executive Research Forum translates these ideas into a practical set of guidelines with which police can identify. Hence, this four-step model—scanning, analysis, response, and assessment (SARA)—has been widely adopted by police departments as a strategy for addressing neighborhood problems. In a similar vein, Chicago developed its own five-step problem-solving model (in the context of other changes) to stimulate police officers to move beyond reactive, incident-driven patrols and to begin the process of engaging the community in a joint problem-solving process. In the research community, several case studies have described variations in problem solving and levels of success (e.g., Capowich & Roehl, 1994; Hope, 1994). While impact successes have been noted, there is considerable concern about process. Some critics argue that some steps in the SARA model have been skipped or ignored, that the police have tended to focus on trivial, easy-to-solve problems (Clarke, 1998), and that they have failed to take seriously the role of the community in the problem-solving process (Rosenbaum, Lurigio, & Davis, 1998).

This brings us to our third principle of community policing—the requirement that police be responsive to citizens' demands when they decide what local problems are and set their priorities (Skogan & Hartnett, 1997). When the police listen to the community, what they will hear, according to community-survey results, is that local citizens are sick and tired of the social disorder and signs of incivility that are observable on a daily basis (Skogan, 1990). Consequently, law enforcement agencies nationwide have begun to crack down on public disorder (e.g., loitering, prostitution, visible drug markets) and signs of physical decay (e.g., graffiti, abandoned autos, garbage). This type of enforcement is consistent with the "Broken Windows" theory (Skogan, 1990; Wilson & Kelling, 1982), which suggests that failure to address these incidents will only fuel a cycle of neighborhood decline and contribute to more serious violence (one broken window, if not repaired, will lead to many broken windows). Certainly, this model suggests that partnerships between agencies are essential to achieve success, and that the police alone are not equipped to stop physical and social decay. The police and the community must work in concert with other agencies to insure that abandoned autos are towed, garbage is picked up, and streetlights are repaired. In Chicago, the formation of these interagency partnerships, under the leadership of the mayor, was a key component of the initial success story (Skogan & Hartnett, 1997). But a key question remained: Were the police able to form solid, working partnerships with local residents in diverse Chicago communities to assist in this process?

The fourth principle of community policing is a commitment to help neighborhoods solve crime problems on their own, through community organizations and crime prevention programs. Over the past twenty-five years, the U.S. Department of Justice, as well as local and state units of government, has advocated a wide array of community crime prevention programs, seeking to educate the public about their role in helping to create safer communities (for a review, see Rosenbaum et al., 1998). Aside from Neighborhood Watch programs, however, local residents have been given few concrete and predictable opportunities to participate in community safety activities. The Chicago CAPS experiment has been an important exception. A distinguishing feature of many CAPS initiatives is the provision of new avenues for citizen involvement in partnerships with police. Residents may be called on to help identify and prioritize neighborhood problems of actions, to get involved in problem-solving efforts, and/or help shape police policies and operations. In theory and ideally, the commitment to responsiveness and information sharing made by police agencies as they adopt community policing will be matched on the civilian side with the enthusiastic involvement of a representative segment of citizens from the community.

In reality, our national experience indicates that, similar to the police, the extent to which neighborhood residents actively embrace community policing is highly variable (see Sadd & Grinc, 1994). From cross-site studies, we have learned not to make the assumption that citizens will necessarily express a high level of enthusiasm about such programs without any prior positive experience. We have also learned not to assume that police and neighborhood residents have a history of mutual respect, despite national polls showing public support for the police. In poor and minority neighborhoods especially, broken promises and police programs that were discontinued or perceived as abusive often mark their history. We have learned not to assume that resident participation in public safety programs will be sustained without serious attention to maintenance activities. Research suggests that community-based organizations are needed to encourage and sustain involvement over the long haul (Podolefsky & DuBow, 1981) and that police may have to involve themselves in helping build this supportive infrastructure (Skogan, 1990).

The problem of citizen participation is complex and goes beyond motivation and behavioral reinforcement to giving citizens the knowledge and skills needed to participate effectively. In essence, research suggests that the public, not unlike the police, must be educated and retooled—a fact that is often overlooked in most community policing initiatives. Community policing not only entails a new way of thinking about problems, but it brings with it an entirely new jargon and new responsibilities for both police and citizens. Thus, well-designed adult education is required before any of the participants can fully appreciate the new roles and responsibilities they are expected to adopt. Furthermore, this model of change assumes that classroom and field instruction will require a substantial amount of "face time" between police and residents in order for trust and cooperation to develop. Whether these desired conditions, prescribed by prior research and theory, can be implemented with integrity in the real world is the subject of this chapter. The Chicago reform initiative—CAPS—represents a major test of community policing in practice.

The remainder of this chapter contains the "nuts and bolts" of how the Chicago Police Department, in conjunction with other city agencies and the community, sought to engage the public in community policing. As suggested above, extant research has left many questions unanswered regarding the role of citizens in the process of implementing community policing, which provides the focal point of this chapter. Many assumptions have been made previously that have not been supported by experience or research. We are left asking, can the police and citizens work together effectively to prioritize problems and develop concrete plans for addressing them? Will success vary by type of neighborhood? What formal and informal mechanisms can be used to draw in the community to the problem-solving process? What specific problems can be expected along the way, and what lessons have we learned that might benefit other communities in the United States and other countries?

We briefly describe our research methodology and then proceed to our findings, conclusions, and recommendations with respect to the community's role in community policing. We examine how citizen awareness can be enhanced through professional marketing and the training of both police and citizens. We describe the formal and informal methods employed to facilitate joint citizen-police problem solving. Some promising beginnings are highlighted, but the difficulties in developing and sustaining these citizen-police partnerships are examined. By shedding light on promising strategies as well as likely pitfalls, we hope this chapter can serve as a guide for other communities that are attempting to bring more "community" into community policing.

COMMUNITY PARTICIPATION IN COMMUNITY POLICING

There is no question of the importance of community participation in community policing. It is inherent in the name—community policing. So what is the formula for getting the community to "buy in"? Unfortunately, there is none, and this is known all too well by the many cities that have experienced great difficulty in getting neighborhood residents involved. As it turns out, getting the community involved in neighborhood-oriented policing in a meaningful, sustained fashion is quite a task.

Just like police officers, community members must be "brought on board," and on the whole, community members do not prove to be readily cooperative. The Vera Institute's study of community policing in eight cities found "all eight . . . sites experienced extreme difficulty in establishing a solid community infrastructure on which to build their community policing programs" (Sadd & Grinc, 1994, p. 31). These researchers concluded that of all the implementation problems these programs faced, "the most perplexing . . . was the inability of the police departments to organize and maintain active community involvement in their projects" (p. 33).

Engaging the community can be just as difficult as involving police officers, and the list of potential problems in sustaining community involvement is just as long as the one on the police side of the equation. While Chicago's efforts are the focus here, and cities' needs and problems differ in the details, there is a logic to community-oriented policing that often leads cities of all descriptions and demographics down the same general path. And so it is for bringing the community onboard.

The Chicago Community Policing Evaluation Consortium has been tracking Chicago's policing strategy, or CAPS, as it is known, since 1993. Our involvement actually began early that year during the program's initial planning stage, and fieldwork began in April of 1993 when the prototype program kicked off in five districts. As the program grew, so did our activities.

Over the years, we have done citywide surveys to gauge residents' awareness of the CAPS program as well as their attitudes about police service and the extent and nature of problems that affect their neighborhoods. We have observed training events, roll calls, all manner of community-police meetings, and powwows among the top brass. We have gone on ride-alongs, done case studies on problem-solving efforts, polled community organizations, and interviewed activists and police personnel alike.

FOUR KEY LESSONS

And after these several years of looking at Chicago's ambitious program, we have learned at least four important lessons about the community's involvement in community policing. The first lesson is the community support must be won. It cannot be assumed that community support will be there, for as was mentioned before, getting the community on board can be as difficult as engaging the rank and file.

The second is that effective community involvement depends on an organized community. Trying to involve random people off the street is not very effective. Lesson number three is that training is as critical for the community as it is for the police. Neighborhood residents are as apprehensive and initially resistant to change as anyone else, and they certainly should not be expected to simply step into their new role without any guidance. Finally, fourth, there is a real risk of inequitable outcomes. The best-off elements of the community will take to community policing pretty naturally, but those who really need it may be last to come on board—if they come on at all.

BUILDING THE PARTNERSHIP

Though it seems at first blush that residents might be eager to get involved in a partnership with their neighborhood police officers, the fact remains that their support must be won, because too many residents of poor and disenfranchised neighborhoods have been disappointed in the past. New programs are announced, and then they disappear when the special funding dries up. Furthermore, sometimes a new chief or mayor will take over and decide to do something different—something that makes it distinctly his or her program. Too often it has been "here today, gone tomorrow."

Residents who basically support the police but struggle to get their attention have also been disappointed too often by outbreaks of nasty misconduct or corruption. They can never be certain that the latest smiles are sincere. They are being told, "this time it's for real!" But their reaction will probably be, "show me"—they are appropriately skeptical. All of this means that getting programs started is a long, hard campaign. Resident involvement can only be gained slowly—one block at a time.

In Chicago, one of the principal ways this is done is by holding about 260 small public meetings—known as beat meetings—every month throughout the city. These are gatherings at which police and residents can hash over the area's problems and focus on solutions to them. An average of forty-five hundred people attend these gatherings every month. The meetings are regular, well known, safe and popular. They are well attended by police. Beat officers assigned to the area come, from all three shifts, as does the sergeant who has "24-7" responsibility for their efforts as a beat team.

ORGANIZED COMMUNITIES

We find that the effectiveness of the program depends upon an organized community. Only organized communities get to the "bottom line," which translates as actually getting involved in problem solving.

Many parts of Chicago are honeycombed with block clubs, civic associations, social action groups, and churches with a strong commitment to the community. Chicago decided to have a community-policing program with lots of public involvement in large part because those groups were already out there and, ideally, their energy could be harnessed to the new program. (This is a typically Chicago way of getting things done.)

We find that residents who are involved in block clubs and other community organizations are more likely to come to meet with the police, and they attend more frequently. Perhaps more important, they are more likely to actually get involved in problem solving, and they do more of it. The types of activities they get involved in range from Saturday morning graffiti paint-outs to negotiating with storeowners about how to alleviate the problem of men gathering and drinking in front of their establishments to working to get things done about decrepit and dangerous buildings.

This type of problem solving is sustained by organizations. Organizations help keep people focused on their collective concerns. They sustain us when we as individuals get tired or burned out. They also can find replacements, so we can take vacations or paint the house. People have to be replaceable, and organizations help find and foster "new blood."

But the problem is that in poor and disenfranchised neighborhoods, organizations representing the people do not have a history of working with the police, or even seeing themselves on the same side. Marshaling the community involves getting their organizations on board.

TRAINING

We have also found that training makes a difference. Another important and distinctive feature of Chicago's program is that there has been large-scale training for both police and for neighborhood residents.

This is quite important, because community policing involves a whole new set of jargon as well as a lot of new ideas. Without training, people will continue to do what they have been told to do: call 911 and hand responsibility for everything over to the police. Community input will be confined to griping about problems and grousing about the fact that police haven't fixed them. Everyone will go away frustrated.

Training was also important in Chicago because the city and the police department created all kinds of new resources for problem solving, and people had to know how to access them and use them. So, during 1995 and 1996 the city and a group called the Chicago Alliance for Neighborhood Safety (CANS) developed a new set of training materials and trained people from all over the city about the new program as well as about their role in neighborhood problem solving. About twelve thousand residents attended at least some of the training, which became known as Joint Community-Police Training, or JCPT.

Training was carried out by teams of police officers and civilians who worked together as partners. They traveled to the beats in the evenings and on Saturdays—whenever local activists thought it would be best to meet. Residents who stayed with the training were able to attend four full sessions while working on an actual problem on their beat between sessions. We found that many who attended training were new participants—not the same old group of experienced CAPS activists. For example, one-third of them had never even been to a beat meeting, so they were indeed new recruits.

The influx of new blood was partly because of a considerable amount of legwork done by experienced CANS community organizers. They fanned out into the neighborhoods in advance to drum up participation. We found that those who attended training got involved in a lot of problem solving. Overall, more than 60 percent of them actually worked on problems outside of the training venue. They got most involved in drug problems, the physical decay of the neighborhood, and problems with specific business establishments.

Being linked to a neighborhood block club was also important for those in training. Just like at beat meetings, residents who came to training who were involved in block groups were much more likely to actually stay involved in problem solving when the training was over. More than 80 percent of trainees who were heavily involved in their community—which translates into being involved in four or more organizations—actually worked on a problem after leaving the training.

The city of Chicago has been pushing hard to organize communities and connect people to beat meetings in order to get problem solving moving faster. City hall created a department called the CAPS Implementation Office, which primarily focuses on marketing and community outreach. The Implementation Office has targeted a number of specific beats that really need help. In some of them, the Implementation Office is providing experienced organizers, while in other places it is working with organizations that are familiar with an area. The organizations are providing staff and supporting involvement in the target areas helping to develop block clubs, strengthen turnout at the monthly beat meetings, and get problem-solving projects started.

Other groups are doing the same thing independently. For example, one group has a special focus on identifying potential neighborhood leaders and grooming them with special training. And these are the right leverage points. Organized people turn out, they keep coming, and they get involved in solving neighborhood problems.

Note that the police in Chicago have not been assigned to do this. Throughout the nation, police have attempted in the past to be community organizers—usually with less-than-satisfactory results. This is another example of the importance of involving other city agencies, civilian employees, and neighborhood organizations in community policing programs, because neighborhood safety has to be everyone's business.

INEQUITABLE OUTCOMES

Finally, evaluations around the country have found that there is a risk of inequitable outcomes to all of this, as well as unequal participation in community policing. Middle-class homeowners and whites who already get along with the police and share many of the same views jump on the program quickly, and historically they have gotten most of the benefits from programs of this type. These groups are also more likely to be well organized already, with lots of effective block clubs, high voter turnout, and downtown clout.

As a result, better-off neighborhoods are the ones that get better off. African-Americans and Latinos, and poor people of all denominations fall behind. It is very important to watch out for this, as well as to figure out what to do about it.

In Chicago, the program has been a real success in the African-American community. But it is done best in the large middle-income part of that community. Conversely, however, many of the shortcomings of the program seem to fall most heavily on immigrant communities, which represent the fastest-growing part of the city.

Our immigrant research has focused mostly on Chicago's Latino communities. There are perhaps 500,000 Latinos in Chicago, mostly originating from Mexico and Puerto Rico. To put it in a nutshell, compared to the city's largest communities, Latinos have been left out. They are less likely to know about community policing, less likely to know that beat meetings are being held nearby, less likely to attend beat meetings, less likely to turn out for training, and less likely to get involved in problem solving.

We have also found that they've enjoyed the fewest benefits from the program. Compared to other neighborhoods, CAPS hasn't made things much better in theirs. It's not that they do not need help; their problems are as bad as any in the city. Latinos consistently identify gang and drugs as their neighborhoods' biggest problems, and those are tough problems.

Compared to others, Latinos in Chicago have even more problems with the physical decay of their communities. Among these problems are graffiti, vandalism, abandoned buildings, abandoned cars, loose garbage and rats in the alleys, and a collapsing infrastructure. Another issue is that beat meetings underrepresent Latinos who live in the beat by 30 to 50 percent. Even when they know about beat meetings, Latinos are less likely to attend.

The representation of Latinos in the original CANS training program was a little better. They still fell short in numbers, but teams of community organizers who worked to get people to come to the meetings supported the trainers.

THE CHALLENGE

So why is engaging the community in a partnership with the police such a challenge? Above all, the two groups do not have a history of getting along. Especially in poor and disenfranchised neighborhoods, residents often have a history of antagonistic relationships with the police. The police may be perceived as arrogant, brutal, and uncaring—not as potential partners. Residents may fear that more intensive policing could generate new problems with harassment, indiscriminate searches, and conflicts between them and the police.

These ideas were very much on the minds of Chicagoans when we surveyed them in the months before CAPS began. Hispanics and African-Americans were almost three times more likely than whites to think that police serving their neighborhoods were impolite, and more than twice as likely to think the police treated people unfairly. About 35 percent of Hispanics felt police weren't concerned about the problems facing people in their neighborhoods, as did 25 percent of African-Americans, but, only 15 percent of whites felt this way.

Another potential obstacle is that organizations representing the interests of community members might also not have a track record of cooperating with police. Poor and high-crime areas are often not well endowed with an infrastructure of organizations ready to become involved. Since their constituents often fear the police, groups representing poor and minority areas can be more interested in monitoring police misconduct and pressing for greater police accountability than being involved in coordinated action with them.

Research on participation in organized crime-prevention programs also finds that they are not easily initiated nor sustained in poorer neighborhoods. Crime and fear stimulate withdrawal from community life rather than involvement. In crime-ridden neighborhoods, mutual distrust and hostility are often rampant. Residents tend to view each other with suspicion rather than neighborliness, and that undermines their capacity to forge collective responses to local problems. They fear retaliation by drug dealers and neighborhood toughs, so programs requiring social contact, neighborly cooperation, or public involvement are less often successful in areas with high levels of fear.

The problem may be compounded when program boundaries imposed by the police department bundle together diverse communities. Under these circumstances, suspicion and fear may divide the area along race, class, and lifestyle lines, leaving residents and the organizations that represent them at odds with one another. They will almost inevitably point fingers at one another over who causes what problems, and there will be pressure for the police to choose up sides. Groups contending over access to housing, municipal services, infrastructure maintenance, and public-sector jobs and contracts may also find themselves battling one another over policing priorities and the ear of the district commander.

MARKETING THE PROGRAM

Clearly it is important to develop a vehicle through which the community can have a meaningful role. Yet only those who've been working with or watchdogging the police are going to be aware of the program at first. Therefore, in addition to holding meetings and forming committees, marketing the program is a vital step. Obvious though that may be, one thing we found is that certain types of marketing work better with some groups than with others—there is no "one size fits all" marketing.

The mainstay of CAPS marketing has been a large media campaign touting the existence of CAPS and beat meetings. The bulk of the media comprised advertisements on the radio, television, and in local newspapers. Television spots were aired during sporting events, such as Bulls and Bears games, and they drew a large number of viewers. The Implementation Office shifted marketing tactics in their advertising campaign away from having sports celebrities as spokespersons to showing real people who have benefited from CAPS. For example, one spot had testimonials of residents who worked with their beat officers to reclaim a neighborhood park that had been taken over by drug dealers and gang members.

The police department, in conjunction with a private production company, produces a television show called "Crime Watch," which airs five times daily on Chicago's cable channels, with new episodes featured every two weeks. CAPS has also been advertised on billboards, mass transit signage, and booths and kiosks at major city festivals, which abound in Chicago in the summertime.

We learned of the significant differences of CAPS awareness among various ethnic groups by conducting—on a yearly basis—a citywide public-opinion telephone survey of adults living within Chicago. The 100-question survey asks residents' opinions on such topics as quality of police service, the safety of their neighborhoods, neighborhood trends, how aware they are of CAPS, and whether they attend anti-crime meetings. The following are some key findings on sources of awareness from 1996, 1997, and 1998 surveys.

- CAPS awareness has increased over the years. In 1996, 54 percent of those surveyed were aware of CAPS. By 1998, 79 percent of those surveyed were aware. The city's marketing campaign clearly made quite an impact.
- Awareness of CAPS was not evenly distributed across racial groups; however, CAPS awareness has reached minority groups previously left out of other community policing programs in other cities.
- Program awareness has increased across all racial groups over the years. African-Americans are proportionally the most aware of CAPS. African-Americans were 8 percent more aware than whites in 1998.
- Latinos are the least aware of CAPS.

After the release of our 1997 report showing that Latinos were less aware of CAPS, the Implementation Office focused on the Latino community, advertising on Spanish-speaking radio and television. Although Latinos were still least aware in 1998, the gap closed slightly. They were only 15 percent less aware than African-Americans compared to 19 percent in 1997.

A language barrier stands in the way of getting the CAPS message out. Latino respondents were given the opportunity to be interviewed in Spanish if they preferred, and as a result, we learned that more English-speaking Latinos were aware of CAPS than were Spanish-speaking Latinos. In 1998, English-speaking Latinos were nearly 20 percent more aware of CAPS than were those who communicate primarily in Spanish.

If, in fact, we had only interviewed in English, we would have found the awareness rates of Latinos to be as high as that of African-Americans—80 percent of both English-speaking Latinos and African-Americans were aware of CAPS. It is the Spanish-speaking population that the CAPS message is not reaching. Awareness of CAPS was highest among the better-off in the communities. For example, homeowners were more aware of CAPS than are renters—11 percent more aware in 1998. Those with more education were more aware of CAPS, with those who graduated high school being significantly more aware than those who did not. The difference in awareness between high school graduates and those with college degrees was insignificant—both at about 80 percent in 1998. The differences were seen between those who do and do not graduate from high school.

As mentioned earlier, the Implementation Office has made great efforts in getting the word out about CAPS, so we asked those who said they knew of Chicago's community policing program how they became aware of it. Far and away, television was the primary source of CAPS awareness, and much more so in 1998 compared to 1997—40 percent versus 27 percent.

Learning via "word of mouth" was the second-largest source of awareness. There was a large increase between 1996 and 1997 and a smaller increase in 1998. Sources of awareness differ by race. Television was still the greatest source among all racial groups, but TV particularly reached Latinos. There was a large jump in 1998, perhaps because of the targeted CAPS advertisements on Spanish-speaking stations.

African-Americans were the racial group that most learned about CAPS from others, and this source improved for the other two groups as well. This is encouraging because this means CAPS is "the buzz"—it's being talked about. Most sources of awareness either increased for each racial group or stayed the same—with the exception of radio. This was an interesting reversal, particularly for Latinos, because in 1997 radio looked to be an effective way to spread the CAPS message. In 1998, rates of awareness through radio dropped for both Latinos and African-Americans even though the CAPS office had targeted English and Spanish-speaking radio stations.

Because of the relatively low number of Latinos involved in CAPS, differences in the way English-speaking and Spanish-speaking Latinos learn about CAPS is of interest. We see that Spanish speakers primarily know of CAPS through free television. As mentioned above, awareness via radio dropped for Spanish speakers.

When analyzing who actually goes to meetings, we found that the two greatest sources of awareness for those who attend meetings were notification through schools, at 30 percent, and from someone else at 27 percent, followed by brochures and flyers and notification through churches, both at 25 percent.

But one thing that has become quite clear to us is that knowing about the program is not the same thing as getting involved: Television, which was such a major source of awareness of CAPS in general, turned out many fewer beat-meeting attendees. Only 14 percent of those who go to meetings learned about CAPS from TV. Television generates a large amount of recognition and provides blanket exposure for those who have the budget for it, but it does not encourage people to go to meetings. Spreading the message via word of mouth and through churches and schools is certainly more time-consuming and less pervasive, but personal contacts make an impact. Our study revealed that people who are contacted in person are the most likely to actually go to a beat meeting. It is probably a very practical medium for hard-to-reach groups, for it reaches out to them where they live, in their language.

The following is a breakdown of what percentage of those surveyed are aware of CAPS, are aware of beat meetings, and go to beat meetings:

- Nearly 80 percent of those surveyed in 1998 knew about Chicago's community policing program; 62 percent were aware of anti-crime meetings being held in their neighborhoods, but only 16 percent went to anti-crime meetings.

- Those who went to beat meetings attended an average of three a year, while 25 percent attended only one; 25 percent attended two; and nearly a quarter attended three meetings a year. Sixteen percent of those surveyed attended six meetings or more a year.

What this means is that there are two types of people who get involved in Chicago's community policing program by attending beat meetings: core members and those on the periphery. Core members are the ones who attend regularly. They are part of the 16 percent who attend meetings more than six times a year. For whatever reason, they get something out of the meeting, whether they are trying to work with the police or they attend merely for social reasons. The other type is residents who float in and out of meetings depending on whether they have any pressing problems, or something that is to be addressed at the meeting brought them there—some type of "heater" situation, such as a shooting or youth getting hurt. This supports the common police officer complaint that only a handful of core residents attend the meetings regularly. The rest are residents with individual problems who stop attending once their problems are resolved.

OUTLETS FOR PARTICIPATION

There are four principal formal outlets for community involvement in Chicago's community policing program: District Advisory Committees, Court Advocacy, Joint Community-Police Training (JCPT), and Beat Meetings.

District Advisory Committees, or DACs as they are known, are composed of residents, business owners, and other stakeholders in the community. As a group, they are supposed to identify broad issues related to crime and disorder and, after doing so, establish priorities and develop strategies to address those issues at the district level. Since the character and problems of each district are very distinct, so are the goals and accomplishments of the DACs. DAC members often head up subcommittees and sometimes represent influential outside organizations. Aldermen, park district employees, and representatives of city, state, and federal agencies may also regularly attend DAC meetings; however, these individuals serve in an ex-officio capacity. There are three mandated DAC subcommittees: Court Advocacy, Senior Citizens, and Domestic Violence. Other subcommittees were to be established "as required to address issues of community concern." Subcommittees were also charged with the responsibility of identifying and researching issues, developing and implementing solutions, and mobilizing community resources.

There are, of course, certain subcommittees common to most of the DACs, such as Youth and Family, Business, Parks, and Education. There are many examples of subcommittees that are specific to the individual needs of districts, too. For example, there is a Hospitality subcommittee in a district with a preponderance of hotels, nightclubs, and restaurants; a Zoning subcommittee in a district where illegal building conversions are prevalent; a Community/Police Relations subcommittee where residents have had an uneasy relationship with the police; and a Gay and Lesbian subcommittee in a district where this demographic group that represents a large sector of the community.

The mandated Court Advocacy subcommittee is composed of community volunteers who track court cases and attend judicial hearings in cases that are of concern to the community. This vehicle for resident involvement in CAPS shows support for victims as well as solidarity against crime. Court Advocacy volunteers generally consult with beat officers or other district personnel to identify cases that negatively affect the quality of life in their district, and the group actively and systematically follows them through the criminal justice system. Court advocacy was actually conceived at the behest of the mayor, before the inception of the CAPS program. As a former state's attorney, the mayor became aware of the need for the community to have a voice in the courtroom because of the great impact that crime and disorder have on the community.

JCPT, taught by sworn officers as well as by civilians, is the CAPS training program that has been underway, in various configurations, for the last several years. JCPT provides classroom instruction to community members on their new CAPS roles and responsibilities. Following the classroom instruction, the project brings police and community members together to apply their training in solving actual crime problems on their beat. As such, JCPT strengthens the community-police partnership and elevates problem-solving skills of both the police and community.

The fourth outlet is beat meetings—the involvement-opportunity for one and all. The essence of beat meetings was explained above, so what follows is a review of a few things we have learned about who attends them and what makes beat meetings work.

In terms of turnout, it is notable that CAPS beat meetings are not a novelty. About sixty-nine thousand Chicagoans attended beat meetings in 1998—that comes out to nearly 4,500 per month. As noted earlier, attendance figures grow slightly every year. African-Americans in not-well-off neighborhoods attend almost two times more than do whites and Latinos. Yet, this is not necessarily good news, because statistically, involvement rates are driven by crime.

As mentioned previously, the language barrier seems to also restrict non-English-speaking Latinos from attending meetings. There is a significant difference in attendance between those Latinos interviewed in English and those interviewed in Spanish. Our research shows that among those who attend beat meetings, those who feel less safe in their neighborhoods attend in significant proportions, while residents who feel least safe do not attend as often, most likely because they are incapacitated by fear—they will not leave their houses. However, those in the less-safe categories attend in larger numbers. Overall there is little variation between the groups; what we are not seeing are large percentages of residents who feel very safe attending most often.

Even though residents of areas with more violent crime problems and residents who feel less safe attend beat meetings in higher proportions, they still represent the better off and more invested in their community.

These residents tend to be over thirty years old, married with children, and own their homes. Attendees tend to be involved in other organizations. We asked interview respondents if they were part of a neighborhood watch group, a PTA/school organization, a block club or community group, or church or synagogue. A large percentage were involved in three or more other groups. Only 6 percent of beat meeting attendees are not affiliated with other organizations compared to 43 percent who were involved in four groups.

Beat meeting attendees have more positive opinions about the police. We have found that the more involved residents are in CAPS, the more positive they are about the job police are doing. That involved residents have more positive attitudes about the police is a "which came first" situation. It is not clear whether CAPS self-selects more positive people or whether the relationships that residents build with police officers through CAPS engender a more positive attitude. Regardless, the net impact is that those who are higher on the "activism scale" are more positive.

MAKING MEETINGS COUNT

We are now left with the question of what makes for more effective beat meetings. To derive this, we sent observers out to examine the dynamics of more than 450 beat meetings. Observers were given information on the elements of a "model meeting," and they used this to rate the extent to which each actual meeting resembled an ideal gathering. The rating scale was based on ten aspects of the meetings.

Based on what our observers saw, dynamics that contribute to more effective meetings fall into three categories: structural features, organizational features, and process features. Structural features that lead to effective meetings are really quite sensible and predictable—meetings should be held on a regular schedule at a regular location. They should be held in all areas of the city, including those in which community groups and leadership are still developing. Effective beat meetings must be held in an environment that is considered safe by residents—perhaps a site that is already a locus for neighborhood activities, like a church or fieldhouse, and the meetings should be regularly and widely publicized.

Organizational features that help make meetings work include having an individual who is always responsible for creating an agenda and leading the meetings. Some type of handouts, like crime maps or lists of top-ten crimes in the area should be distributed and, ideally, reviewed, too.

Discussion of general community information, like announcements of upcoming events, is a helpful process feature. Also within this category is feedback about efforts that have been undertaken in response to issues that were brought up at previous meetings—an accountability function for both residents and police. Reports on problem-solving efforts serve several functions. These discussions help make it clear to participants that attending "pays off"—that they should attend because something actually happens as a result of the meetings. One very easy way to accomplish this is by taking advantage of results that come from city service actions. For example, if residents come to a meeting to complain about a dark and dangerous street corner where suspicious-looking youths congregate, perhaps getting trees that obstruct the streetlight trimmed will make the area seem less foreboding. This action shows residents that if they come with a complaint, something can be done. Neighborhood-oriented policing is not just about solving crime.

Making sure that there are network-building activities at community meetings is also critical. Participants who see each other around, who talk outside of meetings and who attend other meetings together are more likely to get involved in problem-solving efforts. There should also be social aspects to the meetings, like informal discussion over coffee either before or after the meeting, get-to-know-one-another exercises, or development and distribution of phone trees. There has to be some sort of interaction element, and maybe even a little fun.

Finally, there needs to be an action component. This can be as simple as having people sign up to engage in some sort of activity that responds to a matter brought up at the meeting, or merely a call for volunteers. Community members should leave the meeting with a mental "to do" list and know that they will be providing an update on what was accomplished since the previous meeting.

SUMMARY AND CONCLUSIONS

To sum up, here are some things that can be done to encourage community "buy in":

- Create meaningful roles for the community and train residents on these roles.
- Customize program marketing so that it is geared to the various factions of your community.
- Endeavor to get residents beyond the awareness stage. Awareness is not the same thing as getting involved—it is merely an essential first step.
- Focus recruitment efforts on community organizations, because residents who are involved in them are more likely to get involved and stay involved.
- Know what would constitute a model meeting in your community, and be sure to zero in on the components that will help make meetings worthwhile.

REFERENCES

Eck, J. E. & Spelman, W. (1987). *Problem solving: Problem-oriented policing in Newport News.* Washington, DC: Police Executive Research Forum.

Capowich, G. E. & Roehl, J. A. (1994). Problem-oriented policing: Actions and effectiveness in San Diego. In D. Rosenbaum (Ed.), *The challenge of community policing: Testing the promises.* Thousand Oaks, CA: Sage.

Clarke, R. V. (1998). Defining police strategies: Problem solving, problem-oriented policing and community oriented policing. In T. O'Connor Shelly and A.C. Grant (Eds.) *Problem oriented policing: Crime-specific patterns, critical issues and making POP work.* Washington, DC: Police Executive Research Forum.

Goldstein, H. (1979). Improving policing: A problem-oriented approach. *Crime and Delinquency,* 25, 236–58.

Goldstein, H. (1990). *Problem-oriented policing.* Newbury Park, CA: Sage.

Greene, J. R., Bergman, W. T., & McLaughlin, E. J. (1994). Implementing community polling: Cultural and structural change in police organizations. In D. P. Rosenbaum (Ed.), *The challenge of community policing: Testing the promises* (pp. 92–109). Newbury Park, CA: Sage.

Hope, T. J. (1994). Problem-oriented policing and drug market locations: Three case studies. In R. V. Clarke (Ed.) *Crime prevention studies* (pp. 5–31). Monsey, NY: Criminal Justice Press.

Kelling, G. L. & Coles, C. M. (1996). *Fixing broken windows.* New York: Free Press.

Podolefsky, A. & DuBow, F. (1981). *Strategies for community crime prevention: Collective responses to crime in urban America.* Springfield, IL: Charles C. Thomas.

Rosenbaum, D. P., Lurigio, A. J., & Davis R. C. (1998). *The prevention of crime: Social and situational strategies.* Belmont, CA: Wadsworth Publishing Company.

Sadd, S. & Grinc, R. (1994). Innovative neighborhood oriented policing: An evaluation of community policing programs in eight cities. In D. P. Rosenbaum (Ed.), *The challenge of community policing: Testing the promises* (pp. 27–52). Newbury Park, CA: Sage.

Skogan, W. G. & Hartnett, S. M. (1997). *Community policing, Chicago style.* NY: Oxford University Press.

Skogan, W. G., Hartnett, S. M., DuBois, J., Comey J. T., Kaiser, M., & Lovig, J. H. (1999). *On the beat: police and community problem solving.* Boulder, CO: Westview Press.

Skogan, W. G. & Lurigio, A. J. (1994). Winning the hearts and minds of police officers: An assessment of staff perceptions of community policing in Chicago. Community policing in Chicago. *Crime & Delinquency,* 40 (3), 315–330.

Skogan, W. G. (1990). *Disorder and decline: Crime and the spiral of decay in American neighborhoods.* New York: Free Press.

Wilkinson, D. & Rosenbaum, D. P. (1994). The effects of organizational structure on community policing: A comparison of two cities. In D. P. Rosenbaum (Ed.), *The challenge of community policing: Testing the promises* (pp. 110–126). Newbury Park, CA: Sage.

Wilson, J. Q. & Kelling, G. (1982, March). Broken windows. *Atlantic Monthly,* 29–38.

2

Community Partnerships in Affluent Communities

"The Phantom Menaces"

Chief Francis D'Ambra

❖

As Chief of Police at Manteo, North Carolina, I believe that an important part of establishing a sound community-oriented policing philosophy within a police agency requires first and foremost a commitment to organizational change. Much has been written about community-oriented policing as a policing model. Even more has been offered in the way of advice on grant writing for community-oriented programs; and funding has never been more available for any other type of police service than community poling services. However, many of my colleagues in police administration feel that community policing is too soft on crime to be a viable approach in solving contemporary crime patterns. I do subscribe to the notion that successful community-oriented policing does not seem to fit well into a formula pattern. That is, no right or best programs can fit every situation in every police agency in the country. Yes, I embrace the community-oriented model and believe it to be the most effective way the police have of resolving community problems and crime. However, community-oriented policing should never be viewed simply as a program. It is a complex process and philosophy that should radically change the manner in which police services are delivered. It's a different state of mind than the traditional "cuff 'em and stack 'em" perspectives.

My experiences tell me that many police leaders view community-oriented policing as a "program." For example, some agencies will claim a community-oriented model based upon the fact that they have a bicycle patrol unit or a community watch group. Clearly there's more to it than that. It means shifting the basic tenants of policing from the traditional response-driven action to a prevention-driven, service-oriented view. In my view, those agencies who have grasped the true heart and soul of the community policing philosophy are the ones who stand as leaders in the new era of police. For me, this shift in philosophy offers exciting challenges in the new millennium, new areas where police can effectively manage crime problems and social order. How do affluent small communities manage the community-oriented policing concept?

How should a police agency go about the task of building a partnership with the community? One answer is to examine some of the obstacles to community policing efforts and analyze those common problems. Many police agencies, both large and small, have jumped onto the community policing bandwagon, but for many, it has been a journey into the unknown as produced by new avenues of resources from the federal government. For others, neighborhood pressures have spurred on the change. Special interest groups within the community begin to stir. Soon the local media picks up on the community dissention, and before you know it the town council is passing legislation on police programming. Sadly, even more agencies have felt that if a shift from the traditional model was not made there would be virtually no avenue for funding. By this I mean that much in the way of state and federal funding is predicated upon implementing a community-oriented model. Police agencies are entities which are in part dependent on tax dollars for support.

Criminal justice professionals know that their agency depends on the local tax dollar for support and financing. For many individuals who are not in the profession, maybe the idea arises that police agencies should be self-sufficient. This, too, is not the case. Police agencies can neither have fire sales, raffles, fundraisers or the like to derive funds for operation. I believe this fact is the impetus for many of the new ideas and shifts in programming that agencies undergo. This fact may also account for some of the higher-level public scrutiny that police agencies face. For example, as compared with say, a volunteer fire department, which also may be partially tax supported, their spending is not as closely scrutinized by the public as police. The partial versus full tax-dollar funding may account for this.

In more affluent smaller towns, there seems to be an unhealthy interest in local government as a whole. Why, for example do such minor things seem to garner the most attention? Is it that the money is so important? Why would the board of commissioners float a million-dollar sewer bond in thirty seconds but argue over the merits of getting a new "radar gun" for four hours? Could it be that money is the driving factor behind all that we do in government? I hope not, yet I have struggled with this issue for some time. When I put to use the college education that I struggled for many years to complete, I kept arriving at the same conclusion. I would view the relationship between money and community policing, with the expectation of plugging in a formula and getting an answer.

As the town manager reminded me, "Chief," Kermit says, (That's my boss, he's a good guy). "This is just not an algebra problem. You're gonna just have to figure this one out without using a formula." I just did not realize the answer until I fully grasped the concept of community policing. What I found is that people are people. Those who get elected to public office like to discuss, weigh, touch, and feel things and issues that they identify with. I believe that is human nature. When it comes to the ideas that some of us do not understand, we have a tendency to pass over those issues. Unless there is some huge pressing need, there is little to identify with a million-dollar sewer bond. It can be passed or rejected. Usually the consequences for its passage or failure is clear. You will either get the new water tank or you will not. What I have discovered and offer in the remainder of this chapter are problems I refer to as "phantom menaces." Being aware of these phantom menaces and having the ability to address them has allowed me as chief to go a long way toward establishing good police community partnerships in Manteo, North Carolina.

So what is it about the Radar Gun that could possibly occupy four hours of discussion? Enter Phantom Menace Number One: "Chief what do ya need a radar for? If you get one of those things, that means that you'll have to write tickets."

"Yes, Sir," I respond, "we already have one, you know the one we got on a mini-grant ten years ago. But it needs to be replaced."

"Well Chief," he answers, "if you get a new radar gun then your officers will spend all their time making our streets safe from traffic. Then they will want to write more tickets. Then they will want to write more and more tickets even to our visitors who won't want to shop here. Then your officers will have to write more tickets to make up for the other lost revenue of the community."

"Oh and by the way Chief, we have had some complaints about people speeding in the business district, could you have your officers look into this problem and report back to us at the next meeting with how you intend to address the problem?"

Before you know it, four hours have passed and no new ground is gained. What I learned is that perception is fact, regardless if it is true or false. So, in building partnerships with various groups including town council members, a chief must be able to identify their concerns and address them effectively. Bearing in mind that people want to discuss what they can feel, know, and touch, it is not surprising that even affluent towns and cities can come under the gun of political bantering. What can we do about this scrutiny? I believe that whether a chief manages a staff of ten sworn officers or one thousand sworn officers, a police executive can successfully work through this type of obstacle by building partnerships from within. My boss, Kermit, gave me another gem that I reflect on from time to time. He said, "Chief, win their hearts, and their minds will follow." Good advice, even from a town manager. You know, I believe that city managers enjoy an even shorter average tenure than police chiefs do. Regardless, my boss has survived for over ten years. Part of this survival has been because of his ability to sense the "political waters" before diving headlong into the pond. Our management team has strived hard to build upon partnerships within the community. In most cases from our team approach, it has been a matter of capitalizing on partnerships that already existed.

Never! Never! Never make the mistake of discounting the strong political ties that may already exist within a community. Many police chiefs consider politics a taboo that nary a brave soul should enter into. There has often existed the myth that if you enter the political arena, it will surely come back to bite you.

In a small town, whether it is affluent, poor, urban, or rural, politics is its mainstay. In fact, in Manteo, politics is the national pastime. Developing a partnership with the political community can be a driving force behind a successful community-policing program. I say the "political community" for this reason. In many areas of our country, people consider the everyday, business-as-usual crowd, as the political community. This group is not at all, in my belief, the political community. The political communities to which I refer are those bona fide groups who truly wield influence and power. If a city has a solid program to promote, I think that there is great benefit from having true power brokers champion a cause.

There is that group, however, that I just mentioned, the business-as-usual crowd. Enter Phantom Menace Number Two. I call this group "The Parallel Government." This group is usually comprised exclusively of men, most of whom are older individuals.

This group sets up its base of operation at the "whiner diner." Again, this location varies from jurisdiction to jurisdiction. These individuals are your typical regressionists, including retired police chiefs, unemployed and under-employed individuals, real estate brokers, appraisers, active members of the naysayers' league, insurance salesmen, self-employed general contractors. Oh and did I mention retired police chiefs? The usual suspects. This parallel government starts the morning breakfast in full legislative session. Their relentless pursuit of negativity is the crowning jewel in destroying a town's overall economic development plan.

I say this sarcastically. But truly this group cannot benefit any business that intends to make a profit. This same group will ingest some ten to twenty gallons of coffee each morning. The conversation usually begins like this. "Can you believe what that chief is up to now?" "There he goes again, in that damned paper." "When I was the . . ." Or, "Th t department has got to have everything, why do they need walkie-talkies anyway?" Not only does this group legislate on the police department, but also they spread their negativity around.

They appear to be "equal opportunity whiners"—they hate everybody. No one is spared their wrath. Some days it's a police agency, some days it's the Board of Education. But rest assured that they will eventually touch on each and every branch of local government. Yes, even in affluent communities, partnerships must be formed with this group. Though this group is difficult, if you can discover on an individual basis some commonality with members of this group you can still be effective. As with behavior in many groups, the synergy of the group often sways opinion. There are those whose opinion just cannot be changed. Attitudes, beliefs, and perceptions all play a part in the group dynamic. Sometimes those beliefs may have nothing to do with your practices and efforts. I believe that if I can identify a leader among the group, I can develop a certain commonality with that individual. This can translate into a non-appetite for police issues. If there is no hunger for the gossip, there is no reward in its delivery.

Why do race relations play such a large part of police delivery planning? Race relations are truly a key component in the success of community policing efforts. Enter Phantom Menace Number Three. Face it, racism is real. Oftentimes, police administrators believe that minority groups pull "the race card" when dealing with police issues. There may be good reason. How many times I have heard one of my officers call in to central communications that they will be assisting a black male subject? I think that in many common contact situations between police and the public a reference to the person's race is given. It seems that many times this information is not germane to the situation. Nonetheless, it is provided. Does this mean that we're all racist? Certainly not. For some groups, racism is big business. Many a tax dollar has been spent on trying to recompense this great societal ill. Even more time I believe has been spent by governments in developing ways to not look like racists. I do not believe that everyone who makes an unnecessary reference to race is a racist. I say this to illustrate my point that generally we have been socialized into a police culture where police actions, words, and programming, as innocent as they may seem, can be viewed as racism. In my jurisdiction (that is how us southern cops talk, we don't say, "where I live"), our minority population is less than 1 percent. Even in this 1 percent, there are genuine concerns over racial issues.

Are the police racist in their delivery of services? No! But this fact does not mean that police officers can discount the need to be mindful of public perception. Whether it is attributed to racism or just to neglecting a lesser populations' needs, officers must understand that there are certain segments of society who get slighted when it comes to receiving police services. This is not to say that police agencies should invest all of their time, planning, budgeting, and patrolling minority areas just to avoid looking like racists. Police agencies should always try to balance their resources with the needs of the community as a whole. I would say that racism is wrong, but so is sexism, and the many other "isms" that officers sometimes fall into. I believe that building partnerships within the minority community is essential. But it must be real! I don't believe that it is appropriate for officers to throw a minority community a bone! Police agencies and their leaders must be real, honest, caring, and most of all—equitable.

Oftentimes municipal police chiefs have had a run-in with the local sheriff. I believe that one area of much misunderstanding lies in this critical relationship. Enter Phantom Menace Number Four, The High Sheriff. Typically, the local sheriff is an elected position. In my home state, the sheriff is a constitutional office. This fact seems just by itself to endear a certain atmosphere when relating to the High Sheriff. Just the mere connotation of the term "High Sheriff" lends a certain air of credibility to the position and office. Traditionally, the citizenry has seen the role of the sheriff as the only avenue for police services. This is especially true in rural areas and in areas where local police departments are smaller than the sheriff's office. Just the very foundational premise for municipal police is different. For example, municipal officers typically derive their powers and authorities from the state. That is, general statutes, standards, and ordinances establish and govern their power. This is not the case with many deputies who derive authority and power directly from the High Sheriff.

Deputies are extensions of the sheriff and serve at the pleasure of this elected individual. Deputies are expected to be ambassadors for the values and goals set by the sheriff. In North Carolina, the sheriff's deputies are governed and certified through a training and standards division, but those standards may and do vary from criminal justice officer standards. The political process drives the sheriff and the electorate decides who is the sheriff. This can mean that the entire police effort in a given county can change directions virtually overnight. Recently, a line deputy corrected me when I referred in conversation to the sheriff's department. I was told in no uncertain terms that "cities and towns have departments, sheriffs have offices." Does it make a difference? I think so . . . .

Why then do I say that this can be a "Phantom Menace?" Is it just me or does there seem to be some natural conflict between municipal police agencies and sheriff's offices? I believe that many rural counties, the traditional sheriffs' role is acted out in a way in which a certain attitude develops. The attitude that I have identified is portrayed as the deputy believing that he or she is the only police officer in the county. Clearly this is not the case in our world, but nonetheless, attitudes do develop.

Does community policing as a philosophy threaten the traditional role of the sheriff? After all, the community as a whole, especially the electorate, has been the domain of the sheriff. Police departments for years have been burdened with many levels of bureaucracy and governmental red tape. They have only been worried with "just the facts." They have never had time for the community before. Now all of a sudden police agencies enter into the community. This newfound excitement to enter into the community and police might have the effect of alienating the local sheriff's office. The scenario may resemble something like this: The police department develops this exciting new philosophy. Much effort is invested in programming, promoting, and implementing this strategy. The media senses a change in the traditional status quo within the police department. (We will discuss the media later.) Then a great deal of media coverage blankets the market. Invariably, the first comment to be made to the troops by the line deputy is "Who does your chief think he is?" Naturally, being a smaller agency than the county, the line police officer feels a certain level of discomfort with the question. The next comment to be made is "You know that 'stuff' is not really police work, y'all a bunch of social workers." This type of banter can cause a degree of tension between agencies. By the way, I hate to break the news, but police officers are social workers, ministers, priests, and rabbis, doctors, and friends, and big brothers, and big sisters, and counselors, and secretaries, and enforcers. I was always taught that there were two reasons police officers would be ostracized in this world: One was to not meet the standards, and the other was to exceed the standards. Community policing in affluent communities causes an officer and an agency to exceed the standards.

As the scenario unfolds, a police manager's best intentions concerning a community can be subverted by the attitudes a manager counts on most to make the philosophy work. So, how does a manager grow this inter-agency relationship? I have found that when trying to sell a group on a new philosophy, such as the community-policing philosophy, whether it's to the High Sheriff's office or the officers who report to me, that ego has no place in the equation, especially my own. Police managers must be willing to invite surrounding police agencies to participate in this newfound trust established with a community. Every chance a manager has should emphasize the community's participation, including outside agencies because they are part of the community. I believe that a productive police executive needs to be the P. T. Barnum of a community when it comes to community involvement. Is it an easy road? *No!* Those traditional rivalries are always present yet the constituents should never see a police executive become antagonistic. A police manager must be wholly committed to his or her community and eager to accept other agencies as a valued part of the community being served.

Phantom Menace Number 5: The Media Myth. It is quite mythological to think that the media is any easier to deal with in affluent communities. I live in a community where the total county population is roughly 30,000 year-round residents. This population swells to roughly 250,000 seasonally. My community hosts three thriving newspapers, four substantial radio stations, and is regularly covered by five television stations. An unhealthy interest exists in Manteo concerning local government, and it can be assumed that many other agencies have similar situations. For me, it is clear that I can never underestimate the power of the political atmosphere. Maybe my approach is not typical, but I find it best to avoid the media. I don't want to be in a situation where I am misquoted because I do care about the community and about the political leaders of the community. I think many police executives have experienced two common events when approached by the media: (1) Many of them panic rather than commit on a situation. And (2) many others come down with diarrhea of the mouth commenting on everything and everybody. Something about that microphone gives me the willies. I say something . . . I'm not sure what . . . it sounded like words . . . but it turns out to be . . . ballallapalostimus garbage. Or I begin with the suspect's name and end up divulging my mayor's private comment on gun control or abortion. But I never said that . . . Next!

I have learned to give the media only what they need and only what I want them to know. When the wrong question is asked, and it is asked often, I respond with a question instead of a statement. For example, I might ask, the question you really meant to ask is this and the answer to that question is blah, blah, blah. It is not a shut-out, it is not a "no comment," and it is not a black-out. Again, ego has no place in police work especially at the police executive's level. Why do many officers and police managers feel that police business is "secret police stuff"? Most of what the media wants is public record anyway. Why can't executives be friendly toward the press? I do not ever remember hearing that P. T. Barnum ever blocked the sidewalk so a media person could not pass. Unless it is case-sensitive, would violate the law, compromise officer safety or that of the public, or compromise the integrity of the case, I work with the media! Let the media validate and bear witness to the fact that a police department truly desires to have the community involved in solving problems. I guess I ask myself often, are you really committed to involving your community in police affairs? Do I see crime as a police problem or community problem? One of the modern schools of thought in the area of developmental supervision would suggest that if police executives solved people's problems for them then they have no vested interest in sustaining the solution. When the media is involved with a police agency, critical relationships can be laid that build community trust and become a catalyst for community problem solving.

Phantom Menace Number Six: The Rigid Bureaucrat. Why is it that government employees get such a bad name? Let me introduce you to a true bureaucrat. He or she is the government employee who is "by the book." There is nothing inherently wrong with bureaucracy. Bureaucracy can be a very efficient means of operating governmental units. So why is it that the thought of bureaucracy endears such criticisms? By the mere definition of the word bureaucrat, some police managers find someone who is inflexible and rigid when it comes to rules and the organization. I believe that those traits can be good things under certain circumstances. In this sense, the bureaucrat can be a true technician of his or her particular profession. One popular political philosophy would suggest that government and in particular government employees should have no place in the operation of local government. The notion that the populace should govern is widely heard during political debates and during the political seasons. The notion of putting the government directly in the hands of the people however, as apple pie and mom as it may be, in reality can truly make government inefficient and ineffective.

Local political influence and direct citizen involvement can be problematic if it is not managed carefully. In other words, it might be right back to "Chief, why do you need a radar gun?" The chief's job, his or her specialty if you will, is marrying the various components of the organization, building upon them and making the most efficient, effective decisions to make the agency work. That is, the chief is a government bureaucrat!

Here's a story about a local government employee. This guy was a great textbook bureaucrat. He looked at the job each day that awaited him. He took on the day with vigor and enthusiasm every day he worked. Each day he made decisions based upon the rules that the organization set for him to follow. Unfortunately, this employee saw the rules as absolutes, in very black and white terms. He was what I would define as a rigid bureaucrat. One day while preparing to host a rather large concert, he had contracted with some local business owners to cater the event. As the day of preparation progressed, the caterers asked for various items and equipment that they felt that they would need to adequately host the event. The bureaucrat viewed these requests as the caterer trying to skirt the rules, and by God he would have none of it. Now, those requests became innocuous and were viewed with a contentious attitude. Needless to say, very little was done in the way of making a positive impression for the town. More importantly to be studied was the fact that the employee was totally ineffective in carrying out the intent of the organization. I believe that rigid bureaucracy is best saved for God and Country. The rest is negotiable.

Now I am not suggesting that police executives compromise ethics, values, the law, or moral standards, but there is room for some flexibility on the small stuff. When I was in field training as a buck recruit, my training officer would always say to me, "Rookie, don't sweat the small stuff, if you do you'll be dead by fifty." I believe he was right on the mark. After all, police executives are charged with the responsibility of making situations better. Oftentimes, they make decisions without the luxury of vast resources, days to contemplate actions or outcomes, or long sessions of deep breathing exercises. Police executives must make the agency work, efficiently and effectively! That is not compromising standards. That is doing what needs to be done. It is the mark of excellence in an organization and exemplifying true skill in bureaucratic management. It is how to build partnerships in communities. People will not want to partner with an agency that they cannot communicate with. Finding common ground to build upon is essential in any relationship.

One of the most critical partnerships a police executive can nurture in affluent community is the relationship between the agency and other non-police agencies. Phantom Menace Number Seven: The Outside Agency. These relationships can truly be phantom menaces in that they can sometimes be built out of necessity rather than through true benevolent partnering. In small cities and towns, and especially in affluent communities, public agencies can succumb to the complaint du jour from the local press and whiner-diner crowd. This week the complaint is about the board of education, next week it is about the sheriff's office, the following it is social services, but that's been mentioned above.

Then there is the viability issue. Public service agencies compete for grant dollars, clients, and limelight in solving community problems and in addressing community concerns. Each group lends its particular educational bent or expertise to the issue and ends up attacking the problem from another angle. The rub comes into play when these public service agencies overlap with grant dollars, clients, or limelight. Who is most viable in servicing the community? Can social services do it better than mental health? Is it a school issue or one that should involve domestic violence prevention? And where do child protective services, police, and juvenile justice intervention come into play? I have found in working in my area that the best approach is a team effort. These are critical issues in finding success.

An example of overlapping competition I can offer is this: One area of my home state has a judicial district that encompasses seven counties. Part of the district is rural and poor, the other part is urban and affluent. In this environment, political power vacillates between various areas of the judicial district. Additionally, community services there may compete for the same client base. Hence, the rub. Does police service support local service alone, or does it lend support to the service that is district-wide? I suggest both, and not to get caught in the viability game. The important thing to remember here is for me to stay on track with the program. Some organizations with which relationships will be forged may have to deal with the police agency as part of some grant mandate or other governing measure and may truly have no interest in partnering with it to solve problems within the community. They will lend their particular discipline or expertise to the situation sometimes to detriment of community policing objectives. When participating in outside agency relationships I suggest a scenario something like this: If discussing drugs in the community and the representative of the agency that is partnering asks, "Well what about jobs? How are we going to provide jobs?" It might be best to respond with a well-intended representative (AKA, pain in the butt): "Today we are talking about drugs in the community. The jobs meeting is tomorrow at this same time [as you tap on your watch], and you can be chairman of the jobs meeting, but now it's drugs!" These types of outside agency relationships can really stifle a program, so staying focused might be difficult to accomplish from time to time but well worth the energy.

Have I said enough about outside agency relationships? The important thing that I try to remember is that these relationships represent the hallmark of community policing efforts. By establishing solid partnerships with these groups the philosophy of community policing will flourish. I remember that I am not to be overbearing, egotistical, or headstrong in dealing with outside agencies. Despite the fact that many police commanders are entering a playing field where some police programs and services have failed, they know it best to be seen as a team player.

I try to remind myself that I am in a job where there are some several thousand other police executives wondering about many of the same things that I wonder about. I realize that none of us woke up one morning and simply found high-crime rates, social disorder, and urban decay. I do not believe that as a profession, police commanders can afford to sit on their laurels and discuss what a positive impact they had on crime and social disorder over the past forty years. In some areas, police agencies have been winners, and in some areas agencies have been losers! I think that because of the nature and the resources of police work that agencies have ineffectively dealt with the roots of crime and social problems primarily because it wasn't the focus or expectation of an agency. If police agencies become arrogant or condescending in their approach when dealing with outside agencies, can the very people agencies need to partner refuse to help the task ahead for police agencies?

I believe that a big part in measuring the success of community policing lies in the ability of the agency to link people to services that they need to help *them* solve *their* problems. But that's social work, Chief! Yes it is. And if anyone tells me that cops are not social workers, I do not believe that they have a good grasp of what policing in the twenty-first century has become. Even traditional police work has an element of social work. One example can be seen in the vast amount of discretion that a police officer has when interfacing with others. An arrest is not the only option, nor is it always the best option. Being able to recognize an appropriate time for the arrest has merit. What makes community policing effective is the ability that an individual officer has to explore some of the other options available to him or her.

How important is discretion when it comes to community policing initiatives? The wise officer is one who can recognize the threat and apply appropriate action to help resolve a problem. Some call it "proactive" policing. Think of how many injuries to officers could be prevented if, when responding to a domestic call, instead of advising warrants, officers linked people with services. In this fashion, an officer might reduce future service calls in a traditional police manner, which implies, "You called. We came." Police agencies need to hedge their bets and prevent crime from happening.

Board to death! Phantom Menace Number Eight: Just how many boards can a police chief serve on? One, ten, twenty—your guess is as good as mine. One thing is certain: If asked, a chief will serve. Why do chiefs get themselves buried in so much work? People ask for my time to sit on committees and boards, and I give it to them. Nonetheless, service on various boards and commissions is paramount in the furthering of community policing strategies. This is hardly a self-promoting perspective, but rather a chief must believe in the organization and support the agency's objectives. Boards and commissions serve the interest of the organization. They are necessary for the agency to grow in stature, viability, reputation, depth, and credibility. A chief should not serve on a board where he or she has nothing to offer. That is, I will not serve for the glory of being on a committee for the sake of serving.

If I do run the risk of appearing self-promoting rather than organizational promoting, it's time to make other decisions. My mother taught me that if I wanted to be seen, stand up. If I wanted to be heard, speak up. If I wanted to be respected, shut up. I have found much wisdom in those thoughts, especially when it comes to service on boards. I have tried to touch on some of the things that I have found to be helpful and to be menaces. So now I will take my mother's advice and realize that it is time to shut up. I will close with these thoughts. So what do we do in affluent communities to build trust, bolster a police agenda, promote the community policing plan, satisfy constituents, satisfy council members, make people happy, and more?

Finally, we've reached my last phantom. It starts like this: The expectation of most people is that a chief of police can do all things for all people, all of the time. Chiefs are supposed to be super arbitrators, super lawyers, guardians of the light, possess super personalities, super intellects—be supermen and superwomen. Yet, most chiefs are like me, hard-working folks with children to raise and electric bills to pay. Now, many of those folks are police managers, hopefully schooled and seasoned in managerial perspectives since that is what they are, but not necessarily experiences that they enjoy the most. The truth is that most chiefs are in charge simply because they asked for the job without knowing what they were getting themselves into. Generally, most of them were effective and down-to-earth good patrol officers and/or detectives, who knew they wanted to be a cop when they were twelve (or thereabouts) and wouldn't have it any other way. Then they watched their supervisors and often thought the job of chief was easier than anticipated because of the skill level of their mentors. Suddenly, those patrol officers and/or detectives must impartially juggle politically modified budgets, balance personalities and quality service while doing a fire walk over legal codes, hierarchical demands, and political correctness. They must stroll through mountains of paper work while being pushed by bureaucratic redundancies yet pulled by the Babylonian Code of Hammurabi. They must at all times exercise the wisdom of Socrates, tolerate the insanity of some psychologists, judges, and distant dictates, and report to individuals who generally know less about police service than they do. Combining these thoughts with all the phantom menaces mentioned above, enter Phantom Menace Number Nine: Super Chief. And I wouldn't trade my job for the world even if I can't do all of those things I've mentioned.

Each phantom category is an important ingredient in building a strong community policing program. Yet, each dealing effectively with each phantom menace and others I haven't considered, will help build the trust of those served. Each commander like each community shares a single characteristic: They are uniquely American! Without sounding cliché, police executives, like their communities, bring to the table their culture, values, and ideas. All of these work together to make the community function toward the objectives of public order and comfort. That is a very important component in making a community policing partnership successful. Each part of a constituency has a certain flavor that it adds to the community. Each component of an internal administrative function also plays a part in the community as a whole. If I had to say one thing about community policing in affluent communities it would be this: Community policing reflects a philosophy which takes into account the needs, desires, hopes, and abilities of those who serve and those who are served. Sir Robert Peele, who was known as the Father of Modern Policing said that the police are the community. If he was right and the police are the community, then police commanders owe it to themselves to give of themselves to their community and to be consumed in its existence. If those executives see obstacles that resemble any of the phantom menaces I described, and do nothing, I believe those police executives can be self-defeating and their effectiveness will diminish the potential of the community relationship.

Each of these obstacles is real and, of course, varies from community to community and the recommendations suggested, of course, are general thoughts that must be modified to fit specific circumstances. One task of the police is to guide the community closer to reducing their fear of crime, control crime, and to enhance their quality of life standards. That is not to say that my list represents all of the phantoms there are or that my experiences are similar to every commander. Certainly some of my colleagues will and should take issue with many of my ideas offered in this chapter. What is consistent is that most police executives spend more time getting to the other end of obstacles than they do in furthering the comfort of the community. Commanders must effectively and professionally provide police services for their communities in an efficient and practical manner. If they can meld their community and turn diversity into commonality, those communities will thrive and will meet the challenge of a renewed sense of fulfillment. Those communities will learn that they too have a responsibility in public affairs which includes policing themselves. Thus, one of my primary missions as chief, through community policing, is to help a community arrive at this point.

Chief Francis D'Ambra can be reached at dambra@townofmanteo.com.

3

Preparing the Community for Community Policing

The Next Step in Advancing Community Policing

Chief Charles H. Ramsey

❖

The latter part of the twentieth century was a time of tremendous energy and progress in American policing. In a very short period, police departments across America helped define, then implement, a complete transformation in how our communities are policed. The adoption of community policing as the prevailing policing philosophy in the United States was dramatic not just for the speed with which this paradigm shift occurred, but also for the wholesale nature of the changes it entailed—in everything from recruitment and hiring, to training and technology, to strategy and tactics.

Now, nearly two decades into this latest revolution in American policing, community policing is at a crossroads. After spending considerable time and energy in defining community policing, reorganizing the police structure to reflect the shift in philosophy, and experimenting with different strategies and tactics for implementing it, police leaders are left with a difficult, but inescapable decision. Are we satisfied with the status quo when it comes to community policing? Or are American police prepared to take community policing to its next level?

And if police leaders are committed to advancing community policing, just what will that involve? What additional organizational reforms will be needed? And perhaps more importantly, what changes will need to take place in the community to ensure the continued development of community policing? This chapter looks at the future of community policing in America, with a particular focus on the expanded role the community must play as this strategy continues to develop and mature.

INSTITUTIONALIZING COMMUNITY POLICING IN POLICE DEPARTMENTS AND THE COMMUNITY

From its earliest days, "community policing" has been defined by two key concepts: partnerships and problem solving. Over the years, different cities have adopted any number of different names to define their community policing strategies (San Diego has "Neighborhood Policing"; Chicago, the "Chicago Alternative Policing Strategy"; Washington, D.C., "Policing for Prevention"). And different strategies may have emphasized one of the two concepts—either partnerships or problem solving—over the other. But while the labels may vary, and the programmatic emphases may differ from city to city, the bottom line is that the revolution known as community policing has come to be defined by these two principles. Partnerships and problem solving are what make community policing fundamentally different from the traditional policing approaches that American law enforcement practiced for much of the twentieth century.

Under the philosophy of community policing, problems of crime and disorder are addressed not simply by reacting, after the fact, to problems that have already occurred. Rather, crime and disorder are attacked through a problem-solving orientation that, by its very nature, is proactive, systematic and comprehensive. And under community policing, this problem-solving process is carried out not just by the police alone, as previous crime control strategies were. Rather, problem solving requires a partnership of neighborhood-oriented police officers, other government agencies, residents, business owners, and their employees—basically, anyone and everyone with a stake in the quality of life of a community.

After two decades of experimentation with and implementation of community policing, these two concepts—partnerships and problem solving—have become firmly ingrained in the vernacular of almost every police department in the country, along with the communities we serve. The federal government has supported the new policing philosophy to the tune of hundreds of millions of dollars and tens of thousands of new police officers. Community leaders have embraced community policing as a viable and progressive way to give residents a voice in determining the policing priorities in their neighborhoods and a structure for channeling their energy and resources. And police departments have demonstrated their commitment to this new paradigm through eloquent mission statements—backed up by new programs, catchy slogans, sophisticated Web sites, and the like.

But two decades into this revolution, police departments across the country face another, more grim reality about community policing: Defining and espousing the concepts of community policing have proven a lot easier than getting them firmly embedded in our police departments and fully operational in our communities.

That's not to suggest that community policing has not had a dramatic impact thus far. It has. In a very short period of time, community policing has fundamentally changed how American police officers and executives view themselves and their respective roles in the community. Community policing has also significantly changed—and raised—public expectations of what the police can, and should, do when it comes to the old concepts of "serving and protecting." Perhaps most importantly, community policing has coincided with—and, I would argue, contributed to—the steady and significant reductions in crime the United States witnessed throughout much of the 1990s. As crime rates have declined, the underlying concepts of community policing have become validated and the number of people recognizing the promise and potential of community policing has continued to grow.

But while the changes in our basic approach to policing have been dramatic and the drop in crime significant, the fact remains that operationalizing—and, more importantly, institutionalizing—the concepts of partnerships and problem solving remain significant challenges for almost every police department in almost every community. For example:

- Uniformed police officers, especially those in larger jurisdictions with significant demands for service, are still largely "slaves of 9-1-1"—rushing from emergency call to emergency call (and many non-emergencies in between), without the time or opportunity to develop partnerships or engage in sustained problem solving.

- Many residents and other community stakeholders still view their role as being little more than another set of "eyes and ears" of the police—looking out for trouble, and then stepping back and calling in the law enforcement professionals when they see it.

- And in many cases, the concepts of partnerships and problem solving have been reduced to monthly meetings, attended by the same small core group of activists, hashing over many of the same problems.

Despite the shortcomings of community policing, the new philosophy still represents a vast improvement over policing practices of fifteen or twenty years ago. At least police officers are thinking more analytically and strategically—even if they don't always have the time to work on solving problems. At least police and residents are meeting and talking on a regular basis, in a non-adversarial setting—even if those discussions are often little more than "walk-in 9-1-1 sessions."

While it is clear that the full potential of community policing has not been realized, it is equally apparent that there is no turning back on this paradigm shift or on the principles of partnerships and problem solving that are the pillars of community policing. The challenge—for police executives, managers, and officers, as well as community and political leaders—is to make the philosophy work even better in the future. The key to achieving success lies not solely in continued improvements in police organizations and operations, although ongoing internal reforms remains critical. Taking community policing to the next level will require that the community be better prepared and equipped for its role in community policing. Just as police executives helped drive the internal changes in American policing that took place in the 1980s and 1990s, so too will the same police executives need to lead the quality and pace of change in the community in the new decade.

PREPARING THE POLICE FOR COMMUNITY POLICING

For most police departments, implementing community policing up till now has focused largely on getting our own police officers, supervisors, and managers ready for the new strategy. This has involved, first, getting them to buy into the concept (and overcome concerns that community policing would somehow turn them into "social workers," despite Chief D'Ambra's notion in Chapter 2 of this book where he argues that police, are, indeed, social workers). Beyond buy-in, implementation has also involved providing our sworn personnel with the basic skills and techniques they needed, as well as the information and information technology that would allow them to apply those new skills in a real-world setting. This initial phase of community policing—"Community Policing 101"—by necessity has emphasized getting the internal police house in order.

New Mission Statements

Employee buy-in has been approached through a number of different, yet complementary strategies. For example, most police departments have revisited their traditional "serve and protect" mission statements and updated them to reflect community policing's focus on partnerships and problem solving. In Chicago, the importance of the police-community partnerships is reflected in the Police Department's mission statement, which was reissued in 1993 with the implementation of the Chicago Alternative Policing Strategy (CAPS):

> The Chicago Police Department, as part of and empowered by the community, is committed to protect the lives, property and rights of all people, to maintain order, and to enforce the law impartially. We will provide quality police services in partnership with other members of the community. To fulfill our mission, we will strive to attain the highest degree of ethical behavior and professional conduct at all times.

In Washington, D.C., the Metropolitan Police Department's mission statement has been updated twice since the adoption of community policing. The current mission statement reflects the importance of proactive crime *prevention,* not just after-the-fact law enforcement, to policing in our nation's capital:

> The mission of the Metropolitan Police Department is to prevent crime and the fear of crime, as we work with others to build safe and healthy communities throughout the District of Columbia.

While some people may dismiss proclamations such as these as little more than fancy words on a piece of paper (or a Web site), these and other mission statements have served an important purpose in the development of community policing. They have been a highly visible declaration—both inside and outside the police department—of the agency's commitment to community policing and its basic philosophy in how that commitment will be met. As such, they have been critical to buy-in both internally and externally.

Organizational Change

Developing new mission statements to reflect community policing was only the first step in developing employee buy-in. Getting the concept ingrained and operational inside the police culture and organization has consumed a great deal of police executives' time and energy over the last several years. Most departments have had to make significant organizational, structural and policy changes just to bring their agencies into compliance with the principles of community policing and the edicts of their own mission statements. This has involved reinvigorating old concepts such as "police-community partnerships" and developing new ideas such as geographic accountability.

These changes have taken place at both the micro, or beat, level, as well as the macro, or organizational, level. For example, under community policing more and more departments have emphasized the concept of "beat integrity." This has involved not only assigning the same group of officers and supervisors to a police beat (often on the same shift) for an extended period of time, it has also led to new dispatch and differential response procedures that ensure officers can remain on their beats during their tour of duty, and not constantly be pulled to answer calls for service on neighboring beats. Beat integrity, and the sense of continuity it provides, have proven integral to the development of grass-roots partnerships between police and community and the growth of neighborhood-based problem solving. Beat integrity has forced individual officers and first-line supervisors not only to buy into the concept of community policing, but also to accept responsibility for the quality of police service in their particular, geographically defined area. This has been a critical step in institutionalizing community policing within our police organizations.

Some departments have taken this notion of geographic accountability one step further: They have reorganized their entire departments to reflect the importance of managerial accountability that is geographically based. The Metropolitan Police Department in Washington D.C., for example, recently eliminated the traditional bureau structure, in which different aspects of policing were organized by function: patrol, investigations, technical support and administration. In its place, the department has implemented a system of geographic accountability that begins at the police service area (PSA, or "beat") and builds up to the police district, region, and citywide. At each level is a manager who is accountable for the quality of police services and the conduct of police personnel at that level. At the PSA, it is the lieutenant; at the district, the commander; at the region, an assistant chief; and citywide, the chief of the police.

In addition to having greater accountability, each manager at each level now has the full resources to get the job done. Detectives, for example, have been taken out of their own bureau and integrated, at the district level, into the overall community policing operations there. A PSA lieutenant who needs investigative support on solving a problem no longer has to go up and across and down the chain of command to get some help; he or she merely needs to approach the detective lieutenant in that district, with the district commander serving as an arbitrator if there are any disputes.

Other departments have implemented other, creative organizational changes. For example, New York City has bolstered accountability by integrating previously separate transit and housing police forces with the NYPD. San Diego has dramatically expanded the use of volunteers in a variety of capacities as a way to free up sworn officers' time for problem solving. And almost every major city department has made dramatic gains in civilianizing jobs—in areas such as records, personnel, communications, and firearms examination—that were traditionally held by officers.

The adoption of community policing has forced police executives to reevaluate their organizational structures and practices and to implement oftentimes sweeping changes. Departments have also been forced to codify these organizational changes through new directives, new forms, and new basic procedures—a not insignificant task in a large agency. In many cases, agencies have had to loosen their traditional command-and-control management styles to accept new practices such as strategic planning and participatory management.

The bottom line is that this entire process of reengineering the police organization to support community policing has proven to be a long and arduous process—and one that many people grossly underestimated in terms of time and energy. Along the way, many police officers may have felt that community policing was just another fad that they could wait out. To their credit, however, American police executives have recognized the promise of community policing and stayed the course, even if progress was slower than many of us might have expected. The result has been widespread acceptance of community policing as our current paradigm.

Training

If gaining employee buy-in was the first step in the internal implementation process, expanding officers' understanding of community policing was the next critical step. As with other new ideas and concepts, developing officer understanding has been accomplished primarily through training. But unlike other police training programs, training for community policing had to be more expansive, in terms of both content and duration. In the early 1990s, it was not unusual to attend a community-policing seminar and meet officers who had been sent by their chiefs to "learn community policing" so they could implement it upon their return. I would often pity the poor officer who would soon discover that community policing was a little more complicated than something that could be covered in a one- or two-day training block and implemented by a single officer working alone.

One of the great legacies of community policing in America will be the renewed attention it has focused on police training. Not only have individual agencies retooled their training academies to support community policing, but entire new community-policing training facilities have developed at the state, regional, and national levels. For example, federal funds have supported the development of dozens of regional community-policing institutes throughout the country, providing training for agencies that might not otherwise have the capacity to deliver in-depth training.

New and enhanced training facilities have brought new and expanded content areas. Officers today are learning not only the philosophy of community policing and its nuts and bolts, but also such diverse topics as communications skills, problem-solving techniques, community organizing and diversity management, to name a few. Thanks to this new emphasis on training, police officers today understand the new philosophy and are being equipped with the knowledge, skills and abilities they need to implement it.

Information and Information Technology

When people think of community policing, they tend to conjure up old-fashioned images of a police officer walking the beat, helping seniors cross the street, corralling wayward youth and the like. These type of "back to the future" images of community policing are certainly part of the equation. But another important legacy of community policing will be the development of information technology over the last two decades. Community policing has demonstrated that individual police officers on the beat, as well as their supervisors and managers, need access to information that will help them create partnerships and identify and solve problems. The best to provide them with that information is through modern information technology.

Twenty years ago, a police officer was lucky to leave roll call with a printed "hot sheet" of recently stolen vehicles and maybe a wanted poster or two. Today, many officers' squad cars are equipped with mobile data computers (MDCs) that offer access to a wide range of information, including comprehensive data on stolen vehicles, missing and wanted persons, motor vehicle records, criminal history data and the like. Some of these devices are portable, providing officers with constant access to information while visiting a victim's home or walking their beat.

In addition to giving officers access to real-time operational information, new technology developed to support community policing has revolutionized the entire crime analysis function for police departments. Instead of being a back-room activity carried out by only a select few specialists, crime analysis has been moved into the front room of the district station and even into the squad cars of officers through their MDCs. In recent years, several agencies have developed easy-to-use, walk-up crime-mapping and analysis systems that are accessible to everyone from the cop on the beat to the chief of police. In Chicago, for example, ICAM (Information Collection for Automated Mapping) allows officers to create maps, data tables, and other graphics that depict crime on their beats or in their police districts—all with a few clicks of a computer mouse. Now, agencies are working to make this same graphical information available to their officers via MDCs and to the public via the Internet. Under community policing, the old days of pin maps and lengthy (and often dated) computer print-outs have been replaced by information systems that offer widespread access to real-time data.

In addition to MDCs and crime analysis systems, community policing has ushered in other new technologies, including more sophisticated computer-aided dispatch systems, a new non-emergency system (3-1-1), robust records management systems, automated field reporting, radio system upgrades, and new advances in automated fingerprint and DNA analysis. Some of these systems may have developed irrespective of the move to community policing. But the speed with which they were adopted and the breadth of their application were certainly accelerated by the wholesale shift in policing philosophy. Police executives recognized early on that community policing would require that officers had both the information needed to identify problems and the time in the community needed to develop and implement solutions. New technology is beginning to accomplish both: giving officers greater access to information, while also streamlining routine tasks that used to take extended periods of time and frequent trips from their beats to the district station or police headquarters.

New Tools and Tactics

Finally, community policing has brought about new and creative approaches to solving crime and disorder problems. Traditional policing relied almost exclusively on the enforcement of laws. Under community policing, law enforcement remains crucial. But now, officers and communities are turning to a broader range of tools and tactics to address problems.

Some of these new tools and tactics have taken the form of new laws targeting such things as nuisance properties, illegal dumping and other environmental crimes, aggressive panhandling, problem liquor license establishments and other quality-of-life concerns. In many cases, police departments have formed new alliances with other government regulatory agencies or private concerns to enforce these laws. In the District of Columbia, for example, Operation Crackdown is a program created by the Young Lawyers Section of the D.C. Bar Association. Using volunteer attorneys who work with police, community prosecutors, and residents, the program targets the owners and managers of nuisance properties. While the ultimate sanction is the potential filing of criminal and/or civil charges, the program usually accomplishes its goals—elimination of the nuisance and a commitment to make long-term improvements to the property—through voluntary compliance that is generated by the mere threat of legal action. Chicago combines similar legal and quasi-legal approaches with extensive training programs for landlords, on how to screen tenants, improve building safety and evict problem tenants.

Beyond designing and implementing new approaches to law enforcement, police departments have also turned to new internal tactics to support community policing. Bike patrols, once a luxury found only in warm-weather areas, are now routine in almost every major city police department. Storefront mini-stations and Japanese-style kobans have also sprung up in many cities, enhancing policing visibility and providing residents with easier access to officers. The D.C. Metropolitan Police Department has taken this concept one step further. Our department now operates more than a dozen "open-air mini-stations," picnic-table-and-chair sets (complete with umbrellas) that are stationed conspicuously in open-air drug markets and other high-crime areas. Staffed by uniformed police officers, the mini-stations provide the same benefits of storefronts and kobans, but allow police to move the facilities around, as warranted by changing crime problems.

In recent years, then, community policing has spurred innovation in a number of these and other tactical areas. The result has been a dramatic expansion of the problem-solving toolbox that is available to police officers. Whereas in the past officers looked almost exclusively to the passage and enforcement of laws as their primary crime control tools, the resources available to them have gotten larger and more sophisticated under community policing. Through better training and information technology, officers have been able to maximize the effectiveness of these new tools and tactics.

THE COMMUNITY'S ROLE IN COMMUNITY POLICING

Just as traditional policing carved out a very narrow role for the police in addressing crime, it also set forth a straightforward, even restrictive, role for the community. Residents were instructed, first and foremost, to be on the alert for suspicious activity or outright criminal behavior. When such activities occurred, the public was told to call the police immediately and to step back and let the "professionals" solve the problem. This type of passive community role in traditional policing gave rise to the popular expression of the public being "the eyes and ears" of the police.

Over the years, police departments built up elaborate systems and acquired whole new technologies to support this "eyes and ears" role. We put the vast majority of police officers in squad cars, so they could respond rapidly to citizen calls for service. We implemented a uniform, easy-to-remember, toll-free emergency telephone number (9-1-1) for contacting the police. We designed robust radio and wireless communications systems, and we installed sophisticated computer-aided dispatch systems. These and other developments all shared the same goal of making it easier for the public to contact the police in emergencies (and, increasingly, in non-emergency situations as well) and for the police to respond more precisely and rapidly. In some cases, new programs and new technology were created for the community as well, to support their role as "eyes and ears." Neighborhood watch programs and signs were developed, CB and cellular phone patrols were created, and various crime prevention programs (focusing primarily on individual target hardening) were established.

These developments were significant in making the police more efficient in one critical aspect of our work: the ability to respond quickly to public safety emergencies. After all, rapid response to emergencies always has been, and always will be, a unique responsibility of the police. In other respects, however, police and communities have become a victim of our success in 9-1-1–driven policing. For the police, our enhanced ability to capture calls for service and dispatch police cars using modern technology has served to reinforce this reactive approach to crime control as the singular, or at least the primary, role of our profession. For the community, the ease and efficiency of 9-1-1 have served to reinforce the "eyes and ears" role that has now become commonplace, almost cliche. The irony, of course, is that while residents grew increasingly comfortable with this role, they also grew increasingly frustrated with the inability of our 9-1-1 and rapid response systems to keep up with the demands they are placing on those systems.

When the ideas behind community policing were first introduced in the early 1980s, they challenged the wisdom and efficacy of many of these reactive policing concepts—the primacy of 9-1-1, rapid response, eyes and ears, etc. Yet, community policing issued this challenge at the very time these concepts were firmly entrenched in the culture and practice of American policing. Perhaps the biggest impediment to the adoption of true community policing, with its bedrock principles of partnerships and problem solving, has been disrupting the "comfort zone" that both police officers and residents settled into with traditional, reactive policing. A closer examination of the dramatic changes in both perspective and practice of community policing may help explain why getting out of this comfort zone has been difficult.

Under traditional policing, police and residents often spoke about "partnerships." But this concept of a "partnership" was a one-way, one-dimensional relationship epitomized by the "eyes and ears" paradigm. Citizens were partners with the police only to the extent that they provided information to officers. It was still the police who bore the ultimate responsibility for addressing crime. Beyond picking up the phone now and then, the community's role in this "partnership" was extremely limited, if not non-existent. Under community policing, the concept of "partnership" is broadened significantly. The relationship between police and community becomes multi-dimensional. Information flow becomes a two-way street. Perhaps most importantly, the responsibility for public safety becomes shared: the community does play a role—an active and engaged role—in addressing crime and the conditions that breed it.

The changes demanded by community policing are equally significant when the principle of problem solving is considered. Under traditional policing, a crime problem was solved in one way: by arresting and prosecuting the offender. This was complemented at times with rudimentary crime prevention measures that emphasized little more than individual "target-hardening" of homes, autos and other property. Still, enforcement of the law was the primary tool in the problem-solving toolbox. Under community policing, problem solving suggests much more—and demands much more from both police officers and residents. Beyond arresting offenders and removing them from the community, problem solving entails altering the behavior of the victims (through more than just target-hardening) and the environment in which the crime is taking place.

Many departments have adopted the symbol of a triangle—the Crime Triangle—to represent the three parts of a problem that must be addressed through true problem solving: offender, victim and location (or environment). Without "knocking down" at least two sides of the triangle (and preferably all three), crime problems that communities thought were solved with the arrest of an offender will simply reappear. Knocking down various sides of the Crime Triangle cannot be accomplished by the police alone (as traditional problem solving was). Rather, this more robust approach to problem solving requires the types of multi-dimensional police-community partnerships that community policing envisions.

So the switch to community policing has meant a sea-change in the roles and responsibilities of the community when it comes to public safety. The concept of "community policing" sounds enticing to most residents, especially those frustrated by the inability of traditional policing to control crime. But the transition to true community policing—anchored by multi-dimensional partnerships and problem-solving approaches—has proven difficult for many residents. The "eyes and ears" role that had been relegated to them was so simple. Residents understood it, and they were comfortable in filling that role, and that role only.

Police departments, even those committed to community policing, have often perpetuated this limited community role. It is not uncommon for police chiefs, commanders, supervisors and officers to go to a community meeting and enthusiastically tout the benefits of community policing, then turn around and describe the community role in this "new" strategy as being the "eyes and ears" of the police. Our profession tends to underestimate the importance of the rhetoric we use in shaping peoples' ideas and opinions. In addition, when discussing our performance, police departments continue to over-emphasize arrest statistics, special enforcement programs, and other measurements of more traditional policing tactics. We simply haven't come up with a new and appropriate set of community policing measures, so we continue to rely on the tried and true.

Even in those instances where police departments have created new mechanisms to support partnerships and problem solving, we have tended to fall back on old ways. The "beat meeting" offers a good example. Regular (often monthly) meetings between the officers assigned to a police beat and the residents and other stakeholders on that beat have become a fixture of most community policing strategies. These meetings are meant to be a forum for exchanging information, identifying priorities and developing action plans—in other words, a forum for cooperative problem solving. In reality, beat meetings in many cities have become little more than "walk-in 9-1-1 sessions." Citizens come to voice their concerns. The police dutifully record those problems. The police go away, promising to deliver with some action before the next meeting. One can argue that it is still a positive development that police and community are meeting—and talking—on a regular basis. But unless we use these meetings as a forum for engaging one another in true partnerships and problem solving, then we miss an important opportunity to institutionalize community policing and make it work.

Taking community policing to the next level—a level in which the safety of neighborhoods is indeed a shared responsibility—remains our biggest challenge and our greatest hope. Until now, police departments have expended considerable energy and resources in developing the basic strategy and preparing our own people to implement. What we have not done adequately enough is prepare the community for community policing. This is a task that is essential to our success and one in which the police must take a lead role, just as we did in preparing our own organizations for community policing.

NEW APPROACHES

In preparing the community for community policing, police departments must be as thorough, as rigorous and as persistent as we have been in preparing our own members. That means applying to the community the same types of strategies we used internally: generating community understanding and buy-in; providing residents with the knowledge and skills they need to implement the concepts of community policing, making information available to residents through open, cooperative information technology projects; and encouraging community involvement in the new tools and tactics developed for community policing.

Public Awareness and Understanding

The whole concept of community policing defies a single, common definition. The fact that each agency implements the philosophy through different tactics is inherent in the philosophy itself. This has led to a splintered public understanding of what community policing is and what it means to the average resident. Without a strong effort on the behalf of the police to educate the community about what community policing means in a particular city, residents will tend to fall back on what they *think* community policing is. For some residents, that will mean police foot patrols and neighborhood watches. For other residents, it will mean enhanced traditional law enforcement and crime prevention strategies. For still others, community policing will mean specialized programs such as DARE, GREAT, Police Athletic Leagues, and the like.

The bottom line is that left to chance, residents will define community policing by whatever preconceived notions they bring to the table. It will be extraordinarily difficult for police and community to move forward with community policing without a common definition and a common understanding of what that definition means. While this process should be as collaborative as possible, it is up to the police to take the lead in developing and communicating a jurisdiction's definition of community policing.

In the District of Columbia, community policing has been defined not as a single strategy or a loose amalgam of programs. Rather, it has been defined as a concrete, three-part philosophy called "Policing for Prevention." This label reminds officers and residents that the primary mission of public safety is the prevention of crime. The definition of "Policing for Prevention" spells out the specific strategies that will be employed to meet that mission: focused law enforcement, neighborhood partnerships and problem solving, and systemic prevention. Each of these strategies is defined with some precision, and examples of activities that fit within each are provided. Critically important is the concept that while "Policing for Prevention" creates a shared responsibility among police and community, different strategies will require a different level of involvement by each partner. Whereas the police will take the lead role in focused law enforcement, the community and other governmental agencies will have the primary role in systemic prevention efforts.

With a definition of community policing in place, the next step is to communicate it—with the twin goals of raising both awareness and understanding in the community. This is a difficult, long-term, and potentially expensive process, but it is critical to developing the community buy-in and understanding that are essential to community policing.

Chicago has achieved considerable success in marketing its community policing strategy, known as CAPS (Chicago's Alternative Policing Strategy). Chicago's extensive public education and outreach strategy for CAPS has relied on both the mass media and grassroots organizing, and everything in between. A coordinated mass media campaign included both paid and public service advertising for radio, television and newspapers; transit advertising; billboards; information kiosks, and other outlets. The police department also began producing a twice-monthly television program that airs on both the municipal cable channel as well as a local network affiliate. At the grassroots level, outreach was made to churches, block clubs, community organizations, and other entities with a strong presence and history in the city.

These types of comprehensive marketing initiatives are not inexpensive, especially when agencies are competing with thousands of other commercial advertising messages during critical time periods. But the return on investment can be tremendous. In Chicago, public recognition of community policing rose from 53 percent to 79 percent in the two years that coincided with the public education strategy. The largest percentage of residents reported hearing about CAPS through television—both news reports, advertisements and the department's cable program.

Training for the Community

In preparing the community for community policing, raising public awareness—as Chicago and other cities have done quite successfully—is the critical first step. But simply getting residents to recognize that community policing exists and to understand its basic tenets is not enough. Police departments must follow up awareness activities with programs that provide residents with the skills they need to practice community policing in their neighborhoods. As police departments have done with their own officers, skills-building in the community will be accomplished primarily through hands-on training and practice.

American police departments have been involved in community training for many years, primarily through citizen academies and similar efforts. These programs provide residents with valuable information on police structures, policies and procedures and on what individual officers do in serving the community. Typically, they show how 9-1-1 calls are received and dispatched, how arrests and interrogations are conducted, how prisoners are processed, and the like. As such, these training programs have served to reinforce many of the aspects of traditional policing, including the passive "eyes and ears" role of the community. Traditional citizen academies, even when updated for community policing, have not adequately equipped the community with the information and skills it needs to be full, active and engaged partners in problem solving. That type of information-transfer and skills-building can come about only through training for the community that is rigorous and ongoing, and which covers the areas that residents need help with.

To support community policing in the District of Columbia, the Metropolitan Police Department initiated the Partnerships for Problem Solving (PPS) community training program as an alternative to the traditional citizen academy approach to community training. Unlike citizen academies, which typically require residents to come to the police for training, PPS brings the training to the community. Training sessions are held in church basements, community centers, even community leaders' homes. This truly community-based approach not only ensures greater resident access to the training; it also sends a powerful, symbolic message that the police consider the training so critical that they will come to the community to provide it.

PPS training is also rigorous and systematic. In D.C., residents and police officers on each of our eighty-three police service areas (PSAs) are trained together in a comprehensive, five-step problem-solving process. During training, this process is not taught as abstract theory; it is applied to real problems, affecting real people, on the PSA. Through this hands-on approach, residents develop the skills and experience that can be used on other, subsequent problems in the community.

Finally, the PPS training not only develops problem-solving skills but also reinforces the principle of partnerships. Because officers and residents train together, they learn to work together as well. The goal is to ensure that the trust, respect, and comfort that are developed during a controlled setting of training are easily transferred into the "real world" of PSA meetings and problem-solving strategies that follow. While it remains too early to measure the effectiveness of these and other comprehensive community training programs, they do appear to be developing both individual leadership and broad capacity in the community to engage in community policing.

Information Sharing Through New Technology

Awareness of community policing's principles and training in specific skills and techniques are the first two steps in preparing the community for community policing. The next step involves providing community members with the information and information tools they need to implement what they have learned. This requires police departments to freely share information about crime and crime trends, as well as tactics and operations—but to do so without compromising ongoing investigations or the privacy rights of individuals. It requires a commitment on the part of police departments to be forthright and consistent in the information they provide to the community and the speed with which that information is provided.

For many police departments, the sharing of information with the community represents a dramatic change in standard operating procedures. In fact, law enforcement in the United States has a long tradition of *not* sharing information with the community for a variety of reasons—not alarming the community, not wanting to appear ineffective or incompetent, protecting the reputations of city and police leaders, etc. The irony, of course, is that securing information from the community usually has had the opposite effect of actually increasing fear, promoting images of incompetence, and hurting government leaders.

With the explosion of mass media in the late-twentieth century, the issue of secrecy became a moot point. Community members who consume even a moderate amount of television, radio and other mass media cannot possibly avoid the growing amount of news coverage on crime and the increasing sensationalism of the coverage. As competition in the news media intensified during the 1990s, media coverage of crime exploded (even as crime rates themselves declined). It seems as though the network evening news programs devoted an extraordinarily greater amount of time to crime in 1995 than they did in 1990. And while crime coverage has declined somewhat since 1995, it still remained far more prominent at the end of the 1990s than at the beginning of the decade. This trend was even more pronounced in local news, especially local television news. For police departments across the nation, the days of not providing information to the community (or the news media) and hoping no one would even find out are over.

With community policing, information-sharing with the community has become a necessity for all departments, as opposed to a luxury that a department could choose to provide. It only makes sense that we cannot possibly expect to have full, active, and productive partnerships if only one partner has access to information. For community policing to be successful in the future, regular, ongoing, real-time information-sharing must be the standard, not the exception.

The good news is that new technology makes this information transfer easier, faster and cheaper to accomplish. With the World Wide Web and e-mail, police departments can now deliver to residents' desktops specific information about recent crime and crime trends. Third-party organizations that facilitate the exchange of information from police to community have sprung up, and their presence will likely grow in the future. In Washington, D.C., Salt Lake City, and elsewhere, a Web site called *crimereports.com* takes summary incident information—what we used to call "police blotters"—organizes it by community, and sends out e-mails on a regular basis to residents who have signed up for the free service. Archives of these crime reports are available via the Web.

Other police departments have begun providing crime maps on their Web sites. This allows residents to see, in a clear and graphic manner, the same crime trends that police officers can through their internal crime mapping and GIS systems. In addition, community crime alerts, wanted person mugshots and descriptions, and aggregate statistics by community have all become regular features of many law enforcement Web sites.

The result of these and other information-sharing systems is that residents no longer have to wait for a monthly meeting with the police to get information about crime in their communities. Nor do residents have to rely on the morning newspaper or the evening news to get their information about crime (very little of which pertains to their immediate neighborhood). In this new era of information-sharing, data is provided almost instantaneously to the community, and once posted, it is available at all times for residents to reference. As a result, community members are better informed—and, thus, better prepared—when they do attend training sessions, beat meetings or other venues where problem solving is taking place.

New technology is also making it easier and more efficient for residents to provide information to the police—promoting the two-way information-sharing process that is essential to community policing. Various police departments—Sacramento and San Jose in California being among the pioneers—now allow residents to report various non-emergency property crimes via their Web sites. Other departments have established Web- and e-mail-based capabilities for reporting drug tips, graffiti, gang activity, and various other criminal or suspicious events in their neighborhoods. These interactive approaches not only increase the quantity and quality of information that comes to the police; they also free up other police resources from routine administrative matters that can instead be applied to emergency response or proactive policing.

The bottom line for police departments committed to community policing is this. Absent a compelling reason not to (and there are legitimate reasons), information that police departments provide to our members should also be provided to our residents, and it should be provided with similar speed and detail. Only then can we expect our partners in community policing to have the information they need to be fully equipped and engaged.

New Tools for the Community

Just as community policing has provided police officers with a wealth of new and creative approaches to solving crime and disorder problems, so too has it offered new tools for the community. In fact, many of the new tools that have become commonplace in community policing—nuisance abatement, liquor license scrutiny, and others—are effective only when police and community work together on implementing them. For example, Washington, D.C.'s Operation Crackdown, which targets nuisance properties, is possible only because of the volunteer efforts of local attorneys, who are supported by police officers who provide crime reports and residents who provide observational data.

Some of the new community-policing tools are designed specifically for the community, however. One increasingly popular tool is court watch. Under this program, citizen volunteers identify court cases of concern to the community and then attend court sessions in small groups as a show of solidarity against crime in their community and a show of support for their neighbors who have been victimized. In some jurisdictions, court watch organizers, like the victims themselves, are even allowed to present "impact statements" at sentencing hearings—in effect, legitimizing the fact that some crimes and some criminals do indeed victimize not just individuals, but entire communities. In addition to using the court watch tool in criminal courts, some communities have expanded the concept to include housing courts, drug courts and other specialized panels, such as liquor control commissions. Court watch programs not only send a strong message to the judicial system and prosecutors that their actions are being scrutinized; they also keep the community engaged in the criminal justice process beyond the early stages of the process. This serves to further strengthen and extend police-community partnerships.

Another common tool for community members is citizen patrols. Historically a cornerstone of traditional neighborhood watch programs, citizen patrols are being enhanced to support the community's larger role in community policing. Whereas in the past, such patrols were designed primarily to be an extra set of "eyes and ears" for the police, citizen patrols are maturing into a more robust and effective community policing tool. For one thing, residents are doing more than simply providing a community presence and calling police if they see a crime in progress. Increasingly, these groups are using their patrols as an opportunity to inventory environmental or other quality-of-life problems in their communities—things such as abandoned vehicles, burned-out street lights, trash, graffiti, or sneakers strewn over power lines (a sign of gang activity in many communities). These problems are then presented to the appropriate municipal agencies for resolution, often-times through the local police district or precinct.

Other citizen-patrol groups incorporate the faith community in direct outreach to teenagers either directly involved in gangs or other criminal activity or at least at high risk of engaging in this type of behavior. This type of focused, more intensive citizen-patrol effort will likely grow as the faith community and other service organizations come to recognize the common goals they share with the police.

The dramatic growth in the problem-solving toolbox is affecting both police and community. And as the community comes to recognize its new role in community policing, and as it moves beyond its traditional "eyes and ears" role, this toolbox will continue to expand and become more effective.

TAKING COMMUNITY POLICING TO THE NEXT LEVEL

Just what does the "next level" of community policing look like? While it is difficult to know the answer to that question with total precision, we do know some factors that will dramatically influence this evolving policing strategy in the new millennium.

Internally, police organizations will continue to evolve into more technologically savvy and neighborhood-based entities. Accountability—to the police command, municipal leaders, the news media and, above all, the community—will be the watchword for agencies. This new focus on accountability will emphasize the need for results (a reduction in crime and citizen fear) as opposed to simply activities (number of arrests, traffic citations, etc.). Like community policing itself, accountability will also become more and more geographically based. Police officers and their supervisors will have to answer for the results in a very defined geographic area for which they, and they alone, are ultimately responsible. Providing these officers and supervisors with the resources and tools they need to do the job will be among the biggest challenges for police executives.

Perhaps the most significant hurdle in taking community policing to the next level lies outside the police organization. It involves fully preparing the community for its role in community policing and then providing the community with the tools it needs to fulfill that new role. Even though these functions lie outside the traditional role of the police, it is police departments and police executives who must play a major role in meeting these needs. We must be ready to provide the outreach and organizing, the training, the information and information technology, and the new tools that our partners in community policing will need. Without the direct and consistent intervention of the police in these activities, it is likely that, in many cases, residents will slip back into the comfort of the limited and passive "eyes and ears" role that traditional policing carved out for them.

The continued growth and development of new technology will foster this process by making it easier, cheaper and more efficient for residents to access the information they need to fulfill their new roles. But even with new technology, it will still take the energy, commitment and direct intervention of the police in preparing the community for community policing—and helping them, and us, succeed.

4

Creative Community Policing Initiatives in Columbia, South Carolina

Professor Carroy U. Ferguson

❖

To meet the public safety needs of increasingly diverse neighborhoods in cities across the nation, creative and innovative community policing initiatives seem to be required to curb and to prevent crimes and related problems and to bridge the gap between the police and citizens through creative community involvement in policing activities. Community policing is guided by the values of building partnerships, people helping people, and community organizing (Kelling, 1998; Goldstein, 1990). In this light, community policing initiatives in Columbia, South Carolina, are characterized by the concept of "shared responsibility." In this chapter, therefore, the creative and innovative community policing initiatives in Columbia, South Carolina, are examined. This discussion thus focuses on the following questions as they relate to the community policing initiatives of the Columbia Police Department and the City of Columbia, South Carolina:

- What was Columbia's initial challenge for engaging in community policing, and what were the events leading to Columbia's community policing initiatives?
- How did Columbia develop, manage, and operationalize its Comprehensive Communities Program (CCP) as a community policing initiative, what are some of the CCP programmatic activities, and what is the function of the innovative police roles called "police community mobilization officers" and "residential community officers"?
- What are the elements of Columbia's vision for continuing its ongoing community policing efforts and what efforts are being made to continue to establish

community policing as a philosophy jurisdiction-wide, which is reflected through the department's infrastructure?

- What are some of the creative and innovative Columbia Police Department–sponsored outreach programs which promote community policing?
- What are some factors that will help Columbia sustain its community policing initiatives, and what are some general implications or conclusions that can be drawn?

First, however, a brief history of the City of Columbia and the emergence of its police department is provided.

A BRIEF HISTORY OF COLUMBIA, SOUTH CAROLINA, AND ITS POLICE DEPARTMENT

Located in the geographical center of South Carolina, Columbia is arguably the first city, as well as the second planned capital in America. Named for Christopher Columbus after a heated debate in the state's senate, it was founded March 22, 1786 and was built on a site that was then occupied by the plantations of John and Thomas Taylor. At the time of Columbia's inception, Charleston was the capital of South Carolina. However, there were those who lived in the interior of the state who were opposed to having a capital on the Atlantic coast. Columbia was thus considered an alternative compromise. It is now the largest city in South Carolina.

The original town of Columbia was designed as an area of four-hundred blocks in a two-mile square. Speculators and prospective residents were sold half-acre lots and had to build a house within three years of their purchases or they would receive a 5 percent penalty. Columbia received its first charter as a town in 1805, with an intendent and six wardens as the governing body. Columbia became a chartered city in 1854, with an elected mayor and six alderman as the governing body. From its inception, the town grew rapidly, and by 1800, the population was nearing 1,000. By 1816, there were 250 homes in the town, with a population of over 1,000. Early policing issues were related to public drunkeness, gambling, and poor sanitation. These issues were policed by commissioners who comprised the local government until 1797, at which point a new role, a Commissioner of Streets and Markets, was created by the General Assembly to take over these duties.

By all accounts of early Columbia, policing the new town was a hit-and-miss proposition in the early 1800s. By 1808, however, a town marshal was appointed who walked through the town twice a day. On Sundays, in particular, the town marshal would pass through the town, once in the morning and once in the afternoon, to deal with any disorderly conduct or out-of-the-ordinary behavior. The town marshal also served as clerk of the town market. In 1824, an official town guard was created, which involved a form of citizen participation and could be viewed as Columbia's first early gesture toward community policing. The policing duties were then carried out by a small department of ten. The captain was paid $33.33, the sergeant $20.00, and each private earned $18.00. Citizens, however, could buy an exemption for serving in the guard for $5.

When General Sherman marched to the sea in 1865 during the Civil War, the entire city of Columbia, like many other Southern cities, was badly damaged because of all the shelling. Many years would pass, but with the dedication of its citizenry, Columbia eventually regained its prominence and returned to some form of legitimate governance. By the late nineteenth century, Columbia, South Carolina, had recovered to a point of being a cotton manufacturing, agricultural, and industrial center in the South.

In the early 1900s, a police barracks was built behind Columbia's city hall at a total cost of $6,000. The police department consisted of a chief and forty-three officers. Examples of fines that were enforced by the department included: (1) airing your knickers in public (a $1.00 fine); (2) removing sand from the city street (a $5.00 fine); and (3) allowing livestock to run in the city streets (a $10.00 fine). The total operating budget of the department was $44,851. It was during this time that Columbia's police department purchased its first gasoline-powered patrol wagon and a motorcycle, to augment the department's stable of four horses and ten bicycles.

By 1955, the Police Department of Columbia had grown to 147 sworn officers. The department also included a parking patrol force, comprised of 9 female non-sworn officers. Additionally, a new headquarters, located on Lincoln Street, was constructed for the department and the department had its own short-wave radio station (W4XAH). In 1973, the Police Department of Columbia hired its first female sworn officer. In 1980, the city was divided into four patrol districts or precincts. By 1985, a computer-aided dispatch (CAD) was added to the department's communications center. In 1990, a new chief of police was installed. With this transition in leadership, Columbia began to implement in earnest community policing initiatives which directly involved the citizenry in participatory policing efforts. As part of these initiatives, the city was divided into three patrol regions, consisting of two patrol divisions each, and "substations" were initiated in troubled public housing projects. In addition to substations, established later was what were called "Kobans," a Japanese term for a local police substation that is highly visible and accessible to citizens with augmented services. When initially established, Columbia's Kobans were staffed by two police officers and an Urban League program director. It also served as a part-time base for a social worker and a "police community mobilization officer," as well as a part-time base for such organizations as a community block club and the Columbia Housing Authority. By 1997, mobile data computers were placed in police vehicles which allowed officers to have access to a statewide computer network. The department has now grown to include a total of 354 including sworn officers (287), non-sworn officers (44), and part-time school crossing guards (23). The department has an operating budget of $16,169,809. Various buildings also have been rehabilitated to accommodate the personnel. For example, a 100-year-old town hall building, located in a neighborhood called Eau Claire, was rehabilitated to serve as the North Region Police Headquarters. A new police headquarters complex was also relocated to a rehabilitated building previously called the Old Jail House Building, which is adjacent to the older Lincoln Street headquarters facility.

Today, Columbia is a multi-ethnic community. According to the 1990 census and Columbia's Planning Department's 2015 population-growth projections, Columbia is also becoming more racially diverse. Further, it is a city of well-organized neighborhoods. The population of Columbia is comprised of 54 percent whites and 44 percent African Americans. The remaining 2 percent of the population primarily include Asian and Pacific Islanders. Columbia's citizenry of approximately 100,000 live within a four-county area with a population of 500,000 people. The average home in Columbia is valued at approximately $83,000, and the median income of the population is $23,200. Approximately 20 percent of all families in Columbia live below the poverty line, while 30 percent of African Americans in Columbia live below the poverty line. About 45 percent of Columbia's population own their own homes, as compared to a national average of 65 percent. Despite a modest growth in the population since the 1990 census, it is interesting to note that overall the percentage of citizens in Columbia who own their own homes is declining. Like most cities, the population of Columbia is also an aging population.

COLUMBIA'S FIRST CHALLENGE FOR COMMUNITY POLICING INITIATIVES: EMBRACING THE IMPORTANCE OF COMMUNITY INVOLVEMENT

The police are often expected to be "the problem-solvers" in most communities. To become more effective in addressing the substantive problems of the twenty-first century, it is important, however, for police organizations to embrace more creative approaches to policing activities and to recognize the futility of their former self-defeating approaches. Like most law enforcement organizations in America, the Columbia Police Department, prior to its community policing initiatives, was primarily incident-driven in its attempt to be responsive to the public's perceptions about three duties of the police. That is, the public's perceptions about the police are related to the following parameters: (1) response time, (2) visibility, and (3) the reduction of crime rates as reflected, for example, in the Uniform Crime Reports. While recognizing the relative importance of public perceptions and these three parameters, the Columbia Police Department has sought to extend its activities and connectedness with the community through a variety of other kinds of creative community policing initiatives.

Some police organizations are highly invested in incident-driven, crime control measures without, however, consulting those individuals who are their constituents. When community involvement is neglected, the results may not always lead to the desired outcomes. For example, studies in policing such as the Kansas City Preventive Patrol Experiment (Kelling et al., 1974) demonstrated that preventive patrol alone had no effect on reducing crime. Yet, some departments continue to deploy patrol resources just as they did prior to this study, without involving their constituents, the community residents.

In a Kansas City Response Time Study (1977), investigators set out to measure the effectiveness of reducing crime through rapid response to police calls. This study was replicated by Spelman and Brown (1984) in research sponsored by the National Institute of Justice. Both studies concluded that the success of rapid patrol response and the apprehension of criminals were loosely associated, based upon rapid response to police calls. These findings suggest that patrol management depends upon the length of time between the actual time of the incident and the actual time the incident was reported, both of which are beyond the control of the police. The city of Columbia recognized the wisdom in these studies and began to listen to its constituents—the community residents. One result of following the wisdom of the above studies and listening to its constituents was the creation of Columbia, South Carolina's Comprehensive Communities Program (CCP). According to George Kelling (1998), the city's CCP is based upon the city's philosophy of "people helping people" through close collaboration among governmental organizations, representative neighborhood groups, private agencies, and churches. Since Kelling's observations and findings,

Columbia's community policing initiatives have become more professional, yet some of Kelling's statements continue to ring true. Governmental agencies are closely linked to the CCP. In fact, the administrative agency for the CCP is the city's planning department. Also, the lead operative agency in the CCP is the Columbia Police Department. At the heart of Columbia's program are three "police community mobilization officers." These police officers operate out of community-based offices. They link the police, other city government agencies, social service agencies, and citizen volunteers with citizens who are either experiencing serious neighborhood problems or are creating them. Some of these problems are associated with, for example, disorderly conduct, fear, serious crime, and the quality of life in Columbia's neighborhoods.

Charles P. Austin, Sr., Chief of the City of Columbia's Police Department since October of 1990, embraced the importance of community involvement in policing efforts and thus provides the following perspective about and the challenge of Columbia's current community policing initiatives:

> In Columbia, a quiet evolution is occurring as the posture of law enforcement is undergoing dramatic changes. We must be innovative, proactive and aggressive in our efforts, while remaining ever cognizant of the constitutional and civil rights of those people we serve. It is urgent that our citizens join in and help fight crime. The problems all of us face today require shared responsibility between the community and its policing agency. The challenge is clear. We have a responsibility to identify and accurately interpret problems affecting our communities. And, to accomplish that, our role as police must be that of fellow citizens and community members. Total harmony must exist between us to ensure that we provide services which are consistent with the needs of our community (personal communication, 2000).

EVENTS LEADING TO COLUMBIA'S COMMUNITY POLICING INITIATIVES

There were many reasons that community policing was established in Columbia, South Carolina. However, there were primarily four distinct catalysts behind its community policing agenda. These catalysts can be characterized as follows: the crime problem, the neighborhood concerns, the role of churches, and the police leadership.

The Crime Problem

In the 1980s and early 1990s, the crime problem in Columbia, South Carolina, was serious and escalating (see Table 1, Kelling, 1998; Bureau of Justice Statistics, 1998). Using 1984 as a baseline, Part I Index Crimes in 1993 were up by 20 percent, index violent crimes were up by 60 percent, murder was up by 35 percent, rape was up by 62 percent, robberies were up by 49 percent, aggravated assault was up by 60 percent, property crime rates were up by 14 percent, larceny was up by 12 percent, and motor vehicle theft was up by 59 percent. Only burglary rates dropped during the same period by 5 percent. Between 1989 and 1993, arrests of juveniles per year increased from 475 to 1,091, or 130 percent. Violence within the family was also a serious problem. Two thousand and eight acts of interfamily violence were reported in 1993, of which 58 percent were spouse against spouse, 10 percent were parent/guardian against children, and 11 percent were among siblings (Kelling, 1997).

Table 1 shows reported crime data in Columbia, South Carolina, during the period 1985 to 1995. In terms of patterns, violent crimes peaked in Columbia, South Carolina, during the early 1990s: aggravated assault in 1990; and murder, rape, and robberies in 1991. Burglary rates fluctuated with no clear pattern. Larceny-theft peaked in 1988 and motor vehicle theft peaked in 1990.

The Neighborhood Concerns

In the 1960s and 1970s, the city management of Columbia was primarily preoccupied with revitalizing the downtown area and, for the most part, ignored the problems of its residential neighborhoods. According to one of the presidents of a neighborhood association, "When you look at city government and departments in the 1960s and 1970s, you would pick up on the fact that city government really didn't care much about neighborhoods. The mayor was concerned about downtown, trying to make Columbia a 'Capital City.' They didn't worry about neighborhoods. About the mid-1980s, that began to change."[1]

The city of Columbia is made up of a number of neighborhoods (Kelling, 1998). The Eau Claire neighborhood is one such example. Both city officials and neighborhood representatives agree, therefore, that by the mid- to late-1980s, whether by design or benign neglect, Eau Claire had been largely "written off" as a viable neighborhood. First, middle-class whites had fled the area during the 1960s and 1970s.[2] By the mid-1980s, middle-class blacks were fleeing the area as well. According to city officials, these population shifts were a "jolt," alerting city officials that unless they paid more attention to neighborhoods, the whole city would suffer, including the downtown area. Concurrently, according to a neighborhood president, "Neighborhood residents just didn't feel that they had a part in government."

It was then that the president of the Elmwood Park neighborhood managed to develop Columbia's Council of Neighborhoods (CCN). The CCN was a council made up of presidents of neighborhood groups and associations. One mission of the CCN was to find ways to be a participate in governmental processes, including activities such as applying for Housing and Urban Development (HUD) or Department of Justice (DOJ) funds.

> In the early 1980s, the CCN at first was a modest organization. As the current president notes, only six neighborhoods were at the table in the early 1980s. Yet, for citizens, its creation provided an urgently needed voice in local governance. Its overall aims were to prevent conflict among neighborhoods and to provide a united front in dealing with government and in dealing with mutual problems. By 1985, the CCN had grown to represent 20 neighborhoods and was meeting in City Hall. In the words of a neighborhood president,

---

[1]As found in George Kelling's (1998) version of Community Policing in City of Columbia.

[2]The majority of the urban population now lives outside the city limits of Columbia. The competition generated between the inner city and the suburban areas has resulted in a shift that will have to be addressed if the city is to maintain its central role in the region. The number of households in the City was nearly evenly distributed throughout the spectrum on median household incomes. Between 1980 and 1990, the median household income in the city of Columbia increased approximately 87 percent from $12,393 to $23,216. However, this was probably as much a reflection of the "natural" increase and migration accounted for by the growth of Richland and Lexington Counties as the city's growth due primarily to annexations. Annexations since 1990 have accounted for an additional 16,000 people, for an estimated total population of 126,754 persons.

TABLE 1 Unified Crime Report: Columbia, South Carolina

Crime	1985	1986	1987	1988	1989	1990	1991	1992	1993	1994	1995
Population	100,024	100,959	94,320	97,609	95,982	98,052	99,990	99,990	99,929	100,504	104,457
Murder per 100,000	12	11	16	8	12.5	22	25	15	22	19	9
Rape per 100,000	67	101	77	103	119	105	94	89	67	100	82
Robbery per 100,000	389	446	396	448	?	?	687	595	686	571	697
Aggravated Assault per 100,000	931	956	990	1197	1357	1318	1202	1170	1422	1350	1401
Larceny/Theft per 100,000	6016	7418	6958	7887	7110	7563	7912	6529	7316	7531	7559
Motor Vehicle Theft per 100,000	519	563	573	990	1093	1154	1073	516	753	660	841

"By this time, city government and its involvement with people, and money, and programs, and outreach, and staff-support, and everything else, began to develop not so much to run downtown Columbia, but to run the City of Columbia and to look at neighborhoods. Since then, the dollars and the efforts have gone toward answering the question, What can we do for neighborhoods and how can we involve neighborhoods in government? That is the trend that began in the 1980s and influenced how the Comprehensive Communities Program (CCP) was developed." In his words again, "[Government] now listens and responds. In the same way, citizens listen and respond." (Kelling, 1998. p. 25).

According to Kelling (1998), the CCN is now an association of sixty-four neighborhood groups and, at any specific meeting, it attracts presidents of approximately two-thirds of its constituent organizations. Moreover, the relationship between neighborhood groups and city government has matured. At first, many of the meetings between community groups (whether individual groups, clusters of groups, or later the CCN) and city government were largely confrontational. "Why aren't you doing this?" "Why are we left out?" with the city responding defensively. Later, as city government and the neighborhood groups gained experience with each other, the relationship became less confrontational and more collaborative. Additionally, as the CCN grew and city government worked hard to develop priorities in an equitable fashion across neighborhoods, the nature of the relationship among neighborhoods themselves changed, shifting from a somewhat defensive, zero-sum relationship (if you get it, we don't) to one of collaboration in defining priorities.

By the 1990s, the CCN began to develop and to push for its own positive program. It was incorporated in 1993. The city now provides the CCN with a small annual stipend ($3000) for incidental expenses. Of the constituent groups, one-third are incorporated and all have by-laws. Traditionally, leadership of the CCN alternates between black and white representatives. As will be noted below, the CCN was a pivotal force and played a vital role in the development of Columbia's Comprehensive Communities Program (CCP) plan, as it was orchestrated by then deputy chief of police, who eventually became chief of police of Columbia, in conjunction with other city and community leaders.

Since the 1970s, there have thus been a variety of redevelopment activities throughout Columbia. These activities include projects such as the clean-up of public spaces, park improvement, and work with business associations. Five community-based corporations have primarily been involved in promoting these kinds of redevelopment activities: (1) Eau Claire Development Corporation, (2) South Columbia Development Corporation, (3) Columbia Development Corporation, (4) Columbia Housing Corporation, and (5) TN Development Corporation. It should be noted here that the original target neighborhoods for Columbia's Comprehensive Communities Program (CCP) focused on 26 percent of the city's population: 73 percent of the residents in this subset are African American and 26 percent are white. For these kinds of redevelopment activities and others, the city of Columbia's community policing initiatives have been showcased by the National Institute of Justice in The United States Conference of Mayors' publication entitled, "On the Front Lines: Case Studies of Policing in America," and in other articles.

The Role of Churches

Historically, the churches in the city of Columbia, particularly the African American churches, have often played a role in sustaining and transforming the quality of life of its constituents. While technically the churches are not CCP players, they nevertheless "(have played and) . . . play a significant role in developing a truly comprehensive approach to dealing with crime and the quality of life in Columbia" (BOTEC Analysis Corporation, 1998). One observation of Columbia's churches is that there are a number of them, particularly in inner city neighborhoods such as Eau Claire, and they are thriving.

According to Kelling (1998), there were church leaders in the 1960s who formed coalitions such as the interdenominational group called "Shalom" in Eau Claire. From its inception, the Shalom coalition of black and white clergy had a social agenda and included a strong community orientation. Church leaders believed that "to attack crime, the spirit of youth must be empowered," that "the church must make moral statements about what is happening in the community," and that "the church must be in the community and a force in it." The group, for example, exposed early redlining, discrimination, and other housing and development practices that were impacting the Eau Claire neighborhood. The group developed strong links among political leaders, colleges, and churches. Currently, the Shalom group continues to direct its attention toward housing rehabilitation, a parish nurse program, Girl Scouts, prenatal and family missions, and publishing a resource directory for the community residents of Eau Claire.

As city managers of Columbia began to embrace the concept of community involvement, the City of Columbia and churches also began to collaborate to rebuild communities. For example, when a church called the House of Prayer wanted to use its own funds to build housing for the elderly, the city collaborated with the church to reclaim land for the church. The city condemned the land for the church and made it available to the church for purchase so that the elderly housing could be built. The city then built single-family homes on some of the reclaimed land through its redevelopment program. The House of Prayer now stands in the middle of the elderly housing and the new single-family homes. Similar collaborative efforts such as that above have taken place with other churches in Columbia. Other collaborative efforts, for example, have been directed toward housing for elderly parishioners, transforming various crime-inviting streets, building a gymnasium (e.g., the Progressive Church), and rehabilitating buildings to house church offices in the community.

The relevance of the role of churches to community policing is that churches are arenas where many community residents are inspired by church leaders to participate in civic activities. In this context, it is important to note that Chief Charles Austin was well-known and well respected by the church clergy, which bode well for his desire to initiate and implement a community policing initiative for the city of Columbia. Chief Austin was thus in a unique position of visibility and had the support and respect of city leaders, community leaders, and church leaders.

The Police Leadership

Chief Charles Austin, as deputy chief of police in charge of the operations division, was very instrumental in creating the momentum and community support that is now the foundation of community policing in the city of Columbia. For example, in August of 1990, then Deputy Chief Austin was a key player in a cooperative effort with the Columbia Housing Authority (CHA) in establishing a "satellite station" in Henley Homes, a public housing project. The purpose of the satellite station was to maintain order and to reduce crime in and about the immediate area. At that time, Deputy Chief Austin was also known in the community as a minister, which further enhanced his stature and influence with residents. When he became chief of police in October of 1990, the "satellite station" initiative was well received and enthusiastically welcomed by the residents of Henley Homes. Subsequently, public interest prevailed to open other satellite facilities in public housing communities. In Columbia, these included the following public housing communities: (1) Saxon Plaza, (2) Saxon Homes, (3) Latimor Manor, and (4) Gonzales Gardens. In 1991, an evaluation of the impact of these satellite stations was conducted. The evaluation revealed that crime had dropped 16.25 percent within the areas where community policing operations were implemented.

With Chief Austin's dynamic personality, leadership by example, and management style with attention to the concepts and principles of Total Quality Management, neighborhoods and communities were awakened and challenged to step forward and participate in providing public safety. Through the concept of "shared responsibility," businesses, religious organizations, community service agencies, recognized leaders, and residents throughout the city stepped forward to answer Chief Austin's call to duty.[3] The result was and has been the realization of a mobilization effort unequaled in the history of the City of Columbia.

Since the inception of community policing in Columbia, a three-pronged strategy for better police services has been introduced. It currently serves as the foundation of the City's community policing initiative. The three-pronged strategy includes: (1) the decentralization of police facilities by establishing community-based operations through the creation of satellite stations, along with plans for opening a residential officer satellite station; (2) the placement of officers into their own homes in the neighborhoods and communities within the city through a three-time award-winning Police Homeowners Loan Program; and (3) the establishment of community outreach programs to mobilize the neighborhoods and communities into action to solve problems instead of battling symptoms. When Columbia's community policing initiative began in 1990, the department had only 218 police officers. Currently, the city of Columbia Police Department has a total staff of 354 employees, including 287 sworn police officers, 44 non-sworn personnel, and 23 part-time school crossing guards. From 1990 to 1994, in a little less than four years, therefore, there was an increase in staff of 69 police officers. The taxpayers and the support from city officials, along with the chief of police, were responsible for the increase in staff.

COLUMBIA'S COMPREHENSIVE COMMUNITIES PROGRAM (CCP)

The Initial Planning Activities for Columbia's CCP Project

In 1994, the Bureau of Justice Assistance (BJA) invited sixteen sites to apply for both planning and implementation funding to develop and implement a comprehensive strategy to combat crime. It was part of BJA's national efforts to have various communities in different States establish and be part of an agenda for a national "Comprehensive Communities Program"

---

[3]The lead organizations and partners are: City of Columbia Neighborhood and Community Associations; City of Columbia Police Department; Richland County School District One; Carolina Peace Resource Center; Downtown Columbia Merchants' Association; Five Points Merchants Association; Community Service Organizations; City of Columbia Division/Departments; State Criminal Justice Agencies; General Sessions Court; South Carolina Fifth Circuit; Solicitor's Office; and the U.S. Attorney's Office.

(CCP). Columbia, South Carolina was one of those sixteen sites receiving an invitation. Sites were asked to use two defining principles of the CCP: (1) "that communities . . . take a leadership role in developing partnerships to combat crime and violence, and (2) that State and local jurisdictions . . . establish truly coordinated and multi-disciplinary approaches to address crime and violence-related problems, as well as the conditions which foster them. Further mandates from the Bureau of Justice Assistance (1994) were: (1) that each site was to include jurisdiction-wide community policing and community mobilization prevention initiatives in their strategy, and (2) that each site was to create programming, based on the area's needs, in the areas of youth and gangs, community prosecution and diversion, drug courts with diversion to treatment, and community-based alternatives to incarceration.

As noted above, by 1994 most neighborhoods in Columbia were relatively well organized, both internally and among themselves through Columbia's Council of Neighborhoods (CCN) as a viable overarching organization (Kelling, 1998). Additionally, in early 1993, many sectors of Columbia, including governmental agencies, social service providers, private agencies, and community residents, had already participated in an extensive planning process to secure funding from the U.S. Department of Housing and Urban Development for Columbia to become an Enterprise Community. While Columbia did not receive Enterprise Community funding, much was learned from the Enterprise Community planning process that bode well for mobilizing a more refined and retargeted effort for the CCP planning process. In fact, the CCP steering committee included many of the same players as the Enterprise Community steering committee (especially CCN). The planning process was broadened to include expanded representation, expanded geography, and an expanded agenda (the program areas of community policing and youth services).

The new groups that were brought together in the earlier Enterprise Community planning process (e.g., representatives of the school district and the University of South Carolina; county or state social service providers and city service providers; government representatives and neighborhood representatives) were now joined by police and criminal justice representatives. Indeed, the CCP steering committee, which included police and criminal justice representatives, received a great deal of local input through regular meetings in targeted neighborhoods with neighborhood groups. Sometimes Chief Austin was the featured speaker at these neighborhood meetings.

Capitalizing on what it was already doing, Columbia's original CCP proposal sought to build on existing programs and community relations rather than implementing new ones (e.g., a city police department already creating substations, decentralizing authority, and trying to collaborate with neighborhoods and other agencies). Three target areas or neighborhoods were identified as primary foci for Columbia's initial CCP project. The three CCP target neighborhoods were Rosewood, Eau Claire, and Waverly. The original CCP proposal called for programmatic activities in the following areas: (1) community policing; (2) alternatives to incarceration; (3) drug court; (4) conflict resolution; (5) diversion; and (6) Boys and Girls Clubs.

BJA funding was thus targeted for the following areas: (1) community policing implementation ($990,00), including funding for eight neighborhood police officers, a job task analysis, training, the leasing and maintenance of a Koban, youth employment, and automation; and (2) community mobilization and other CCP components ($825,751), including funds for diversion ($225,000), youth employment ($100,000), job assistance ($10,000), drug court ($200,000), parent program funding ($10,000), neighborhood program funding

($45,000), anti-violence programs ($50,000), and administrative costs. The official starting date for Columbia's CCP was October, 1994. However, Columbia did not receive BJA notification in regard to funding until October, 1995. The end date for the project was thus extended to September, 1997. Today, other funding sources, primarily through the City's Planning Department, sustain Columbia's ongoing community policing initiatives.

THE MANAGEMENT OF COLUMBIA'S CCP PROJECT

As previously noted, Columbia's CCP project and continuing initiatives were and are directly administered by the City of Columbia's Planning Department, with the Columbia Police Department serving as the "cornerstone agency of the CCP effort" (Kelling, 1998). The initial "chain of command" in descending order for the project was as follows: (1) Mayor (Bob Coble); (2) City Manager (Hadley Miles); (3) Assistant City Manager (Leona Plaugh); (4) Planning Director, City of Columbia (Chip Leland); and (5) Grants Coordinator, Community Services Department (Marshall Johnson). Other initial key players in the project included: (1) the Chief of Police of the Columbia Police Department (Charles Austin); (2) the Coordinator of Community Policing for the Columbia Police Department (E. T. Young); (3) the Director of Community Service (Richard Semon); (4) Community Liaisons, Community Development (Roland Smallwood; Eric Cassell); (5) Columbia's Council of Neighborhoods and neighborhood churches; (6) other representatives from city agencies (i.e., police, housing, planning, and school departments); and (7) three police community mobilization officers (Angel Cruz; Milton Frederick; John Sloan) as the frontline implementers of the community policing initiatives. The three police community mobilization officers were and are supported by "residential police officers," now numbering fifteen (five in each of the three targeted areas), who work primarily as law enforcers, but in a community mode. While much of Columbia's police plans focused on either strengthening administrative processes or changing organizational structures, the core of Columbia's CCP effort was and is its community mobilization program, staffed by three police community mobilization officers. The police community mobilization officers were and are jointly supervised by Columbia's Police Department (Coordinator of Community Policing) and Community Service Department (Director of Community Service).

Today, there are three newly appointed police community mobilization officers who consolidate their role in Columbia's anti-crime strategy. The original three police mobilization officers have been reassigned, but because of their effectiveness and accomplishments, they often continue to serve as troubleshooters for other community-related problems in the greater Columbia community. While a special emphasis of the original three police community mobilization officers was on youth, an expanded focus for the new police community mobilization officers is on linking promising youth to senior citizens with special skills through apprenticeship activities.

ACTIVITIES OF THE POLICE COMMUNITY MOBILIZATION OFFICERS AND RESIDENTIAL POLICE OFFICERS

The role of the police community mobilization officers was and is the most innovative aspect of Columbia's community policing initiatives and CCP efforts. Each of the police community mobilization officers lives in the targeted neighborhoods and has a separate office in the assigned neighborhood. Although they are clearly known as police officers, they usually work in plain clothes. The role entails mobilizing and empowering residents to become more actively involved in CCP efforts and implementing activities to reduce crime and related problems. While the style of a police community mobilization officer may differ, the range of activities in which they engage is quite noteworthy. The strategy of community outreach to mobilize neighborhoods and communities into action to solve problems, therefore, frames the nature of the police community mobilization officers' role and activities. Over the course of the CCP initiatives, police community mobilization officers have engaged in a variety of activities:

- running rap sessions in the schools
- addressing street problems (e.g., abandoned cars and illegal car repairs) and traditional hazards (e.g., abandoned housing or buildings)
- speaking at schools and community meetings, or lecturing at local colleges and universities, or conducting workshops
- training other police departments
- training and certifying young girls as baby-sitters
- working on youth employment issues
- managing traffic problems
- sponsoring, overseeing, and/or coaching athletic activities, including football teams and cheerleading
- developing neighborhood legal clinics
- organizing community clean-ups and dealing with other quality-of-life issues such as drainage
- dealing with loitering, break-ins and neighborhood drug problems
- organizing boys and girls groups
- obtaining school bus service for young children who are exposed to traffic hazards
- counseling elementary and older students with school problems
- creating summer intern programs for youth
- helping citizens influence police response to calls for service
- serving as a substitute teacher in one instance
- working with graduate students to develop a community resource book and an address book for a neighborhood citizens group
- writing reference letters to schools and potential employees for community volunteers
- developing a cadre of volunteers to help deal with problems in various neighborhoods.

Residential police officers work very closely with the police community mobilization officers. Residential police officers are community foot patrol officers and have beats in the neighborhoods which span various areas. According to a report by BOTEC Analysis Corporation (1998), these foot patrol officers are known in the neighborhoods as people and as enforcers of the law and have been credited by some citizens with helping to keep crime low, traffic under control, and property values up. Anecdotal information suggests that the residential police officers enjoy the respect of many citizens who have come to know them as people and as police officers who care about the quality of life in the neighborhoods.

CCP COMMUNITY-BASED, PREVENTION-ORIENTED PROGRAMS WHICH SUPPORT COLUMBIA'S COMMUNITY POLICING INITIATIVES

Emerging out of Columbia's CCP efforts were a number of community-based, prevention-oriented programs designed to support the community policing initiatives. Preventive program activities thus have emerged or have been created in the following areas: (1) parenting; (2) adolescent pregnancy prevention; (3) domestic violence; (4) youth diversion program; (5) recreational programs; (6) drug prevention; (7) conflict management among youth; (8) youth employment; (9) alternatives to incarceration; and (10) drug court. The intent of these activities is to focus on resolving problems rather than focusing on symptoms that result in people engaging in criminal behavior.

In terms of parenting, in October of 1996, Columbia's Family Service Center, in collaboration with the Columbia Housing Authority, the Boys and Girls Clubs, the Baptist Medical Center, and the Volunteer Action Center of the Midlands, began a mentoring program for parents in family skills. The theme of the program was "Survival Training for Parents." The first site for the community-based program was Henley Homes. In January, 1997, a similar program was begun at Latimor Manor Homes. Participants in the program tend to be women younger than thirty-five years old, who are at or below the poverty level.

In September of 1996, Planned Parenthood of South Carolina began its "Rising Stars: Teens Together for a Healthier Future," a pregnancy-prevention program for adolescents. The first group meetings took place at Latimor Manor Homes. Group discussions for this program focus on self-respect, life decisions, refusal skills, abstinence, human sexuality, and pregnancy and HIV/AIDS. Other activities include field trips and social activities, as well as mentoring and discussions with the police community mobilization officers and residential police officers.

In collaboration with Richland Memorial Hospital, Sistercare started a domestic violence prevention program in November of 1996. The program created a family violence task force, trained police in domestic violence, trained the judiciary in domestic violence, and worked to increase public awareness about domestic violence. Medical personnel and volunteers were trained in domestic violence and subsequent assessments were provided by Sistercare staff and volunteers.

In September of 1996, the Columbia Urban League expanded a youth diversion program that is widely viewed as successful (BOTEC Analysis Corporation, 1998). In this program, volunteers, under the supervision of professional Urban League staff, provide aggressive mentoring for young persons who have some history of trouble with the law or otherwise. The volunteers intervene daily with the youth whenever and wherever there is a need, including school, home, and the courts. In terms of recreational programs, the Boys and Girls Clubs received two $50,000 grants which were used to create or extend recreational programs in city parks. One city park where a new recreational program was initiated was Drew Park. A city park where an established recreational program was extended with CCP funds was located in Lorick Park.

In October of 1996, the Lexington/Richmond Alcohol and Drug Abuse Council started a program called "Fighting Back." The purpose of the program is to organize youth and to provide them with activities that helps them to reject drugs. It is also a program that is designed to help youth to find support among each other in dealing with resistance to drugs.

In October of 1996, Dr. Richard Miles started a Peer Mediation Program in Columbia's Richland County School District I. This is a district-wide program. District I includes seven high schools and nine middle schools. In starting the program, a two day training workshop was scheduled in January of 1997. Individual school program facilitators were selected to participate in the training and the subsequent implementation of the program. By 1998, a Peer Mediation Program had been implemented in twenty schools and was touted as a model by the South Carolina State Department of Education and highlighted on "The Nielsen Report" on South Carolina ETV.

In terms of attempts to provide youth with employment through CCP, the city of Columbia has a Youth Employment Program which provides matching funds to both summer and after school work experiences for youth. CCP funds were and are thus matched to create opportunities for youth employment. Approved in December 1996 for Columbia's CCP plan was the Department of Juvenile Justice's program called "Passport for Success: An Alternative to Juvenile Incarceration." This program is a highly structured, community-based program for juvenile offenders. The program includes peer group and family training; training, experiences, and rewards for positive behaviors; sanctions that include restitution; testing, assessments, and education to prevent substance abuse; education in regard to discipline skills; and activities for environmental awareness and an appreciation of community service.

In October of 1996, a drug court was started under Judge Joseph Wilson. The purpose of the drug court program is to provide mandatory treatment for minor drug offenders who voluntarily enter the program. Participants attend either Narcotics or Alcohol Anonymous meetings twice a week and group therapy three times a week. Rehabilitative services are provided by the Lexington/Richland Alcohol and Drug Abuse Council or the Lancaster Recovery Center. Participants in the program appear before the judge every two weeks to discuss their progress. If a participant in the program is truant or fails a drug test, s/he will receive either intermediate punishments by the judge or be remanded to traditional court procedures.

ORGANIZATIONAL PICTURE AND OTHER PROGRAMMATIC ACTIVITIES THAT CURRENTLY FRAME COLUMBIA'S ONGOING COMMUNITY POLICING VISION

The Current Reorganizational Picture of Columbia's Police Department

The ongoing community policing efforts of the Columbia Police Department is currently supported by a continuing process to reorganize the department's infrastructure in such a way as to provide the necessary tools and personnel to implement community policing jurisdiction-wide. Although it is a continuing process, much has already been done to reorganize the department. Currently, there are three patrol regions (North, Metro, and South) within the department and various infrastructure units within the department, each with its own unique, yet interrelated purpose, goals, and objectives. According to the Department's Multi-Year Plan and goals for FY 1998/1999 through 2000/2001 (see Appendix 1).

The objective of the new organizational structure was to set the overall framework for further establishing an infrastructure within the Department to support jurisdiction-wide community policing initiatives. The Department plans to continue to develop and enhance an internal organizational and management structure that is in accord with community policing concepts and principles (Trojanowicz and Carter, 1988). Based on various reports, the department apparently recognizes that the entire organization must change to reflect the philosophy and mission of community policing before jurisdiction-wide community policing can become a reality. More sworn personnel, therefore, must be moved out onto the streets to support such a jurisdiction-wide initiative, and the responsibilities and mindsets of police officers, first-line supervisors, and mid-level managers must change from an incident-driven tradition to policing.

Community policing thus requires much more than simply decentralizing operations. It requires meeting with citizens at the grassroots level (Goldstein, 1990). The foundation must be laid to support such an effort. Officers must know what is expected and what is to be measured in terms of the qualitative duties and responsibilities associated with community policing. Traditional policing often focus on the more quantitative duties and responsibilities of officers (e.g., number of traffic tickets issued). The officer must have a career ladder on which he or she may progress in his career, rather than gather concern from carrying out duties that set him or her apart from his or her peers. The officer must know what promotional opportunities are available.

With the leadership and direction of the chief of police and the cooperation of city administration, the department has developed a multi-year plan with an emphasis on enhancing internal organizational and management structure to be in accord with community policing concepts and principles (Trojanowicz and Carter, 1988). For example, the organizational rank structure and internal management mechanisms such as policies and procedures are being revised to reflect the jurisdiction-wide philosophy of community policing. Job descriptions to reflect a change from traditional policing responsibilities to those of community policing are being revised. A planning component to achieve this end is a job task analysis. The City of Columbia Police Department contracted a firm to conduct a job task analysis of the department. The goal of the task analysis was to identify the department's components of community policing and to operationalize the functions according to position and rank within the Department. The responsibility of the firm also was to seek information from community groups and residents by eliciting their comments on expected responsibilities of community police officers.

Strong cooperation from the City of Columbia's personnel department is required to further enhance the changeover from traditional policing to community policing jurisdiction-wide. Examples of the police officer's new responsibilities include:

1. to make door-to-door contacts in neighborhoods
2. to develop familiarity with leaders in their area of assignment
3. to work with citizens to identify and plan to resolve problems
4. to assist in organizing the neighborhood/community
5. to teach residents how to address community problems and conflicts

6. to work general assignments, including investigations within their area of assignment
7. to conduct regular crime analysis profiles for the assigned neighborhood/community
8. to maintain constant communication with residents informally and through organized meetings
9. to enforce criminal and civil code violations
10. to work with other city agencies; and
11. to network with community service agencies to solve neighborhood problems.

Performance evaluation are in the process of being revised to reflect the change of duties. The department is thus continuing to shift away from its performance evaluation criteria utilized by police supervisors, which was established in early 1984. Emphasis on outcomes and quality of services are to be the prevalent criteria for evaluation, rather than the total number of residents served, calls answered, and/or tickets issued. The revised performance evaluations will provide the foundation to reward individuals who have demonstrated expertise as a community police officer. The revised performance evaluations, over time permeated by concepts, principles, and practices of community policing, will be used in the promotional process. Without the internal infrastructure in place, (i.e., revised policies and procedures, revised job descriptions, performance evaluations, revised promotion criteria), however, the product evaluation of community policing operations will be extremely difficult.

The organization and rank structure has been revised by the department to reflect a flattened decentralized hierarchy, which is necessary to facilitate greater freedom of communication and to promote decision making and problem solving at the line officer's level. As noted, the department has decentralized into three regions instead of the two previously in operation. The Criminal Investigations Division is to be further decentralized and strategically placed into each region according to the demand for services. With the exception of the Crime Scene Identification Unit and the Major Crimes Unit, the investigations component will become part of District Operations. On-the-job training will stress the generalist approach amongst police officers rather than the specialist approach. Officers placed jurisdiction-wide into specified areas are to have the freedom and the responsibility to work a wider range of job tasks and to solve problems often left to others.

Instrumental in the reformation of the organization is a continuing review of the Department's needs and justifications for retaining all specialized ranks (i.e., master police officer, corporal, investigator I, II, III) while providing rewards for excellent job performance with a career ladder.

The outcomes anticipated from a jurisdiction-wide community policing initiative and the department's multi-year plan are as follows: (1) reduced crime; (2) reduced fear of crime; (3) increased public safety throughout neighborhoods; (4) increased citizen involvement; (5) improved efficiency of local and federal taxpayers dollars through the provision of adequate internal infrastructure to implement community policing; (6) effective utilization of existing resources through the prioritization of manpower through management of workload; (7) realignment of community policing services boundaries recognizing the importance of customized services for neighborhoods and communities; and (8) investment and commitment of the Department from the Police Homeowners Loan Program into neighborhoods and communities by allowing police officers affordable housing opportunities within the City.

ELEMENTS OF THE VISION FOR CONTINUING TO IMPLEMENT COLUMBIA POLICE DEPARTMENT'S JURISDICTION-WIDE COMMUNITY POLICING OPERATIONS

I. Community Policing Through Decentralization

According to the department's multi-year plan and in accord with the ongoing reorganization of the department, a primary goal of the Department is to continue to implement community policing operations jurisdiction-wide. The intent is to reduce the overwhelming demand for law enforcement services, reduce crime, establish and maintain public safety in the streets and neighborhoods of the City of Columbia, and to mobilize residents to help themselves in maintaining and preserving the safety of their communities. To continue to accomplish this goal, a specific objective of the department continues to be to reallocate and distribute personnel according to manpower availability, number of calls for service, and targeted neighborhood and communities, based upon crime analysis and socioeconomic risk factors.

The City of Columbia Police Department, according to a diagnostic evaluation of the city's neighborhoods and communities, has determined the best possible placement of personnel. The department has planned to place an additional twenty police officers into jurisdiction-wide community policing. Fifteen police officers were requested from the Comprehensive Communities Program (CCP) Plan, three police officers from an Enterprise Community Application, and two from a Drug Elimination Grant from the Department of Housing and Urban Development (HUD) through the Columbia Housing Authority (CHA). The deployment of the police officers is based on census tracts with high levels of criminal activity. These are called "hot spots." According to the study, eight census tracts areas comprising five neighborhoods were identified as "hot spots" during the needs assessment phase of the plan.[4] The twenty police officers are to remain on a fixed assignment for a minimum of two years, and are to be assigned to four satellite stations, and one resident officer station, yet to be acquired. The Department has invested $60,000 into the community resident officers satellite station utilizing funds awarded from the Ford Foundation under the Department's Police Homeowners Loan Program.

The "hot spots" to which the twenty police officers are to be assigned are as follows: (1) the Greenview satellite station (five police officers under Comprehensive Communities Program [CCP] funding); (2) the Allen-Benedict Court section of Columbia (three police officers, one under Enterprise Community funding and two under funding from HUD); (3) the Martin Luther King Park/Five Points satellite station (four police officers, one un-

---

[4]The census tracts identified in Columbia, S.C. as "hot spots" in descending order of criminal activity are: 13, 10, 11, 9, 14, 26, 5, 107.03. Greenview includes census tract 107403; Allen-Benedict Court includes census tracts 10, 11, and 9; Martin Luther King Park/Five Points includes census tracts 13 and 14; Henley Homes includes census tract 26; Colonial Heights includes census tract 5. Crime rates in each of these areas were as follows: Greenville Teenview (violent crime, 130; domestic violence, 13-1 drug trafficking, 179); Allen-Benedict Court (violent crime, 601; domestic violence, 89; drug trafficking, 77); Martin Luther King Park/Five Points (violent crime, 360; domestic violence, 49; drug trafficking, 147); Henley Homes (violent crime, 160; domestic violence, 38; drug trafficking, 11); Colonial Heights (violent crime, 158; domestic violence, 36; drug trafficking, 9).

der Enterprise Community funding and three under the Comprehensive Communities Program (CCP) funding; (4) Henley Homes (three police officers under CCP funding); (5) the resident police satellite station proposed for Colonial Heights (five police officers, one under Enterprise Community funding and four under CCP funding). Each of the locations is to have the dedicated officers to provide twenty-four-hour coverage. Previously there was not enough manpower in these areas for twenty-four-hour coverage. The additional officers will provide an officer to citizen ratio of one officer for every three hundred eighty-seven residents. The department's multi-year plan calls for officers to be assigned as representatives to an established neighborhood(s), community group(s), business district(s), and/or merchants association(s). Department personnel are to organize and mobilize each of their assigned communities into action to formulate and implement a "customized community safety plan." With the participation and assistance from police, residents, and the designated "community organizer," the customized plan is to identify and target problem-solving strategies, both short-and long-term, to readily address needs and wants of the communities. The "police community mobilization officers" are to continue to provide the necessary non-municipal referrals to residents within neighborhood areas to solve community problems. Over the two year assignment, the police officer is to assist in the implementation and evaluation of each neighborhood's/community's customized plan. Such efforts include seeking assistance from and providing support to address initiatives in the U.S. Attorney's Anti-Violence Program. The advantage of a customized plan approach is the effective and efficient use of scarce resources. More often than not, a saturation of community services without specific identified needs is a waste of resources that could be utilized in another neighborhood and community.

The community police officers have and will continue to have the flexibility to make adjustments to their work hours within the shift assignments. In the future, the need for community policing actions will be determined both by the demand for calls for service and by the customized neighborhood/community plan for law enforcement services. Training is essential for the realization of this initiative. Current officers are to be retrained to be in accord with the community policing doctrine and to be deprogrammed from an incident-driven traditional policing style. Skills and techniques are necessary in nonviolent conflict resolution, community organization, program management, and the management style associated with community policing. As best can be determined, the department is well on its way in doing this kind of retraining.

The department, in collaboration with the Carolina Peace Resource Center, trains community police officers in nonviolent conflict resolution and mediation. The Carolina Peace Resource Center obtained a grant of twenty-five hundred dollars for the training of twenty-five police officers. Again, the goal of the training is to assist community police officers in acquiring the skills and techniques necessary to mobilize residents throughout the city under the concept of shared responsibility and to take a lead role in developing a customized plan for each neighborhood and community for the delivery of police and crime prevention services. These kinds of training activities has helped in the department's goal of decentralizing and implementing community policing jurisdiction-wide.

The department, with the cooperation of Cablevision Industries, Inc. and Richland County School District I, will continue to utilize the local cable channels (City of Columbia Channel 2 and RCSD1 Channel) to advertise the many community policing/mobilization programs and opportunities offered by the City of Columbia Police Department to residents throughout the city. The information channel informs residents and youths about ongoing crime prevention programs in their neighborhoods, scheduled meetings, crime prevention tips, athletic activities, social events, and opportunities to share information with other neighborhood and community groups. Experience throughout the planning process indicated a lack of public awareness of the multitude of programs and services offered by the department. According to Chief Austin, fulfilling the need for an additional twenty police officers to staff the existing district and satellite stations throughout the City of Columbia will go a long way in decentralizing and implementing community policing jurisdiction-wide. He notes that the additional manpower will free up police officers' time currently devoted to answering calls. Communities may then be better served through time devoted to conducting proactive operations such as directed patrol. The additional manpower will also provide the means necessary to place officers in a particular area for an extended period of time, to become the recognizable face, the fixture of the neighborhood/community. This cannot be accomplished presently, because of the current demands for services and the lack of available manpower to staff existing district and satellite stations. The strategy is that once community policing is implemented jurisdiction-wide, it will ease the burden of calls for service. The focus and attention will then be on problem-solving and drafting action plans with residents, businesses, churches, and community service organizations. In other words, the focus will be on helping others to help themselves. Theoretically, the fewer calls for service, the fewer the number of officers needed to answer calls. In turn, there will be available manpower to dedicate to proactive community policing activities.

Visibility is to be increased with the purchase of eight additional vehicles, which will be marked "community policing." One new vehicle will thus be assigned to each of eight satellite stations. For added security, vehicles are to be made available to officers participating in the City's Police Homeowners Loan Program to enable them to drive to and from their assignments. Further, availability of manpower will be increased with the utilization of mobile data computers which will be linked to a central records management system. The completed capabilities will allow officers to access information in the field, without having to be tied to a vehicle, or to a satellite, district station, or regional headquarters. Currently, the allocation and distribution of manpower and resources have been reorganized entirely into a patrol function by regions, districts, and satellite stations. Reorganization has served the needs of community policing without tying resources to Central Headquarters.

Patrol resources, therefore, are now community-based, allowing for the implementation of community policing operations. Capital improvement monies, initially earmarked for the improvement of Central Police Headquarters, already have been redistributed to fund the acquisition and the renovation of facilities throughout the City of Columbia. District stations have been relocated to better sites, and older district stations have been renovated and reopened as satellite stations. Additional satellite stations, therefore, have been opened in the following community areas of the City of Columbia: (1) West Beltline Avenue (District station), (2) Hyatt Park (converted District station), (3) Harbison subdivision (joint jurisdictional station between Columbia Police Department and the Lexington County Sheriff's Office), (4) Greenview Park, Woodhill Mall (District station), (5) South Millwood (Regional Headquarters), (6) Taylor Street (District station), (7) Fernandina Road, and (8) Martin Luther King Park/Five Points. And, as mentioned, three Kobans currently exist in Columbia at the Gonzales Gardens community, Henley Homes, and Saxon Homes. Two future Kobans are planned for Lady Street and the Eau Claire community.

II. New Ways to Manage Calls for Service

One of the Department's major objectives in its multi-year plan is to manage, prioritize, and coordinate calls for service in new ways. In order for the officers to maintain a proactive presence within their assigned area(s), it is essential that the department attempts to manage the factors that govern the many calls for service by providing alternatives to the incident-driven style to which the citizens have become accustomed (Goldstein, 1990). Supervisors have the responsibility and authority to re-route calls for service.[5] Call prioritization for the effective and efficient use of officer time is essential in decreasing the number of repeated calls for service. Part of the process for developing new ways to manage calls for service is public education. The management of calls received by the dispatcher can make or break the workload demands of patrol and wreck the amount of time allotted to proactive community policing activities. The personnel assigned to communications in the department are currently undergoing continuous training to improve the prioritization and dispatching of calls for service within the city.

Officers assigned to the communities are responsible for managing calls for service through referrals that are non-law enforcement related. For these kinds of calls, "community organizers" will be available to residents upon referral from police officers to handle the multitude of services that are available within the community. The concept of shared responsibility is that the residents have as much interest in the reduction of crime and in establishing personal safety as the police officers who are assigned to the area. A corollary objective of the department which relates to new ways to manage service calls has been to reconfigure police districts and patrol beats to conform to established neighborhood and community boundaries. The department's multi-year plan reconfigures the six police districts and patrol beats throughout the city to conform to the sixty-four established neighborhoods in the Columbia Council of Neighborhoods within the city limits.

III. The Police Homeowners Loan Program

A major objective in the department's multi-year plan is to continue to place officers into the communities they serve by offering affordable housing opportunities through the Police Homeowners Loan Program. An integral part of community mobilization is the presence of a resident police officer who lives within the neighborhood who has a vested interest in establishing and maintaining public safety. An incentive to police officers to encourage them to purchase homes within the city is the Police Homeowners Loan Program. As noted earlier, Columbia's Police Homeowners Loan Program has received three awards for its innovation: (1) the 1993 Innovations in State and Local Government Award, sponsored by the

---

[5]The following is an illustration of the City of Columbia Police Calls for Service: Emergency Calls-1992(14,514); 1991(13,472); 1990(13,440); 1989(13,779); 1988*(8,340); Non-Emergency Calls-1992(13,440); 1991(13,549); 1990(12,388); 1989(1,847); 1989(7,093); Violent Calls-1992(6,857); 1991(6,894); 1990(6,163); 1989(5,362); 1988(3,176); Property Calls-1992(25,495); 1991(26,653); 1990(25,442); 1989(26,057); 1988(17,854); Other Calls-1992(93,258); 1991(85,785); 1990(80,583); 1989(82,286); 1988(50,411); TOTAL CALLS-1992(153,564); 1991 (146,353); 1990(138,016); 1989(139,331); 1988(86,874). *Partial data was available-Represents eight (8) months only.

Ford Foundation and the John F. Kennedy School of Government at Harvard University; (2) the Audrey Nelson Award (a National Community Development Award); and (3) the South Carolina Municipal Association Award. The Boston Police Department and the Philadelphia Police Department are using Columbia as the model to develop their own programs to encourage police officers to take up residence within their cities. The program is designed to provide affordable low interest loans to police officers in exchange for continuous law enforcement services in targeted neighborhoods. Police officers and their families choose the home. The relationships established through neighbor to neighbor contact runs deeper than from an officer who only calls door to door in the neighborhood. The eight vehicles requested in the plan will be assigned to the officers participating in the program. The vehicles marked "community policing" will provide visibility to the residents within the neighborhood, thereby establishing a sense of security. Currently, there are fifteen police officers participating in the program. Partnerships throughout the neighborhood empower residents with the tools and resources needed to improve conditions and to eliminate/ displace the criminal elements and reduce criminal opportunities. In accord with community-based policing philosophy, there has been a 15 percent reduction in overall crime within the target area as a result of the Program. Nine area lending institutions have offered financial commitments to the city of Columbia, providing up to 50 percent of the loan at 7 percent for twenty years. The city of Columbia finances the remainder of the loan at 1 percent for a total mortgage interest rate of approximately 4 percent over the life of the loan. Included in the Police Homeowners Loan Program is funding to renovate and remodel the residence for up to 110 percent of the property value. The Program also covers closing costs that can be financed into the mortgage. The resident police officers enjoy the advantages of accumulating home equity at an incredible rate compared to a conventional thirty year mortgage. The officers also enjoy moving into a house that has been renovated to their satisfaction, including updated energy-efficient heating and cooling systems and upgraded insulation to qualify for a reduced utility rate. Officers in the program also receive a marked police vehicle to drive to and from work assignments, and are eligible to receive a five-hundred-dollar bonus at the end of each year for living within city limits.

IV. The Dedicated Resources for Community Policing Operations (Source: Columbia Police Department)

The city of Columbia and the police department, in particular, has dedicated at minimum of approximately one-third (32%) of the annual budget to creative community policing activities. The funding for the multi-year plan will assist the department in continuing to realize the goal of jurisdiction-wide community policing. Table 2 gives a general overview of the current dedicated resources for community policing operations. The city of Columbia annually spends $122 per resident on law-enforcement services. The officer to population ratio before the implementation of community policing was one officer for every 481 residents.

From 1990 to 1994, there was an increase in the city population of more than 17,198. However, in 1994, the officer to population ratio was one officer for every 402 residents. This kind of picture suggests that the city of Columbia was and is committed to its community policing initiatives.

The department attempted to implement jurisdiction-wide community policing two years ago, but realized that the current organizational structure, given the substantial avail-

TABLE 2   Dedicated Resources for Community Policing Operations

	Outside	In-Kind	Budgeted Funding
Personnel/Staff	$2,538,450	$92,137	0
Programs/Services	$888,020	$202,579	0
Capital Outlay	$656,076	$344,979	0
	$656,076	$3,771,449	$296,716
Office of the Chief of Police			$1,349,317
District Operations Division			$1,641,975
Criminal Investigations Division			$874,691
Administrative Services Division			$858,252
			$4,724,241

ability of dedicated resources, could not support such an effort. Communication and operational objectives were ineffective and the community policing function was placed back into a centralized unit to salvage the progress achieved since 1990. Currently, the physical decentralization of the department has been achieved, but it is still without a complete infrastructure to support jurisdiction-wide community policing.

Currently, the City of Columbia Police Department operates community policing within the public housing areas. The community policing effort within Columbia's public housing areas consists of one sergeant and eight officers each in four public housing communities: (1) Henley Homes; (2) Latimor Manor; (3) Saxon Homes; and (4) Gonzales Gardens. Within these public housing areas, the officers initiate problem-solving activities and are allowed to make decisions concerning day-to-day operations. The officers are thus evaluated on their ability to mobilize residents to take responsibility for changing the environment of their community; this is the concept of "shared responsibility." As mentioned earlier, there are presently sixty-four established neighborhood and community groups within the city of Columbia's Council of Neighborhoods.

V. Creative and Innovative Department-Sponsored Community Outreach Programs Which Promote Columbia's Community Policing Initiatives

Community outreach programs are offered by the department in conjunction with other agencies. These community outreach programs encourage residents to become involved in community policing efforts in a variety of ways. Through community outreach programs, residents are encouraged: (1) to participate in their Neighborhood Watch Program, (2) to serve as volunteers within the police department, (3) to attend a Citizens Police Academy in order to familiarize themselves and their neighbors with the difficult tasks confronted daily by law enforcement officers and the mechanics of crime prevention programs offered by the department, (4) to provide feedback/input to supervisors on the performance of police officers, (5) to participate in court watch programs, (6) to prepare agreements specifying work to be done within their neighborhoods/communities, ranging from curbside trash collection issues to street lighting, and (7) to work with police in identifying and resolving community or neighborhood problems.

Examples of community outreach programs sponsored by the City of Columbia Police Department are:

A. "Police In Chairs" for Neighborhoods in Crime (PICNIC)   Through this outreach program, police officers identify and target particular streets that experience drug trafficking activity. The police officers, as well as residents in the community, then literally set up lawn chairs along the illegal commerce route of drug dealers to displace the activity elsewhere. Through this outreach effort, strength and zero tolerance for illegal activities and violence are deployed within the community.

B. The Citizens Police Academy   The Citizens Police Academy is a program of citizens and law enforcement officers, designed to familiarize citizens with various aspects of community law enforcement. It is a free ten evening course, which is conducted by the Columbia Police Department and is in operation at the department's training center. Any citizen within the city of Columbia can participate in the academy. The academy focuses on administrative philosophy, internal policies, and guiding principles of law and ethical conduct governing the delivery of police service in Columbia's neighborhoods. Upon graduation, residents have extensive knowledge of the department's daily operations, knowledge of the responsibilities of all employees from police officer to senior administrative staff, familiarization with law enforcement policies and procedures, street survival skills, and knowledge of the various crime prevention and education programs sponsored by the department. A shortened version of the basic academy training is also presented to new police officers. The training is an attempt to establish an enhanced relationship between the citizens and their police department. It furthers the department's agenda of getting the needed citizen assistance required by police to do an effective job and creates an arena to dispel common myths.

C. The Citizens Police Academy Alumni Association   The Citizens Police Academy Alumni Association is a voluntary organization of interested Academy graduates who assist the department through a variety of activities, including assisting at special department events and promoting ongoing group and individual projects that benefit the community. The Alumni Association works to promote and improve community relations, to provide continuing education, to increase community involvement, and to assist and support the Columbia Police Department and other law enforcement agencies.

D. Student Crime Prevention Mobilization Program   Through education and practical applications, the Student Crime Prevention Mobilization Program is designed to develop police, student, and community partnerships, which tests the concept of shared responsibility. Over the school year, the Department teaches a one-semester class called "Teens, Crime, and the Community" (TCC), a prevention and conflict resolution curriculum, at all four area high schools with a combined enrollment of approximately 180 students. Through this mobilization program, students coupled with community residents, police officers, and the Fighting Back organization, also seek to identify needs, problems, and resources in the community. These parties work together to plan and implement Student Action Projects to alleviate problems. Further, students and residents participate in the Department's Teen Talk Show called "The Seed Show." It is a half-hour television program with a call-in format. Students can call in to discuss their proposed projects and associated peer concerns. Ten minutes of each of the twelve programs, six each school semester, is devoted to "Chief on Call," a call-in segment featuring the Chief of Police.

E. Landlord Accountability Training   In this program, residents are trained with the assistance of local attorneys on the methods for identifying and initiating small claims court action against illegal activities at substandard rental housing facilities. Residents are trained to develop cases, utilizing the assistance of police to take action against a landlord to force the cleanup of neighborhoods. If necessary, the case may go to court. The results of court action may include: (1) the removal of tenants at the landlord's expense, (2) the cleanup of property according to resident and police specifications at the landlord's expense, (3) the demolition of the building, (4) fines levied against the landlord with the funds being distributed among the residents listed in the suit, and/or (5) the possession of property for common use by residents.

F. City of Columbia TV Channel 2/Richland School District I Television Channel
In this program, the department in conjunction with the City of Columbia Department of Public Information and the University of South Carolina School of Journalism develops projects for air on the RSD1 Channel and City of Columbia Channel 2. Topics for projects include holiday safety tips, latchkey kids programs and information, places identified as safe havens, victim assistance services, topics of particular interest to neighborhood/community groups, and a call-in format for citizens to ask questions and provide feedback to city officials and administrations to include, but not limited to the mayor, city manager, police chief, assistant city managers, city division/department heads, and city council members.

G. Teen Pregnancy Center   In this program, the department carries out cooperative efforts with the Teen Pregnancy Center, located at Saxon Plaza, the Columbia Housing Authority, and the Department of Health and Environmental Control. The program assists and provides support to teenage mothers.

H. Elementary and Middle School D.A.R.E. Programs   The elementary school and middle school D.A.R.E. (Drug Abuse Resistance Education) programs are a joint venture between the Department and Richland County School District I. Through this program, officers teach drug resistance education in every elementary and middle school within the city limits, including the private schools. As a preventive program, the aim is to equip youth with the skills to resist peer pressure to experiment with and use harmful drugs. D.A.R.E. lessons focus on: (1) providing accurate information about alcohol and other drugs; (2) teaching students decision-making skills; (3) showing students how to resist negative peer pressure; and (4) giving students ideas for alternatives to drug use.

I. School Safety Patrol Program   The School Safety Patrol program, in cooperation with the Columbia Housing Authority and Richland County School District I, recruits at-risk middle school youth to patrol and secure the school hallways, literally turning the bullies and troublemakers into positive role models upon completion of four hours of training. The students are provided belts for identification and utilize teamwork and a chain of command to report infractions. The students are expected to display themselves in a professional manner at all times and not to become involved in verbal or physical altercations with other students.

J. School Safety Initiative   The School Safety Initiative, an agreement between the Department and Richland County School District I, provides working space for police officers to come into the school during school hours to work and mingle through the hallways before school, between classes, and after school. Officers are encouraged to come in and eat lunch at the school to establish a police presence through non-traditional roles. The goal of this program is to eventually certify police officers to substitute teach classes in the schools in subjects other than D.A.R.E. and community crime prevention.

K. The Crime Stoppers Programs and the Department's Web site   The department has initiated a number of Crime Stoppers Programs. One program is the Security Surveys Program. On-site Security Surveys, which include an examination of physical facilities and surrounding property, are provided by trained police officers at no cost to businesses and residential communities of Columbia. Recommendations are given to minimize criminal opportunity and citizens qualify to have approved deadbolt locks installed. A second program is a citywide Neighborhood Crime Watch Program. The department assists neighborhoods in developing and maintaining Crime Watch Programs and maintains permanent lines of communications with all Crime Watch groups. The department further has designed a Personal Safety Program to aid women in reducing the risk of becoming a crime victim. In this program, women learn how to protect themselves at home, on the streets, and in their car, traveling to and from work, shopping centers and school. A similar program has been designed for seniors and for the handicapped. In a corollary program, police officers teach business employees what to look for, what to do, and how to handle various aspects of shoplifting and armed robbery situations. Another Crime Stopper Program is the McGruff Child & Adult Program. McGruff, a crime fighting dog, is used as a technique in teaching children about strangers who may pose a threat to their safety; the program covers a number of topics to assist children in avoiding danger. In this light, an Officer Friendly Program is also conducted in kindergartens up through the third grade to provide students, parents, and teachers with opportunities to learn about law enforcement through visits by Officer Friendly. Yet another Crime Stopper Program is Operation C. A. T. (Combat Auto Theft), a voluntary program designed to help in the fight against auto theft by having the owner to sign a waiver giving police the right to stop his or her vehicle during the hours of 1:00 A.M. and 5:00 A.M. And, finally, the Department maintains a Web site which provides information about the department, educates the public with crime stoppers tips, and explains the various Crime Stoppers Programs.

SUSTAINMENT OF COLUMBIA'S COMMUNITY POLICING INITIATIVES: AN EVALUATIVE PERSPECTIVE AND CONCLUSION

According to Kelling (1998), "Columbia's commitment to community policing appears to be complete. Implementation was initiated prior to CCP funding . . . and sustainability is not really a question" (p. 30). Columbia's Multi-Year Plan suggests that police and city officials are continuing to look for ways of transferring community mobilization functions to community police officers. Since 1990, when a new chief of police with a strong community policing vision was installed, the Columbia Police Department has steadily moved to implement community policing, not as a program, but as a strategy of policing a city. At the core of Columbia's community policing initiatives are "police community mobilization officers" and "residential police officers," who reside in city neighborhoods with the assistance of an innovative low interest Police Homeowners Loan Program. Through substations, Kobans, reorganizing the department's infrastructure, a variety of creative and innovative police-initiated community outreach programs and police-initiated community organizing activities, and collaborative initiatives among police, social service agencies, schools, and the community, Columbia appears to be on a committed and sustained course of jurisdiction-wide community policing.

Based on various evaluative reports (Kelling, 1998; BOTEC Analysis Corporation, 1998; interviews; federal and local documents and reports), some of the factors that have and will continue to help the City of Columbia and the Columbia Police Department to sustain its community policing initiatives are as follows: (1) the chief of the Columbia Police Department, Charles Austin, is highly respected throughout the community and enjoys considerable local political, social, and media support for his community policing vision; (2) Columbia's neighborhoods are well-organized both internally and among themselves, through the Columbia Council of Neighborhoods; (3) churches have maintained and expanded their presence in Columbia's inner city neighborhoods, playing an active role in its reconstruction; (4) there is an impressive level of coordination and cooperation among city agencies, especially among police, housing, planning, and school departments, as exemplified by the city's planning department being the administrative body for Columbia's CCP effort, the police department being the lead agency, and the Columbia Council of Neighborhoods being an overarching community agency in the city's community policing initiatives; and (5) the city's size seems to make many of its problems manageable in terms of a community policing philosophy and strategy. The primary shortcoming in Columbia's community policing initiatives seems to be in not having enough "police community mobilization officers" and "residential police officers."

A systematic evaluation of Columbia's community policing initiatives, using network analysis (Knoke and Kuklinski, 1982; Heinz and Manikas, 1992) and multidimensional scaling techniques (Kruskal and Wish, 1978), confirmed that Columbia seems to have established a common vision for community policing among police and community leaders, bureaucrats, and citizens. The elements of longevity of contacts and familiarity among key players appear to be important factors. Implications or conclusions that can be drawn from this analysis are as follows: (1) for community policing to work, key players from police, city, and the community must be brought together to develop a common vision and a plan of implementation; (2) a broad community atmosphere must be created for establishing community policing among police department personnel, city officials, community residents, schools, and public and private social service agencies; and (3) sufficient resources, for example in the forms of trained "police community mobilization officers" and departmental infrastructure supports, must be made available to successfully implement community policing.

REFERENCES

BOTEC Analysis Corporation CCP Survey, 1998. Provided by the Columbia, SC Police Department from their archives.

Bureau of Justice Assistance's (1994). Washington, DC: Department of Justice. [On-line]. Available: http://www.ojp.usdoj.gov/BJA/

City of Columbia Police Department Multi-Year Plan, FY 1998/1999 through FY 2000/2001.

Goldstein, H. (1990). *Problem-oriented policing.* New York: McGraw-Hill.

Heinz, J. P. and Manikas, P. M. (1992). *Networks among elites in a criminal justice system.* Law and Society, 41, 297–315.

Kansas City, Missouri Police Department. (1977). *Response time analysis reports.* Washington, DC: National Institute of Law Enforcement and Criminal Justice.

Kelling, G., Pate, T., Dieckman, D., and Brown, C. E. (1974). *The Kansas City preventive patrol experiment: A technical report.* Washington, DC: Police Foundation.

Kelling, G. (1998). Columbia's Comprehensive Communities Program: A Case Study. Provided by the Columbia, SC Police Department from their archives.

Knoke, D. and Kuklinski, J. H. (1982). *Network Analysis.* Beverly Hills, CA: Sage.

Kruskal, J. B. and Wish, M. (1978). *Multidimensional Scaling.* Beverly Hills, CA: Sage.

Spelman, W. and Brown, D. K. (1984). *Calling the police: Citizen reporting of serious crime.* Washington, DC: National Institute of Justice.

Trojanowicz, R. C. and Carter, D. (1988). *The philosophy and role of community policing.* Community Policing Series No. 13, Flint, MI: National Neighborhood Foot Patrol Center.

United Conference of Mayors. (1992, September). Columbia's community policing program in public housing. *On the Front Lines: Case studies of Policing in America's Cities* (pp. 13–17). Washington, DC: National Institute of Justice.

APPENDIX 1

I. THE OFFICE OF THE CHIEF OF POLICE

The goal of the Office of the Chief of Police is to provide the delivery of police services to all citizens of Columbia by means of the efficient operation of the Department through planning, organizing and directing departmental activities. The Office of the Chief of Police assures that law and order are maintained in the City of Columbia. The Chief of Police provides direct oversight of Special Events and the Victim Assistance and Internal Affairs Operation, provides a forum to obtain, collect and respond to citizens public safety requests, provides organizational leadership and establishes organizational Espirit de Corps, manages and directs organizational activities to meet needs, investigates citizen complaints, manages and expends resources to meet public safety needs, inspects departmental operations and procedures, establishes organizational accountability, and corrects deficiencies.

A. Citizens Support Services Unit

The Citizens Support Services Unit is under the command of the Inspector. The Inspector reports directly to the Chief Of Police. The Citizens Support Services Unit is responsible for the coordination of Special Events, the Internal Affairs function, and the Victim Assistance operations. Special Events includes, for example, Chats with the Chief, Employee Open Forums, and the establishment of Kobans. In terms of a community policing initiative, one 1999/2000 objective for this unit was to establish and open a new Koban for a total of three Kobans in the City of Columbia by June 30, 2000. That has already been accomplished and two future Kobans are to be established, one on Lady Street and the other in the Eau Claire community.

II. ADMINISTRATIVE INVESTIGATIVE SERVICES BUREAU

A. Training Unit

The Training Unit consists of the Training Coordinator, Secretary, and an officer that is temporarily assigned. The Training Coordinator reports directly to the Major of the Administrative/ Investigative Services Bureau. The Training Unit provides South Carolina Criminal Justice Academy formal cadets with training.

B. Criminal Investigations Division

The Criminal Investigation Division is responsible for the investigation of Part I crimes and includes the identification, location and apprehension of suspects and the recovery of stolen property. Active investigations may be initiated into other areas as deemed necessary by the Chief Of Police. Some of the activities of this unit includes: investigating criminal cases assigned to the Division; providing polygraph examinations for criminal investigations and prospective police department employees; providing photo-imaging services for investigative personnel; monitoring pawn shops to identify and recover stolen property; extraditing prisoners; investigating all reported missing persons; providing personnel for Federal task forces; narcotics investigations; preparing and processing juvenile petitions as required; appearing for court hearings related to the prosecution of cases made; coordinating and managing the Crime Stoppers Program; preserving and collecting forensic evidence; and chemical testing of narcotics.

C. Police/Administrative Services Division

The Police/Administrative Services Division is the core Administrative component of the Police Department. The Police/Administrative Services Division is comprised of the Fiscal Resources Unit, the Planning and Research Unit, the Crime Analysis Unit, the Evidence/ Property Unit, and the Records Unit. Some of the activities of this unit include: preparing and submitting grants to support department operations and programs; manage federal grants; entering incident and accident reports into the computer system; issuing licenses and permits; providing customer service to citizens and other law enforcement agencies through crime analysis requests, records requests, public information requests, and return of property; preparing internal crime analysis reports; analyzing crime data by crime type, frequency, time of day, day of week, location, victim, and suspect; preparing internal research reports; conducting department program evaluations; conducting annexation impact studies; managing and issuing policy and procedure manuals; requisitioning, purchasing, and issuing department supplies; maintaining inventory to ensure operational readiness; disposing and destroying evidence items dispositioned for destruction; maintaining entered evidence items in a secured location in order to preserve case integrity; returning found property to rightful owners; and auctioning unclaimed found property and bicycles.

III. SUPPORT SERVICES DIVISION

The Columbia Police Department's Support Services Division is responsible for supporting departmental operations in the delivery of police services. The Support Services Division is comprised of the Community Services Unit, Traffic Unit, Mounted Patrol Unit, Personnel Unit, Telephone Response Unit, Maintenance/Repair Section, and Fleet Management Section.

A. Community Services Unit

The goal of the Community Services Unit is prevention of crime through education and elevated awareness of the community in techniques which lessen the potential for crime and to provide the citizens of Columbia with Safety Programs, establish Crime Watch Zones, conduct residential and commercial security surveys, conduct presentations on numerous topics to community, school, church, and civic groups, and conduct and participate in child safety events and seminars.

B. Traffic Unit

The Columbia Police Department's Traffic Unit is responsible for providing enforcement of traffic laws and the investigation of all fatal motor vehicle collisions that occur within the corporate limits of the City.

C. Mounted Patrol Unit

The Mounted Patrol Unit is responsible for enforcement of laws and promotion of community policing philosophies. The Mounted Patrol officer's high visibility serves as an excellent community relations contact, a deterrent to crime and as an effective means to crowd control.

D. Personnel Unit

The Personnel Unit is responsible for processing and maintaining files pertaining to potential and existing employees, and is responsible for payroll of the entire department. The unit provides a number of personnel services to all members of the department and is the liaison with all other Units.

E. Telephone Response Unit

The Telephone Response Unit (TRU) is responsible for receiving citizens' complaints and general information requests, as well as completing incident reports on selected offenses by telephone and maintaining manual filing systems. TRU would serve as a back up communication unit for police community mobilization officers, residential police officers, and other staff.

F. Maintenance/Repair Section

The Maintenance/Repair Section is responsible for supervising a crew of jail trustees engaged in the performance of a variety of tasks. These tasks include, but are not limited to maintaining and repairing departmental equipment and facilities, as well as the grounds.

G. Fleet Management Section

The Fleet Management Section is responsible for two hundred departmental vehicles' maintenance, primary liaison with Fleet Services and other City departments. Inventory and maintenance record management is stressed throughout the department to insure preventative repairs.

IV. NORTH REGION COMMUNITY POLICING OPERATIONS BUREAU (NORTH PATROL REGION)

The Columbia Police Department's North Region is responsible for providing services and special operation to handle criminal activities in the northern area of the City of Columbia. Its mission is to improve the quality of life for all citizens by communication and interaction with the community. Some of the activities include: 24 hour, 7 days a week uniform patrol for the northern area of Columbia; criminal investigations; and narcotic and vice enforcement. Services are provided through aggressive patrol strategies, problem solving, and crime prevention methods.

V. DISTRICT OPERATION METRO REGION (METRO PATROL REGION)

The Columbia Police Department's Metro Region is responsible for providing continuous uniform and investigative police service within police Districts II and III to include narcotic and vice operations. The Metro Region is comprised of a Community Patrol (Districts II & III), an Investigative Unit, a Crime Prevention/Environmental Design Officer, a Special Operations Unit, and a Koban Unit.

A. Community Patrol

The goal of the Community Patrol is to provide continuous police services to the community 24 hrs a day, 7 days a week. The officers in the community patrol continue to maintain a valuable link between the communities and the Columbia Police Department. This Patrol

Division is also part of a more comprehensive COMMUNITY POLICING BUREAU for all three Patrol Regions, under the command of the Inspector.

B. Investigative Unit

The goal of the Metro Region Investigative Unit is to provide expedient investigations into all assigned cases to the unit. Investigators are to be committed to exhausting all means possible to insure that their cases are investigated and cleared to their fullest extent.

C. Crime Prevention/Environmental Design Officer

The goal of the Crime Prevention Officer is to institute a strong effort toward citizen education and prevention in the areas of residential and commercial burglaries. On a daily basis, the officer reviews all reports of both residential and commercial burglaries.

D. Special Operations Unit

The goal of the Special Operations Unit is to monitor all Part I suppressible crimes within the region. This is done by the use of crime analysis reports and other regional indicators.

E. Koban Unit

The goal of the Koban Unit within the Metro Region is to perform community assessment of current crime delinquency and statistics, neighborhood needs, and existing programs through surveys and home visits. They will also provide and organize after-school, mentor and non-school support programs.

VI. COMMUNITY POLICING OPERATIONS BUREAU (SOUTH PATROL REGION)

The Columbia Police Department's South Region is responsible for twenty-four hour uniformed police service and criminal investigations and narcotics enforcement for the southeastern area of the City of Columbia. The mission is to improve the quality-of-life and build a sense of personal security through an interactive relationship with community residents.

5

The Value of Measuring Community Policing Performance in Madison, Wisconsin

Michael F. Masterson and Dennis J. Stevens

❖

Community policing has been a strategy practiced by the Madison, Wisconsin Police Department since the early 1980s. Measuring police performance, however, is a recent experience for them. This chapter describes the experiences of the Madison Police Department (MPD) as they measured community policing performance in some of their challenged neighborhoods. One mission of the MPD was to better understand the needs of the residents in the neighborhoods through their own experiences. Measuring police performance is not an unusual practice since many police agencies have studies conducted by consultants and volunteers. The MPD could have drawn professionals and volunteers from the University of Wisconsin at Madison.[1] However, what makes this study unique is that measuring police performance in Madison, Wisconsin, was conducted entirely by police personnel.[2] It is the hope of the MPD by reporting their experiences that other agencies will be encouraged to utilize a similar methodological design to measure performance in their communities, too, as the advantages far outweigh the disadvantages.

---

[1]The University of Wisconsin is the home of retired professor emeritus and one of the architects of community policing, Herman Goldstein.

[2]Captain Michael F. Masterson provided the leadership for the Madison Police Department to develop, conduct, and evaluate their community policing initiatives. In the interest of sharing information so others may learn, Captain Masterson routinely writes about contemporary police issues, in this case Madison's success of measuring community policing performance.

Three lessons were learned from the Madison study. First, by listening to the individuals in the community, the MPD enhanced police decision-making practices, which, in turn, better served crime control issues through quality police services. Second, the MPD is only one of many participants that shape the meaning of quality police service. That is, it is the voice of their clients, through what they see, hear, and experience that should ultimately influence the levels of police service. Finally, MPD police personnel have greater opportunities to develop community policing initiatives and enhance some of their police skills when they conduct the research themselves.

OBJECTIVES OF THE MADISON POLICE DEPARTMENT

The Madison Police Department has a long history of adapting and being responsive to changing community needs. In the mid-1980s, the department initiated a principal component of their community policing strategy by creating "neighborhood police officers" and incident-based surveys. These neighborhood officers were individually assigned to a handful of areas which were already the source of high calls for service and violent crime. The resident populations in those areas were typically lower income and ethnically diverse, living in older, aging rental properties and apartment complexes. The neighborhood officer's job included becoming well-acquainted with the residents—a job description relationship which is not generally part of a response- driven model of policing. Incident-based surveys were a good barometer in measuring service delivery and were started in the department as the result of the quality management movement inspired by Dr. Edward Demings in the early 1980s. Their shortfall was that they did very little to help identify crime and quality-of-life problems facing our neighborhoods then and those which Madison would soon experience.

Some of the community problems identified through neighborhood officer initiative included drug and alcohol abuse, low academic performance, lack of employment opportunities and job training, conflict, poor housing and disruptive tenants, inadequate recreational programs, and undeveloped neighborhood leadership. Today, MPD's neighborhood officers are assisted by county social workers, state probation agents, and city building inspectors, all working from the same neighborhood offices. These decentralized networks have allowed the teams to focus on serious neighborhood problems that contribute to the effects of crime, dysfunctional families, and social disorder. Many of these notions find congruence with policing experts who argue that the police should not deal with crime alone, and they should seek neighborhood participation within a problem-oriented approach (Goldstein, 1979; Kelling and Moore, 1988).

In the early 1990s, Madison's high crime rate neighborhoods were suddenly deluged with the arrival of massage shipments of crack cocaine. As a means to contain the street-level violence which became prevalent, the Neighborhood Intervention Task Force was created to supplement the efforts of patrol and neighborhood officers. The mission of the task force, referred to today as the Dane County Narcotics and Gang Task Force, was to interdict and prevent trafficking of street-level drug sales. In the spring of 1992, the Task Force's efforts were enhanced when the City of Madison was recognized as one of sixteen Weed and Seed sites by the United States Department of Justice. Subsequently, a grant was awarded to help fund and facilitate "weeding out" those responsible for the drugs and violence within the Weed and Seed designated neighborhoods so that "seeding" efforts could occur in hopes of making the neighborhoods once again self-sufficient. The community policing efforts of neighborhood officers was, in theory, to be the bridge between weeding and seeding.

A variety of measures were used to assess and evaluate MPD's Weed and Seed efforts. Hundreds of drug charges and convictions, thousands of dollars in recovered drugs and drug money, seizure of drug houses and assets, and the removal of numerous guns from neighborhood drug entrepreneurs have been good traditional indicators of taskforce productivity. Yet, something seemed to be missing from the evaluation component. Do they see the same improvements that the MPD sees? Do perceptions differ from one neighborhood to another? Where should future problem-solving strategies be directed? In order to assess resident perceptions, non-traditional evaluation mechanisms were developed including the use of neighborhood officers and police recruits as interviewers. The consultants and volunteers would have to wait until social order returned.

MEASURING POLICE PERFORMANCE

There are many ways to measure police performance. For instance, there is a day-to-day monitoring by the police of their operations. This kind of evaluation is routinely conducted by many police agencies. Traditionally, police departments measure arrests, patrol stops and citations, calls for service, response time, complaints against officers, and/or dollar amounts of confiscated contraband and property such as drugs, weapons, and cash. These practices continue and are used by a wide variety of individuals to determine the level of police service provided by an agency.

The principal mechanism for determining police effectiveness has historically been counted and measured in numbers. This practice can be described as bean counting. Ironically, police agencies have never provided a tangible product that lends itself to so easily being counted. That is, since police agencies deliver a service, and in keeping their communities safe are a principle part of those duties, why do police agencies continue to place a heavy reliance on reports that count things? One reason might be because most people understand the results of those measurements easier than other results. That is, monthly arrest data, case numbers, tickets issued, revenue generated, hours spent on foot patrol, and hours spent attending community meetings lend themselves to being easily quantified and measured. Perhaps the best example of nationwide standardization of categorizing reported crime is the Uniform Crime Report. Measuring perceptions, on the other hand, is relatively new to policing. Police agencies today are discovering the impact of these new measurements. Subsequently, agencies are recognizing that what they do and how well they do it is inherently subjective and personal to those who receive their services. Resident perceptions about quality-of-life issues such as fear of crime and police responsiveness are genuinely as important as crime numbers and, therefore, agencies might want to consider them as part of the equation.

Another kind of evaluation is based on explicit methodologically conducted research by professional researchers (who could be officers trained in research designs). This explicit or standardized method of measurement refers to observing behavior (directly and indirectly) and testing claims about causal relationships.[3] The results of standardized measures aid in making informed decisions about the future of police strategies by informing policy makers, for instance, how strategies should be changed, how community members experience police intervention, and how well police intervention relates to expectations of the community.

This thought is consistent with Brodeur (1998) who argues that professional research procedures can tell police administrators or policy makers when a police initiative or strategy is meeting its goal. These procedures can also help better understand police performance for purposes of accountability, that is, both how a department is progressing toward a collective goal and how individual officers are conducting their day-to-day business of providing police services (Oettmeier and Wycoff, 1997). Performance assessment is crucial for achieving accountability and for verifying how productive both public and grant dollars are spent. What it comes down to for police agencies in the twenty-first century is that they become facilitators as opposed to enforcers especially when they advance community policing initiatives (Skogan, Hartnett, DuBois, Comey, Kaiser, and Lovig, 1999; DuBois and Hartnett, 2001). Police agencies can not nor should try to reduce the fear of crime, control crime, and enhance the quality of life standards for their constituents, alone. As former Police Chief of Charlotte, North Carolina, Dennis Nowicki (1998, p. 265) clarifies, "We no longer want to diffuse a problem, we want to solve it." With that said, the question arises as to how police agencies should gather data to aid them in making decisions about police services that might include deployment, tactical limits, and hiring and disciplinary guidelines among officers. How should information be gathered about other issues such as levels of social order and social problems from the perspective of the individuals whom the agency serves? The MPD believes they have one answer—the police agency should develop, conduct, and assess the findings of their own neighborhoods. Officers could be trained as researchers to fulfil this obligation (Stevens, 1999b).

Community policing constitutes the police as professional experts, argue Ericson and Haggerty (1997), because they possess abstract knowledge about risk that is valuable to others. And, one source of that knowledge is through practical evaluation techniques. Professional research in the last two decades has produced significant findings for evaluating police organizations (Stephens, 1996). For instance, in research assessing the community policing initiatives of nine police departments in the United States, the strongest recommendation made was that departments should rely on practical research to help them determine their intervention outcomes in order to provide better police service through community policing initiatives (Stevens, 2001).[4] However, professionally measuring police performance takes a great deal of time and expense to administer. However, the contributions of explicit methodological procedures can help police leaders develop innovative

---

[3]For an in-depth discussion on cause and effect relationships, see Champion (1993).

[4]The police agencies evaluated were Broken Arrow, OK; Camden, NJ: Columbus, OH; Fayetteville, NC; Harris County, Precinct 4, TX; Lansing, MI; Nashville, TN; Sacramento, CA; and St. Petersburg, FL. Some of these agencies did little to professionally evaluate their community policing initiatives and as one result, failed often. For some of these agencies that failed, little could have saved them since there were many factors deterring a community policing philosophy. Yet it was believed that those agencies might have been better prepared for their failure had they exercised a professional methodological system to aid them in understanding where the pit falls were within their city government among their community members prior to initiating a community policing policy (Stevens, 2000a).

ideas on leadership, help them organize the workplace, and aid in efforts to prevent crime, deliver services, and resolve neighborhood problems.

The former Police Chief of St. Petersburg, Darrel Stephens realizes the necessity of applying practical techniques in an evaluation of police performance in order to determine how a police agency is meeting the needs of the people they serve. As Eck and LaVigne (1994) articulate, the need to measure police performance is imminent:

> The amount of research on law enforcement matters continues to grow, as does the number of police agencies that volunteer to participate in research efforts. However, law enforcement agencies cannot afford to wait for someone else to publish studies or to wait to be asked to participate in research. They must assume the initiative and conduct studies that directly address pressing concerns. Certainly, in the area of police problem solving efforts, it is the agency's obligation to research and analyze the effectiveness of these efforts. (p. 64)

EARLY MEASURING INSTRUMENTS

In Madison, in an effort to better understand the perception of the individuals who were recipients of neighborhood officer services, it was hoped that the results from an incident driven survey could be used as a tool to improve customer relations and measure their satisfaction levels.[5] That is, the MPD wanted to know if they were on the path of continuous improvement and were meeting the needs of their customers.

In 1987, the MPD developed an incident-driven questionnaire through trial and error and finally mailed it to residents who had contact with the department through an every fiftieth case-numbered report. The survey solicited resident experiences that related to: officer concern, helpfulness, knowledge, fairness, and solving problems. The survey also asked the respondents how often the officers made them feel safe, what levels of officer conduct they witnessed, officer response time, and their overall impression of the quality of service they received. A few years later, the MPD increased the sampling frequency to include every thirty-fifth case-numbered report. This survey was mailed to complainants, witnesses, victims, and arrested persons.

---

[5]Incident-based attitudinal surveys have flourished since the early 1980s and can be universally applied to almost every police agency including urban and rural, state and county. The Massachusetts State Police have created a similar survey available on their Web site. Incident-based surveys as described and used are valuable in providing organizations with basic perceptions of how they are doing. They also have many limitations. This particular type of survey presumes an isolated contact with a lone employee, when in fact, citizens may have dealt with multiple employees from various ranks and positions. Their response may have been unduly influenced by just one of those employees. It may have been the civilian call taker at 911 Communications Center, a detective conducting a follow up interview, a records clerk or a police officer. Another disadvantage is that incident-based surveys are completed by a limited number of citizens with whom an agency has a short term contact thus excluding the overwhelming majority of residents. Some unions representing police employees hold a healthy level of skepticism on incident based surveys because they have the potential to be misunderstood by the public as a means to complain about the actions of an officer or to be abused by management.

Overall, a similar questionnaire was used for five years. Annual newsletters carried the results of the studies with neighborhood officers and residents alike. Some of the findings included:

- Witnesses reported professional conduct of officers as higher than all other categories and solving problems and their response time were reported as low.
- Customers requesting information reported response time, officer concern, and helpfulness among the highest-ranking categories.
- Individuals arrested reported officer knowledge, professional conduct, and officer concern as high categories, but solving problems as reported as low.
- Victims reported solving problems and putting you at ease as lower than all other respondents, but professional conduct higher than all other respondents. Fairness was reported as among the lowest of their responses.

Other departments across the country were also involved in assessing police performance, but most used consultants and volunteers. For instance, Lincoln, Nebraska, in partnership with a leading polling and consulting organization, developed a telephone survey to collect citizen perceptions of police services. The Quality Service Audit was developed as a way to validate a new, success-based talent selection system for police applicants and to provide community oriented police officers with relevant feedback about the quality of their contact with citizens (Citta, 1996).

Eventually, the Lincoln Police Department used new recruit officers to conduct the interviews by telephone. In this way those recruits became familiar with the department performance indicators and citizen expectations of service more efficiently than in riding along in a police cruiser. Each officer conducted approximately one-hundred interviews in an eighteen-week period calling citizens who had received a citation, been involved in a traffic accident, and/or reported being the victim of a crime. Lincoln Police leaders used the feedback to identify and improve departmental systems and procedures that might have been barriers to delivering quality service and to determine training that helped elevate officer performance.

DISCOVERING GREATER UTILITY IN SURVEYING

Some police agencies were exploring a larger organizational issue about acquiring a matrix of important information including perceptions of fear, citizen satisfaction levels, contact with police, service and program expectations, evaluating alternate response methods, community involvement and neighborhood problems and their severity. This exploration is a departure from the past as historically police agencies have relied on traditional, hard indicators when attempting to measure agency performance, (e.g., response times, total numbers of calls for service, number of arrests, citations, contacts, dollar amounts for property stolen, recovered, etc.). Yet with the evolution of community policing, police leaders discovered traditional measures were ineffective as indicators of community policing or problem-oriented outcomes.

As more police administrators questioned the usefulness of traditional measures that were generated solely through incident responses to assess agency performance, there was a policy move to adapt problem-oriented policing strategies, at some level or another, to address substantive community problems. The concern was not necessarily focused on evaluation since implementation consumed the energies and resources of most departments. Today's police literature is routinely reporting a greater number of examples of simple survey techniques as being conducted to provide police leaders with data about their partnership outcomes. For instance:

> In a recent analysis of 15 Texas police agencies employing general survey methods, 10 agencies were administering mail surveys to measure attitudes of residents toward local police service, but only one had extended the scope of the survey to identify neighborhood problems (Surveys of Citizens' Attitudes, 1996).

> Surveys in the Reno, Nevada Police Department serve as report cards from residents about police performance and image, extent of citizen fear, concerns about crime and quality of contact with department members. In the Peppermill Pop Project, for instance, residents, business owners, and property managers were asked to identify the number one crime problem; could it be solved or reduced; and, what they could do to improve the neighborhood (Kirkland and Glensor, 1992).

> The St. Petersburg, Florida Police Department used a community-wide survey to identify citizen perceptions of neighborhood problems since 1991. Their survey instrument measured citizen perceptions on a variety of quality-of-life indicators and quality of police service (professional conduct, helpfulness, concern, etc.) Comparing 1994 survey results to 1991's baseline, St. Petersburg police leaders observed significant improvement in resident perceptions on these and other issues (Stephens, 1996).

> The Spokane, Washington Police Department, in collaboration with Washington State University, mailed a questionnaire to a random sample of city addresses to assess the public's attitudes toward police services from 1992 [521 respondents] to 1994 [1,134 respondents]. Results such as perceived improved service delivery; reduced fear of criminal victimization; and, increased citizen interest in working with the police were believed to be evidence of progress in the department's community policing efforts. The longitudinal survey also assisted police officers in identifying specific problems by individual neighborhoods and monitored trends over time (Thurman and McGarrell, 1995).

> In March 1994, the Peel Region Police, using an independent marketing research firm, mailed survey questionnaires to over 10,000 randomly selected citizens. The survey, which included opinions and attitudes on community safety, police/citizen relationships and community-based policing, is the most extensive survey effort ever conducted by a Canadian municipal police agency (Benchmark Study, 1994).

> Decatur, Alabama applied the concept of surveying the city's public housing tenants in evaluating the department's effectiveness in reducing crime. They asked questions on resident's fear of crime; impressions of police; opinion of how effective police were in controlling neighborhood crime; and what problems or concerns should receive priority status (Dutton, 1998).

In 1991, the Madison Police Department's evaluation design changed to putting officers on the front lines of data gathering. That design was influenced largely by being designated as a Weed and Seed site funded by the federal government. This new design, contrary to most agencies who utilized consultants and/or volunteers, consisted of face-to-face, officer-to-resident interviews during which the questionnaire was completed. This design continues today in Madison for the most part and is responsible for over eighteen hundred interviews in nine different neighborhoods conducted by Madison police officers. Some of the questions addressed by these officers pertained to perceptions of crime and safety, victimization, fear of crime, neighborhood conditions, effectiveness of police, involvement of property owners, particularly managers of large apartment complexes, and the extent to which residents themselves are willing to get involved in dealing with the problems of the neighborhood make up the core group of questions which have been asked of residents in each of the previous surveys. There were also questions on how reasonably citizens believe the police were treating them and how effective they felt the police were as they conducted their duty.

SURVEY METHODS

Recent questionnaires designed by the MPD solicit responses concerning resident longevity in the neighborhood, their desire to move away, availability of youth programming and day care, likes and dislikes about the area, and their single greatest need for their neighborhood. Some open-ended questions provide the department with additional opportunities to strike up a conversation and exchange ideas on solutions to improve the area's quality-of-life along with probing for information on what residents know about current crime activity in the neighborhood. Officer-interviewers were encouraged to have a conversation with the study participants and ask questions that were not part of the questionnaire.

In order for the police and the residents to combine forces to combat crime and the fear of crime, the police need to hear the good and the bad first hand, and residents need to explain themselves as they wish in a nonconflictual relationship. Agencies need to hear the experiences of residents from their own mouths. They need to hear their community problems and their ideas about how to solve them. They need to help prioritize them in order to aid in solving them in an orderly fashion. Finally, and equally important, the MPD needs to determine the willingness of residents to become active partners with them in helping to solve those problems. Without community involvement, the future of Madison's neighborhoods remains bleak and continuation of the concept of community policing might remain suspect.

What is the best method of obtaining those objectives? Consultants? Volunteers? Police officers can utilize the skills of an evaluator in investigative duties. That is, the investigative skills of an evaluator would be welcomed by most officers since many of them, especially patrol officers, have not completed academy investigative training as of yet and this represents a perfect opportunity to advance their skill levels. In training circles, this might be called a "two-fer": Teach cops methodological techniques in order to be better investigators. Understanding how investigations are conducted gives insight into survey methodology as the two areas largely follow a similar model.[6]

For instance, when a serious crime is reported, an investigator establishes an investigation process based on a theory of the crime: who did it, what crime was committed, where

---

[6]This is consistent with educators who argue that police offices make excellent students especially if the subject matter deals with police related topics or is for personal use (Stevens, 1999b).

had the crime taken place, when had it occurred, how had it happened, and what motive drove the offender. It's a process known to researchers too as they identify the problem to be studied, build a hypothesis and test claims about causal relationships. A theory, as developed by an officer or a researcher, is an integrated body of assumptions, propositions, and definitions that are related in such a way so as to explain and predict relationships between two or more variables. Both the officer and the researcher attempt discovery through a systematic, objective process where the tools used to gather evidence are guarded for validity (are they measuring what they think they are measuring?). Also, both investigators largely utilize deductive reasoning where typical assumptions are made and conclusions are drawn that appear to be logically connected with those assumptions. For example, "All men are mortal. Aristotle is a man. Therefore, Aristotle is moral." During an investigation, any event that needs to be explained provides a foundation for deductive theory building. Through data gathering and analysis, investigators learn whether their deductions are valid. If the data suggest those deductions should be questioned, further testing or gathering of evidence is necessary. These ideas are consistent with Dean Champion (1993), who advances the thought that even if findings support certain deductions, further testing is ordinarily conducted, since investigators want to be certain of their conclusions in order to accomplish their mission. If they're police officers, they're building a case for their recommendations—a conviction—and if they're researchers, they're building a case for their recommendations, too. The sequential steps of a criminal investigation process closely parallels basic survey methodology where a scientific "ear" is developed which helps investigators to listen to the participants, in this case, residents of the neighborhoods whom police officers are sworn to serve and protect.

LET'S GET STARTED: DEVELOPING A NEIGHBORHOOD STUDY

Below is a suggested list of activities that police investigators might want to consider, as they move through a system of discovery. However, a number of other methods might lead an investigator to similar outcomes. Therefore, this list should be viewed as a tentative working game plan but certainly not as an absolute or final list.

1. Identification of the problem.
2. Construct a working casual hypothesis to test.
3. Review what other departments and other relevant sources have done concerning the identified problem and/or hypothesis using the web as part of the search.
4. Identify sample population.
5. Choose a survey design: questionnaire, in-person interview, telephone interview, observation, and/or combinations of these and other methods.
6. Build a survey instrument and/or develop topic questions to ask during interviews.
   A. User-friendly wording.
   B. Scaling.
7. Pre-test survey instruments and survey process.
8. Determine date, method, time of distribution, and method of collection.
9. Make decisions about where data are to be stored and/or transcribed to computer grids for instance.
10. Analyze data.

    A. Develop typologies.

    B. And/or frequencies of events.

11. Report and discuss results.

12. Develop conclusions based on the results.

13. Determine priorities.

14. Get recommendations about solving the problems discovered.

15. Begin the process of solving those problems.

16. Review and summarize how survey process could be improved.

Developing a survey for questionnaires and/or topic questions for interviews might be important if those are the designs a department wants to follow. A brief overview might include suggestions that when questions are asked, there should only be one question in the statement. For instance, it would be confusing to ask: How often do you witness drug sales by gang members on your block? The problem is that there are two questions asked in this statement, not one. Questions and answers (when closed-ended) should be simple, precise, and understandable statements. It is helpful to have a resource, i.e., an officer, or another person, who is knowledgeable of the technical elements of survey development, to ensure that the instrument is measuring what it is intended to measure.

One productive method is that only one person should write the questionnaire and topic questions. Input should come, however, from a wide variety of others such as district team leaders, neighborhood officers, detectives, officers, residents and other city staff teams who work with identifying possible issues on which the department is interested in soliciting feedback. Here are some of the issues Madison police leaders identified:

- How satisfied are citizens with services they received?
- What are the neighborhood problems and to what extent do they impact residents?
- What are the residents' perception of fear?
- What is the effectiveness of apartment complex managers/owners?
- How effective have the police been in responding to problems?
- How well do police officers treat residents?
- How organized and committed are residents to work with police?
- Are there sufficient programs for youth?
- How optimistic are residents for their neighborhood's future?

Survey objectives should always have a purpose. The MPD focused on the goal of improving neighborhood livability.

The second part of building the survey is to create a measurement scale that might assist in quantifying the attitudes of residents. As with other surveys, a scale of 1 to 4 was selected for many of the questions. Using descriptive words that correspond with a point scale helps the respondent to qualify their perception. For example, 1 = very safe, 2 = somewhat safe, 3 = somewhat unsafe, 4 = very unsafe. In the area of problem identification, the MPD selected a scale that identified the severity of the problem as: 3 = big, 2 = some, 1 = no. The MPD didn't complicate matters by trying to gauge feelings by quantifying them on a 1 to 10 scale. Most of the questions used in recent MPD surveys were phrased to illicit a response or frequency. The MPD developed their own survey then found an instrument created by the Institute of Social Analysis for the National Evaluation of Weed and Seed Sites. It's very comprehensive, and with minor tailoring, was adapted for use in Madison. The survey instrument was further modified in the summer of 1996 through 1998. It represents a substantial improvement over the original survey the Madison Police Department used in 1991, but contains similar core questions used in their first and succeeding surveys allowing them to see how attitudes have changed since incident surveys were used and to perform mean average trend analysis by individual questions and by neighborhood.

Finally, the MPD tested the survey on a number of residents prior to conducing the larger survey to insure that questions made sense. This was the opportunity to check with others to insure clarity of questions contained in the instrument and determine the amount of time it takes to complete. The MPD also asked the thirteen neighborhood officers to pretest the survey with residents in their areas too and results were compared and changes were made to accommodate any deficiencies.

DISTRIBUTION OF QUESTIONNAIRE

During the summer months of 1995, the Madison Police Department administered the resident survey employing the same methodology as in the past (personal interviews). Drug and Gang Task Force officers, neighborhood officers, supervisors, commanders, and MPD interns made up the thirty-five-member survey team which went into the nine different neighborhoods that comprise the two larger Madison Weed and Seed areas. Survey team members were given a target goal for each neighborhood, then set out on foot to locate residents. (Incidentally, this process is referred to as accidental sampling. Information is easy to obtain but may make it difficult to draw conclusions that will be typical of the larger population). Residents were contacted as they walked about the neighborhood, occupied their homes, recreated in community centers, or simply waited at a bus stop. It was also worthwhile to note that surveys were even completed by known gang members and persons previously arrested by officers. They were provided a copy of the questionnaire and each question was then read to them. Survey team members reported it took approximately fifteen minutes to complete each interview, with some reportedly longer than twenty minutes.

Overall, there were four evaluation sections consisting of 1461 participants in those studies. The average age of the respondents was 34, 33 percent were male, 55 percent were black, 22 percent had been victims of crime, and 90 percent of them were renters as opposed to owners of their homes. The MPD analyzed the survey by specific neighborhood. Comparisons were made and the results were publicized. While the results of those studies are important, space dictates that only one of those sections consisting of 382 participants be emphasized below.

BENEFITS OF SELF-ADMINISTERING SURVEYS

Can officers conduct a reliable interview? Are participants less likely to be critical of police activities and police efforts to resolve neighborhood problems when interviewed by a cop? Of the 382 questionnaires completed during a survey of Madison neighborhood residents, 295 were administered by uniformed police personnel and 78 were administered by student in-

terns (from the University of Wisconsin) and Americorp volunteers. Task Force and neighborhood police officers responsible for completing the large majority of resident interviews
were dressed in either full military police uniform or in casual plain clothes with police badge,
department identification, and weapon in plain view. When presenting past survey results,
questions have been raised as to whether interviewer response bias was found during data
analysis. Typically, those inquiring believed residents would be biased by the "police contact"
giving answers that might be different than if the interviewers were not police officers. Therefore, the MPD reviewed the results produced by police officer interviewers versus volunteer
interviewers. Upon comparing means to questions, little difference was found in the data.
However, as the officers completed the questionnaire with the participants, the respondents
tended to give information to the officers about quality-of-life and social order issues whereas
with the other interviewers who were not officers, those issues rarely emerged. Nonetheless,
the MPD's findings did not support the assertion that having a uniformed armed officer asking residents questions coerces participants to reply with what they believe the officer wants
to hear out of fear of retaliation or abuse of his/her authority. Here's a summary of what the
MPD learned from a test when residents were interviewed by police officers as compared to
those interviewed by interns and volunteers. In sum, participants were more likely to report:

- A greater concern that their children would be hurt while playing in
  the neighborhood.
- Less satisfaction with their neighborhood as a place to live.
- Less optimism about whether the neighborhood will improve over the next year.
- Parking, public drinking and intoxication, gang activity, and graffiti as more of
  a problem.
- Drug sales, drug usage, drug addiction, possession of guns and weapons, vio-
  lence, fighting, and assaults all to be more of a problem.
- More negative assessments of the effectiveness of rental property owners and
  managers in dealing with neighborhood problems, and of the extent to which
  residents were organized and committed to improving neighborhood conditions.
- Seeing residents as more fearful of retaliation from working with police.
- More negative perceptions about the overall physical appearance and cleanliness
  of the neighborhood, or whether neighborhood conditions would improve over
  the coming year.

It is difficult to interpret the effect of possible interviewer bias on the survey results.
Residents can be viewed as telling police officers neighborhood conditions are a lot worse
than they really are or they relish the opportunity to tell the officers what they feel is happening in hopes something can be done to improve neighborhood conditions. Residents interviewed by a young student intern or Americorp volunteer may possibly view them as
having little interest, ability, or authority to affect change or improvement in the neighborhood. Subsequently, the interview lacks the intensity which would occur if residents believed their responses would contribute to creating positive change. If a significant difference in means had occurred between officer and intern/volunteer interviewer responses to
the questions pertaining to "MPD effectiveness in the neighborhood" and perceived "rea-

sonableness" with which officers "treat people," perhaps a more serious case could be made for questioning the interpretation of these survey results. Although we must be vigilant that a possible interviewer bias may exist when armed, uniformed officers conduct in-person surveys, there are apparently advantages of having officers conduct the survey which outweighs any potential disadvantages.

WORKING WITH RESULTS

While MPD's results are cause for some celebration, they also alert the MPD that much work remains to be done in the city's most challenged neighborhoods. The agency learned a lot about surveying when they extensively used an incident-based customer survey (1987 to 1991) to provide feedback on officer performance. That survey's design involved mailing a single form to individuals listed in every thirty-fifth case-numbered report asking them to rate the quality of the service they received as a victim, witness, arrested person, and so on. The MPD sought feedback based on seven officer performance dimensions and elected to showcase the survey as an organizational mantelpiece. The MPD compiled the results, prepared fancy graphs, shared it with the organization's membership on a quarterly basis, but seldom followed through on the areas identified as needing improvement by their customers. In retrospect, it had limited value as the department used it, but was not a bad idea at the time. It has proven to be a valuable learning experience. The MPD learned to use feedback to fulfil their mission. The MPD now recognizes and appreciates the true value of surveys—analyze the data, then use it to develop strategies to improve the lives of the people they serve and the personnel of the department.

BENEFITS OF POLICE INVOLVEMENT IN SURVEYING NEIGHBORHOODS

Members of the Dane County Narcotics and Gang Task Force, along with neighborhood officers, have been responsible for conducting face-to-face interviews of residents over the past years. Their duties involve aggressive law enforcement and interdiction strategies directed at drugs and gangs. Needless to say, depending on when and to whom you speak to, many residents hold a wide range of strong feelings.

Ironically, these officers are deeply involved in asking residents questions pertaining to the livability of their neighborhoods. The neighborhoods in question have a high-density population made up primarily of African Americans. These areas regrettably experience significantly higher violent crime, ten times the rate when compared to the city as a whole, which means a proportionately higher number of victims, offenders, and police interaction. There are indicators that crime has been reduced in these communities and that the fear of crime among the residents is less today than five years ago. In part, residents can see officers as they engage in the research process and many of them welcome officers into their homes and back yards to discuss matters. Residents know the names of the officers and the officers know them and their family members by name, too. Clearly, relationships of these types help raise the quality of life among residents. This thought is consistent with the literature pertaining to community policing partnerships (Skogan, 1998; Trojanowicz & Carter, 1988).

CONCLUSION

Although officers may not readily admit it, surveying presents a tremendous opportunity to visit with and talk to people who are constantly struggling to improve their living conditions and the neighborhoods they live in. Conducting interviews with law abiding individuals is unusual in the sense that officers interact more often with law breakers. Surveying through questionnaires or interviews or both is a small, meaningful way of helping to minimize inappropriate perceptions about the public held by some officers and equally important, it helps to minimize inappropriate perceptions held by the public about the police. Citizens are presented with a caring, helping image of the police and through nonconflictual interaction, the public gains confidence in the officers and the officers gain confidence in the public. Building rapport with community members has much to do with their opinion about police activities. That is, when a department has a relationship with community members, the community tends to support police decisions more often even when those decisions include utilization of police tactical units (Stevens, 1999a).

Then, too, officers learn their part of their policing through the interviewing process. For instance, they develop, firsthand experience in building rapport with individuals but under favorable conditions. Rapport allows for the use of interrogation approaches that are less obvious and that will minimize conflict, argues Don Rabin at the North Carolina Justice Academy (1992). Through the interview process, officers can refine their techniques toward valuable interrogation tools.

The most important benefits of using police officers to conduct surveys suggests that the involvement of uniformed police officers could in the long run reduce crime and the fear of crime by enhancing citizen attitudes toward police, independent of any information they gain or what the police do with it.

It has been the experience of the MPD that if their challenged neighborhoods become safer and better organized, their residents are far more likely to be more outspoken, better educated about issues affecting their lifestyles, and more willing to discuss problems within their community. Furthermore, it allows the leadership of the department to assume the role of a facilitator more than an enforcer, a position that some argue is a goal of police leadership relative to a community policing posture (Skogan, 1998). There is the thought that if those early studies in the late 1980s were police officers in the field, they could have been able to predict the advent of the huge cocaine problem about to engulf some of the high risk neighborhoods. That is, officers are trained to anticipate problems, and they have a legal responsibility to address anticipations of unlawful conduct—consultants and volunteers are not seen by residents as having neither the responsibility or the authority to make things change for the better (Stevens, 2000).

Overall, the MPD believes that social order can be accomplished when community members participate in police decisions. Gaining neighborhood input is best left to police officers since there is much to gain for everyone involved. Compelling evidence has been presented that demonstrates the typical community member would be more honest with an officer than others. Strong neighborhood associations, their visible and trusted leadership, an active community center, and the active presence of police officers all contribute to a well-informed and involved community that is more likely to identify problems, report them to authorities, and work with the department to solve those problems. Then, too, officers who are less experienced than others can learn to rely on some of the information provided by the community and the bridge narrows between the "them and us" or phased another way, that thin blue line gets smaller (Stevens, 2000, 1999c).

On the other hand, in a crime ridden neighborhood, residents are often afraid and rarely willing to discuss issues. They believe that reporting them to police will not make a difference. Apathy is firmly rooted in those who have lost hope and a desire to find a better way of life for their families. Police agencies cannot let that happen. Agencies require a greater presence and a higher visibility beyond investigating a crime or making an arrest. Surveys are a personalized way to listen to citizen needs in times other than when enforcement issues are mandated. Surveying gives officers the opportunity to build a coalition of support from citizens as they work together in strengthening relationships.

Through surveying the MPD is learning to incorporate the needs, concerns and ideas of residents to help improve neighborhood livability and enhance their quality of life by identifying and evaluating problems, increasing personal safety and moving them closer to being self sufficient. Officers, too, are realizing immeasurable benefits of increased respect, confidence and support of the people they serve in helping to make neighborhoods a better and a safer place to live. Surveying is a means to that end.

Captain Michael Masterson can be reached at MMASTERSON@ci.madison.wi.us
Dennis J. Stevens can be reached at dennis.stevens@worldnet.att.net

REFERENCES

Benchmark Study. (1994, March). Peel Regional Police Survey of Attitudes and Opinions. Brampton, Ontario.

Bittner, E. (1974). A theory of the police. In H. Jacob (Ed.), *Potential for Reform of Criminal Justice.* (pp. 17–44). Beverly Hills: Sage.

Brodeur, J. P. (1998). *How to recognize good policing: Problems and issues.* Thousand Oaks, CA: Sage.

Champion, D. (1993). *Research methods for criminal justice and criminology.* Upper Saddle River, NJ: Prentice Hall.

Citta, J. (1996). Police department surveys to help police officers grow. [On-Line], Available: www.communitypolicing.org

DeLeon-Granados, W. (1999). *Travels through crime and place.* Boston: Northeastern Press.

DuBois, J. and Hartnett, S. M. (2001). Making the community side of community policing work: What needs to be done. In Dennis J. Stevens (Ed.) *Policing and Community Policing.* Upper Saddle River, NJ: Prentice Hall.

Dutton, D. (1998, May). Don't forget to ask your customers what's most important to them. *www.communitypolicing.org/exchange/e20_98/dutto.htm*

Eck, J. E. and LaVigne, N. G. (1994). *Using research: A primer for law enforcement managers.* Washington DC: Police Executive Research Forum.

Ericson, R. V. and Haggerty, K. D. (1997). *Policing the risk society.* Toronto: University of Toronto Press.

Goldstein, H. (1979). Improving policing: A problem-oriented approach. *Crime and Delinquency,* 4, 236–258.

Kelling, G. L. and Moore, M. H. (1988). *Perspectives on policing.* Washington, DC: National Institute of Justice.

Kirkland, R. and Glensor, R. (1992). *Community oriented policing and problem solving department report.* Reno, NE: Reno Police Department.

Nowicki, D. E. (1998). Mixed messages. In Geoffrey Alpert and Alex Piquero (Eds.) *Community Policing,* (pp. 265–274), Prospect Heights, IL: Waveland Press.

Oettmeier, T. N. and Wycoff, M. A. (1997). Personnel performance evaluations in the community policing context. In Geoffrey Alpert and Alex Piquero (Eds.) *Community Policing,* (pp. 275–306), Prospect Heights, IL: Waveland Press.

Peel Regional Police Survey of Attitudes and Opinions. (1994, March). *Benchmark Study.* Brampton, Ontario.

Rabin, D. (1992). *Interviewing and interrogation.* Durham, NC: Carolina Academic Press.

Skogan, W. G. (1998). Community participation and community policing. In Jean-Paul Brodeur (Ed.), *How to recognize good policing: Problems and issues.* (pp. 88–106). Thousand Oaks, CA: Sage.

Skogan, W. G., Hartnett, S. M., DuBois, J., Comey, J. T., Kaiser, M. & Lovig, J. H. (1999). *On the beat: Police and community problem solving.* New York: Westview Press.

Stephens, D. W. (1996). *Community problem oriented policing: Measuring impact, quantifying quality in policing.* Washington DC: Police Executive Research Forum.

Stevens, D. J. (2000). The threat of civil liabilities and probable cause arrests. *The Police Journal,* LXXXV (3).

Stevens, D. J. (1999a, March). Police tactical units and community response. *Law and Order,* 47(3), 48–52.

Stevens, D. J. (1999b, December). Do college educated officers provide quality police service? *Law and Order,* 47(12), 37–41.

Stevens, D. J. (1999c) Corruption among narcotic officers: A study of innocence and integrity. *Journal of Police and Criminal Psychology, 14*(2), 1–11.

Stevens, D. J. (2001). *Case studies in community policing.* Upper Saddle River, NJ: Prentice Hall.

Surveys of Citizens' Attitudes. (1995). Telemasp Bulletin. Huntsville, Texas: Texas Law Enforcement Management and Administrative Problem, Bill Blackwood Enforcement Management Institute of Texas.

Thurman, Q. and McGarrell, E. F. (1995, June). Findings of the 1994 Spokane Police Department Citizen Survey: Final report, Washington State Institute for Community Oriented Policing, Spokane, Washington.

Trojanowicz, R. C. and Carter, D. L. (1988). *The philosophy and role of community policing.* East Lansing: National Neighborhood Foot Patrol Center, Michigan State University.

6

Perceptions of Community Policing Across Community Sectors: Results from a Regional Survey[1]

Kent R. Kerley**

❖

It is a truism that police occupy a uniquely difficult position in the criminal justice system. As the most visible part of the criminal justice triumvirate, police agencies bear primary responsibility for crime control. Despite voluminous research suggesting that police can do little to affect victimization rates, the general public still expects police to accomplish the elusive goal of controlling crime (Bayley, 1994; Eck and Rosenbaum, 1994; Skogan and Hartnett, 1997). If police are to accomplish this difficult task, they need the trust and support of the general public and, in particular, minority communities. In addition, they must establish effective working relationships with leaders in local government and local non-governmental organizations (NGOs).

With these considerations in mind, and as an alternative to traditional reactive policing strategies, the community policing movement began in the early 1980s. The basic tenet

[1]Funding for this research was provided by grant number 97-PR-M@X-0405, awarded by the Office of Community Oriented Policing Services, United States Department of Justice. Points of view and opinions contained within this document are those of the author and do not necessarily represent the official position of the U.S. Department of Justice. The author thanks Dennis J. Stevens for his assistance in organizing this work and John M. Scheb II, Heith Copes, and Lori A. Hill for their insightful comments on an earlier draft of the paper.

**Direct all correspondence to Kent R. Kerley, Department of Sociology, University of Tennessee, Knoxville, TN 37996, kkerley@utk.edu.

of community policing is that crime control is best accomplished as a joint venture between community residents and police personnel.[2] According to the philosophy of community policing, officers should seek to be more proactive and conciliatory in their policing and less reactive and punitive. In terms of organizational structure, departments are
encouraged to move away from hierarchical and militaristic structures, and toward decentralized and "flatter" structures. Finally, community policing counsels officers to seek the
input of residents and to involve them in policing initiatives, thus increasing trust between
the two. It is hoped that these improvements will then eventually lead to reductions in
crime rates and fear of crime (Cox, 1996; Eck and Spelman, 1987; Goldstein, 1987; 1990;
Kelling, 1987; Kelling and Moore, 1988).

Whether community policing strategies actually are leading to changes in these variables continues to be debated (Bayley, 1994; Cox and Fitzgerald, 1996; Lyons, 1999;
Maguire, 1997; More, 1998; Oliver, 1998; Skogan and Hartnett, 1997; Williams, 1998).
Overall, results of the new strategies are lackluster and vary depending on the areas in
which they are implemented. These weak results lead many authors to conclude that community policing may exist more in rhetoric than in reality (Eck and Rosenbaum, 1994;
Moore, 1994; Greene and Mastrofski, 1988). The argument is that many police departments
are adopting the rhetoric of community policing, in part to avail themselves of federal
grants, but are making few changes in their organizational structures and the tactics of their
officers (Dantzker, 1999; Maguire, 1997; Moore, 1994). Some even argue that many police
departments are using the rhetoric of community policing to mask efforts to create police
paramilitary units (Kraska and Kappeler, 1997).

In this chapter, no pretense is made of providing a resolution to the debate over the
potential efficacy of community policing. There is, however, a contribution to the discussion by investigating perceptions of key community policing issues across the three most
important groups needed for community policing programs to be successful. These groups
are local law enforcement leaders, local government officials, and leaders in community
non-governmental organizations (NGOs). Using data from a survey of three thousand members of these elite groups across the Southeast region, I investigated perceptions regarding
familiarity with community policing, extent to which community policing is utilized, police
training needs, police-minority relations, and the focus of community policing training.

POLICE AND COMMUNITY RESIDENTS

The relationship between police and the general public is a key issue in the policing literature (Carter and Radelet, 1999). Historically, this relationship has often been one of tension
and conflict. Many commentators have noted the failures of police agencies to adjust to
changing times and shifting urban contexts (Crank, 1994; Cox and Fitzgerald, 1996; Das,
1987; Moore and Kelling, 1983). Many studies of policing in the United States reveal that
the hierarchical, militaristic features of traditional policing, coupled with the use of aggressive, reactive policing tactics have served to alienate citizens and have done little to
ameliorate existing social problems (Crank, 1994; Bayley, 1994; Eck and Rosenbaum,

---

[2]See Bartollas and Hahn (1999), Goldstein (1987; 1990), Kelling (1987), Kelling and Coles (1996),
Kelling and Moore (1988).

1994). This was especially true during the time of extreme political and social unrest of the 1960s. The government-sponsored Knapp and Kerner Commissions concluded that police often exacerbated existing conflicts between police and members of racial minority groups (Cox, 1996; Cox and Fitzgerald, 1996; Das, 1987; Gaines, Kappeler, and Vaughn, 1999; Moore and Kelling, 1983; Skolnick and Bayley, 1986). For myriad reasons, the public has historically been at least skeptical and often distrustful of police.

Many researchers locate the causes of the generally strained relations between police and the general public in the structure of police organizations (Bayley, 1994; Das, 1987; Maguire, 1997; Skolnick and Bayley, 1986; Skolnick and Fyfe, 1993). On this issue, Moore and Kelling (1983, p. 50) note that "the pursuit of a professionalized, politically neutral police force—narrowly focused on 'serious crime' and relying on new technologies—eventually weakened the bonds between private citizens and the police, and shifted the burdens of enforcement to a public agency that could not succeed by itself." The failure of police to control crime and the general perception of police as aggressive, forceful and even corrupt led to widespread alienation of the general public. Interestingly, many studies find that despite strained relations with citizens, police tend to overestimate the strength of these relationships (Eck and Rosenbaum, 1994; Greene, Bergman, and McLaughlin, 1994; Alpert and Dunham, 1988). Recognizing the limitations of traditional policing strategies, community policing advocates argue for the creation of partnerships with citizens and community leaders to address crime issues (Goldstein, 1987, 1990; Freidmann, 1992; Fielding, 1995; Kelling and Coles, 1996; Kratcoski and Dukes, 1995).

POLICE AND MINORITY RESIDENTS

The historical tension between police and the general public is even more pronounced when relationships between police and racial minority groups (e.g., African Americans) are considered. An already strained relationship between police and minority members became even more polarized during the civil rights movement of the 1960s. Although many contend that the relationship has improved dramatically since that time, there remains widespread distrust of police by minority members (Bartollas and Hahn, 1999; Carter and Radelet, 1999; Skolnick and Bayley, 1986; Skolnick and Fyfe, 1993). There are certainly good reasons for this continued distrust. Many police departments continue to use tactics such as saturated patrols of minority neighborhoods and criminal profiling. These tactics, combined with aggressive handling and differential treatment of minorities, serve to proliferate tension that is already present (Bayley, 1994; Cox and Fitzgerald, 1996; Roberg and Kuykendall, 1993). National incidents (and reactions to them) such as the Rodney King beating in Los Angeles in the early 1990s and the more recent beating of Abner Louima by New York Police Department officers serve as reminders that police-minority relations continue to be strained in many areas and remain an important issue for law enforcement leaders to consider (Cox and Fitzgerald, 1996; Lyons, 1999; Skolnick and Fyfe, 1993).

As with their relationship with the general public, police tend to overestimate the strength of their relationship with minority groups. Despite strong evidence suggesting that police need to address issues of racial tension in specific communities, police often ignore this and continue operating in an isolationist manner. For example, in their study of police and minority residents in Miami, Alpert and Dunham (1988) found that despite long-standing tension between police and minority residents, police perceived that the relationship was strong and thus did not pursue solutions to existing problems. The movement toward community policing, at least rhetorically, offers some methods in which to address strained police-minority relations.

WHERE ARE COMMUNITY RESIDENTS IN COMMUNITY POLICING?

One of the main tenets of community policing is that police form partnerships with community residents to identify and address community crime problems (Brudney and England, 1983; Friedman, 1994; Skogan and Hartnett, 1997). To date, however, few community policing programs have led to significant increases in police-community interaction and resident involvement (Greene, Bergman, and McLaughlin 1994; Skogan, 1994; Wycoff, 1994). Overall, community policing programs have had weak effects on police-community relations and the stimulation of community processes (Kerley and Benson, in press; Rosenbaum, 1987; 1988; Sadd and Grinc, 1994; Skogan, 1994; Thurman, 1995).

Creating and sustaining community involvement in a community policing program (or any community anti-crime program) is, of course, inherently difficult (Rosenbaum, 1987; 1988). Some argue, however, that police leaders and officers make this task even more difficult when they alone identify community crime problems and develop community policing programs, and then expect residents to become involved. Buerger (1994), for example, argues that rather than empowering community residents to address crime problems, police often attempt to place residents in an ancillary role of simply helping meet pre-ordained crime control objectives. By identifying the problems themselves and expecting community residents to participate in efforts to address them, police proliferate the perception of themselves as insular and unresponsive to community residents (Buerger, 1994). The result of this tendency for police to develop community policing programs without extensive resident input is that they often identify problems that community members do not see as salient, yet expect them to participate in solutions and are surprised if they do not (Cardarelli and McDevitt, 1995; Cox and Fitzgerald, 1996; Eck and Rosenbaum, 1994; Guyot, 1991; Moore, 1994; Moore and Kelling, 1983; Roberg, 1994). Instead, as Friedman argues, "the community must have a voice in the forums that define community policing itself, must be a ready and knowledgeable ally to the forces of reform, and, in the neighborhood, where the benefits are supposed to be delivered, must have a serious part in implementing solutions as well as nominating problems" (1994, p. 263). Clearly, if community residents do not identify the problems, it is difficult to involve them in crime control efforts. Police leaders must make efforts to confer with local residents to identify and address crime problems if community policing programs are to be successful (Fielding, 1995; Friedman, 1994; Roberg, 1994; Skogan and Hartnett, 1997).

On the other side, police often argue that it is in their best interest *not* to work closely with community residents, especially community leaders (Carter and Radelet, 1999; Cox, 1996; Guyot, 1991). Long-standing criticisms of police for being corrupt led them to seek a neutral, "professional" model of policing and to resist local government and community influence (Das, 1987; Guyot, 1991; Lyons, 1999; Moore, 1994; Roberg and Kuykendall, 1993). Police leaders may fear that greater communication will increase the perception and likelihood of corruption and provision of favors to key community or government leaders

(Carter and Radelet, 1999; Guyot, 1991; Lyons, 1999; Moore, 1994; Skogan, 1994). Professional policing goals of crime control through patrols, rapid response, and criminal investigation would thus be compromised if police were to sustain interaction with community and government leaders or if civilian review boards were established (Carter and Radelet, 1999; Oliver, 1998; Roberg, 1993). Perhaps it is because police have the unique position of being responsible for crime control that they often prefer to set the agenda for crime control and expect local communities to adjust to their policies. Police, often admittedly, are generally resistant to change as well as to threats to their authority as the main providers of crime control (Reed, 1999; Skogan and Hartnett, 1997). Greene et al. (1994, p. 93) for example, note that "police organizations have been some of the most intractable of public bureaucracies, capable of resisting and ultimately thwarting change efforts." In the present era of community policing, Moore (1994, p. 286) suggests that many law enforcement leaders now "worry that policing is heading 'back to the future' and that some of the important gains that the police have made in becoming less corrupt and more professional in their key law enforcement roles will be lost." This creates an interesting dilemma as many of the principal goals of community policing run counter to the ideals of police professionalism, yet police departments are expected to embrace the community policing philosophy.

WHERE ARE LOCAL GOVERNMENT AND NGO LEADERS IN COMMUNITY POLICING?

Just as involvement of community residents in community policing programs has been limited, so too has involvement of leaders in local governments and NGOs. In most empirical studies, the role of these leaders and their perceptions of community policing have received little attention. Instead, most studies rely on surveys of police line officers and members of the general public. It is argued that perceptions of local government and NGO leaders are crucial because they are in key positions to work with police leaders to identify and address community crime problems as part of a community policing program (Kerley & Scheb, 1998).

Although perceptions of policing by leaders in local governments and NGOs have been infrequently included in empirical research, their importance is certainly recognized in the literature. Trojanowicz (1994) and Moore (1994) argue that effective community policing programs must involve active participation of police, community residents, social agencies, political leaders, and media (what they refer to as the "Big Five"). In a later work, Trojanowicz and Bucqueroux (1998) add the business community as a sixth important entity to consider. Their combination of social agencies and business leaders constitutes what I refer to as non-governmental organizations (NGOs).

Many others also emphasize that for police to be more effective in crime control, efforts must be made to form partnerships with community leaders and local government leaders (Bayley, 1994; Friedman, 1994; Roberg, 1994; Skogan, 1994). For example, Brudney and England's (1983) concept of the "coproduction of order" involves the police building stronger relationships with members of the general public and with leaders of elite groups such as local governments and NGOs (see also Williams, 1998). Brudney and England argue for an "emerging conception of the service delivery process that envisions direct citizen involvement in the design and delivery of city services with professional service agents" (1983, p. 59).

As noted previously, the movement toward community policing began in the mid-1980s with the promise of changing police organizational structure, making police more proactive and less isolated from the public, and creating new partnerships between police and residents as a more effective means of crime control. Regardless whether the new programs have achieved these goals and whether they exist more in reality than in rhetoric, they surely have become ubiquitous. Since the passage of the 1994 Violent Crime Control and Law Enforcement Act and the creation of the Office of Community-Oriented Policing Services (COPS), over $8 billion have been distributed to law enforcement agencies nationwide to develop community policing programs, and over 100,000 new officers have been hired (Dantzker, 1999). Recent surveys estimate that nearly 85 percent of all U.S. policing agencies either have community policing programs or are in the process of implementing them (McEwen, 1995; Thurman & Reisig, 1996).

Because of the widespread attention that the community policing movement has received among both criminal justice academicians and practitioners, an investigation of perceptions of key community policing issues across the three main groups involved (law enforcement leaders, local government officials, and leaders in non-governmental organizations) appears timely. Such an investigation will shed light on whether differences exist across these three elite groups in their perceptions of community policing and may also indicate areas where further research and policy changes are needed.

Sample and Methods

Data for this study are derived from a mail survey conducted by the author and colleagues in March to April 1998 through the Social Science Research Institute (SSRI) at the University of Tennessee, Knoxville. One of the primary purposes of the survey was to assess the level of interest among community leaders in policing, local government and NGOs across an eight-state region of the Southeast[3] in participating in a new training institute to be housed at the university (Kerley & Scheb, 1998). The new institute, known as the Southeastern Community Oriented Policing Education (SCOPE) Institute, is funded by a grant from the Office of Community-Oriented Policing Services, U. S. Department of Justice.

A multistage purposive sampling design based on known population variance and geographical dispersion of cities in the region is used in this study. First, the four largest cities representing each region of the eight states were selected. Next, for each major city, two additional cities with a population of at least 10,000 and within a 100-mile radius of the major city were selected. Then, in the four largest states, one additional city was identified for inclusion in the study for a total of 100 cities.[4] Within each of the 100 targeted cities, I selected 10 police leaders, 10 local government officials, and 10 NGO leaders to receive the survey instrument. Thus, the sample consisted of 1000 police officials, 1000 local government officials, and 1000 community leaders in NGOs across an eight-state region of the Southeast.

---

[3]States included were Alabama, Arkansas, Georgia, Kentucky, Mississippi, North Carolina, South Carolina, and Tennessee.

[4]It is likely that a random sample of all cities in the eight-state region would have produced a sample similar to ours. However, because we wanted to ensure that the selected cities were evenly dispersed geographically across each state, and because we only wanted to include cities with at least 10,000 residents, we employed the method elaborated.

Within each of the three groups, there were targeted persons in key leadership positions. For police leaders, I sampled leaders in city and county police agencies such as chiefs, sheriffs, assistant chiefs, chief deputies, and captains. Only 5 percent of the respondents are below the rank of sergeant. Local government respondents are also in key leadership positions in their communities such as mayor, city manager, county executive, city attorney, county attorney, judge, probation-parole officer, school superintendent, and parks and recreation director. Finally, my NGO respondents are leaders in community non-profit and service agencies such as YMCA, Boys and Girls Club, United Way, Chamber of Commerce, Salvation Army, American Red Cross, NAACP, ministerial associations, child and social welfare agencies, and community action groups.

For survey distribution, I used Dillman's classic three-wave total design method. All 3000 persons in the sample received an initial mailing consisting of a cover letter, questionnaire and self-addressed, stamped return envelope. Ten days later, all 3000 persons were sent a postcard reminder, and two additional weeks later, persons who had not yet responded to the survey were sent another full mailing. All 3000 initial questionnaires were mailed to respondents at the beginning of March, 1998 and data collection was finished by the end of April. The overall response rate for the survey was 49.4 percent ($N = 1482$) and all 100 of the targeted communities in the eight-state region are represented in the data. Specifically, 639 respondents are law enforcement leaders, 378 are local government officials,[5] and 465 are community leaders in NGOs.

In terms of questionnaire content, the survey was designed to measure several variables related to community policing including familiarity, extent of use, experience of leaders, departmental usage, location in department of programs, assignment of officers, needs for training, police-minority relations, and receipt of grants. In this chapter, the focus is on five key variables from the larger survey. These are familiarity with community policing, extent to which community policing is utilized, police training needs, police-minority relations, and the focus of community policing training.

Results

Sample demographics, broken down by respondent type, are displayed in Table 1. Police respondents are overwhelmingly male (92 percent), middle-aged (83 percent are in the 36 to 55 range), and white (84 percent). On the whole, they are reasonably well educated, with only 1 percent reporting that they did not finish high school. Local government respondents are not as overwhelming male (80 percent) and are somewhat more diverse in terms of age, but 75 percent still fall into the middle-aged category. In terms of racial composition, they are very similar to law enforcement respondents (85 percent white). The biggest demographic difference is that these respondents have the highest level of education of the three

---

[5]Although local government leaders are a specialized group, their response rate is somewhat low. One principal reason is that while verifying the title reported on the questionnaire with the title in our sample database for all respondents, we discovered that, for local government leaders, approximately 10 percent of their returned surveys had been passed from them to their respective police leaders. To avoid potential bias and because we surveyed those same police leaders, we eliminated all local government questionnaires that were completed by police leaders.

TABLE 1   Demographic Characteristics of the Sample by Group

	Police	Local Govt.	NGOs
Gender			
% Male	92	80	60
% Female	8	20	40
Age			
% 18–35	10	8	16
% 36–45	41	30	31
% 46–55	42	45	36
% 56–65	7	13	14
% Over 65	0	4	3
Race			
% White	84	85	82
% African American	15	14	17
% Other	1	1	1
Education			
% Did not finish high school	1	0	0
% Graduated high school	34	5	14
% Graduated from college	42	33	50
% Earned advanced degree	23	62	36

groups. Specifically, 62 percent report advanced degrees, as compared with 23 percent of police respondents. Finally, respondents from the NGOs manifest slightly more demographic diversity. This group is 60 percent male, 67 percent middle-aged, and 82 percent white. In terms of education, these respondents are, on the whole, more educated than police respondents but less educated than local government respondents.

FAMILIARITY WITH AND USE OF COMMUNITY POLICING

To tap general knowledge of community policing among the three groups, I first asked respondents how familiar they were with the concept of community policing. As indicated in Table 2, 85 percent of police respondents indicated that they were "very familiar" with the concept. However, only 45 percent of local government respondents were very familiar with the concept and 12 percent reported that community policing was "not at all familiar." For NGO respondents, only 21 percent reported being very familiar with community policing, and 31 percent reported being not at all familiar. Chi-square analysis performed on this variable for the three groups indicates strong statistically significant differences in familiarity with community policing across the three groups (sig. at $p < .001$). In the test of strength of association, Lambda results also reveal a strong statistical association between

TABLE 2   Familiarity and Use of Community Policing by Group

Familiarity with community policing*		
	Police	Local Govt.	NGOs
% Not at all familar	0	12	31
% Somewhat familiar	14	41	45
% Very familiar	85	45	21
% Not sure	1	2	4

*Chi-Square = 525.87 sig. at $p < .001$
*Lambda = .255 sig. at $p < .001$

Extent to which community policing is employed in respondents' communities*		
	Police	Local Govt.	NGOs
% Not at all	3	2	4
% To a limited extent	46	52	34
% Extensively	51	32	18
% Not sure	0	14	44

*Chi-Square = 397.86 sig. at $p < .001$
*Lambda= .165 sig. at $p < .001$

familiarity with community policing and group (sig. at $p < .001$). These results may indicate a failure of police agencies to educate community leaders on community policing programs.

Next, I asked respondents for their perception of how extensively community policing is being employed in their communities. Again, the modal responses vary across respondent categories (see Table 2). For police respondents, 51 percent reported that community policing was being used "extensively." For local government respondents, however, only 32 percent perceived that community policing was being used extensively and 52 percent suggested that community policing was utilized "to a limited extent." Only 18 percent of NGO respondents reported that community policing was used extensively, 34 percent said that it was used to a limited extent and, interestingly, the majority (44 percent) indicated that they were "not sure" of the extent of the usage of community policing. As seen in Table 2, Chi-square analyses and Lambda measures of association for this variable also show significant statistical differences across the three groups (sig. at $p < .001$). These results also suggest a failure of police to involve local community leaders in community policing programs. Because community policing is centered around increased communication among leaders in policing, local government, and NGOs, it would be expected that local government and NGO leaders would at least be aware of the various community policing programs being implemented in their communities.

TABLE 3   Perceptions of Police Training Needs by Group

Areas of Training	% reporting a need for "a lot" of training		
	Police	Local Govt.	NGOs
Second languages*	58	36	32
Computerized mapping*	44	28	17
Crime analysis software*	44	24	20
Using the Internet*	42	25	16
Cultural diversity*	35	55	51
Communications skills*	35	53	44
Building community partnerships*	31	49	44
Conflict resolution*	35	42	36
Dealing with ethical issues*	29	35	38

*Indicates statistically significant differences across the three groups for the area of training at $p < .001$

NEEDS FOR POLICE TRAINING

To continue the investigation of differences in perceptions of policing across the three groups, I gave respondents a list of potential police training needs and asked them to indicate whether law enforcement agencies in their communities needed "a little," "some" or "a lot" of training in each area. Table 3 lists the top three areas (police, local government, and NGO) where each group reported that "a lot" of training was needed for their local police agencies. Police respondents perceived the greatest training needs to be instruction in using the Internet, computerized mapping, crime and operations analysis software, and second languages. These training needs reflect a concern with technical skills that will allow officers to more effectively complete their jobs.

In sharp contrast, local government and NGO leaders chose nearly identical areas where they thought the most police training was needed. Specifically, they perceived that their local police agencies need more training in humanistic skills such as cultural diversity, communications skills, building community partnerships, conflict resolution, and dealing with ethical issues. Chi-square analyses indicate statistically significant differences across the three groups in these perceptions of training needs (see Table 3). Specifically, the largest differences were between police responses and those of local government and NGO leaders.

These results are consistent with previous research and seem to suggest a distinct police value system concerning needs for training that is in direct opposition to that of local government and NGO leaders (Maguire, 1997). Also from these results, it appears that law enforcement leaders may assume that their officers already possess strong communications and other humanistic skills, and consequently report the greatest need for training in technical skills that they feel will help their officers be more effective in crime control. Conversely, the two civilian groups, local government and NGO leaders, perceived that police need to first focus on humanistic skills such as increasing communication and problem solving skills before focusing on technical skills.

TABLE 4   One-Way Analysis of Variance for Perceived Level of Trust Between Police and Minorities by Group

	Police	Local Govt.	NGOs
Mean	6.81*	5.20*	4.80*
Std. Dev.	1.63	1.99	1.91
ANOVA (BETWEEN)			
$F = 183.345$			
*SIG. AT P $< .001$			

POLICE-MINORITY RELATIONS

Next, I explore the issue of relationships between police and members of community minority groups. As noted previously, this relationship has historically been one of tension often leading to major conflict. Unlike other surveys on this topic, I was able to compare perceptions of leaders in law enforcement on this issue with those of local government leaders and community leaders in NGOs. Specifically, I asked respondents to evaluate on a scale of 1 to 10 (where 10 is highest) the level of trust that exists between police and minority residents in their respective communities.

I use a one-way analysis of variance procedure to test for differing perceptions across the three groups. As reported in Table 4, I found significant perceptual differences across the three groups (sig. at $p < .001$). Police respondents provided a significantly higher estimation of the level of trust than respondents in the other two categories (mean = 6.81). Respondents from local governments reported a significantly lower mean than law enforcement leaders (mean = 5.20) and NGO leaders reported an even smaller amount of trust between police and minority residents (mean = 4.80).

To specifically analyze whether all means were significantly different from one another, I conducted post-hoc multiple comparisons following the ANOVA procedure. Results (not presented in tabular form) indicate statistically significant differences across all three comparisons (all mean differences sig. at $p < .003$), with the largest differences between police and local government leaders and between police and NGO leaders. These results are similar to those of previous studies and support the contention that police leaders tend to overestimate the amount of trust that exists between their agencies and local minority residents (Alpert & Dunham, 1988).

To account for the potentially confounding effects of race on perceived police-minority relations, I add respondents' race to the analysis of variance procedure conducted for Table 4. This two-way analysis of variance of police-minority trust by group and race is summarized in Table 5. Results indicate that only among the NGO respondents is there a statistically significant racial difference in perception of police-minority trust (sig. at $p < .05$), and given the size of the sample, this racial effect is not strong. Thus, I conclude that the differing perceptions of police-minority relations appear to be driven more by respondents' structural positions within the community than by race.

TABLE 5   Two-Way Analysis of Variance for Perceived Level of Trust between Police and Minorities by Group and Race*

	Police			Local Govt.			NGOs		
	ALL	W	NW	ALL	W	NW	ALL	W	NW
Mean	6.81	6.85	6.64	5.20	5.22	5.13	4.80	4.89	4.41
Std. Dev.	1.63	1.59	1.81	1.99	1.94	2.10	1.91	1.90	1.91
	ANOVA (WITHIN)			ANOVA (WITHIN)			ANOVA (WITHIN)		
	$F = 1.289$			$F = 0.093$			$F = 4.065$		
	SIG. = .257			SIG. = .760			SIG. = .044**		

*W indicates White and NW indicates Non-White
**Indicates statistical significance at $p < .05$

FOCUS OF COMMUNITY POLICING TRAINING

Finally, to add a qualitative dimension to this study, I asked respondents a series of open-ended questions pertaining to training in community policing. One of these questions is especially relevant to the present analysis (but see Kerley & Scheb, 1998 for others). Specifically, respondents were asked "What is the most valuable thing a training institute in community policing should provide?" My intention was to determine what types of issues the three groups saw as salient for community policing training programs. Similar to the results of the quantitative analyses, I observed significant differences in responses across the three groups.

Over one-third of police respondents reported that a community policing training institute should provide information on how to "package" community policing so that all officers in an agency will "buy in" to the idea and see it as a viable alternative to traditional policing. There was some concern for training officers to involve community leaders and residents in community policing, but the theme from most police leaders was how to involve their own officers in the programs. One police leader provided a good overview of this intra-agency focus as s/he stated that:

> the training program should provide a historical perspective for establishing the need for COP (community-oriented policing). Officers need to be made aware that COP can be integrated into their daily tasks, and that problem solving strategies can be implemented as well. The concept needs to be thoroughly taught to supervisors so they are cooperative and attuned to their officers' innovations.

Only about one-fifth of police respondents reported that an institute should emphasize humanistic skills such as communications, cultural diversity, and conflict resolution. For those one-fifth concerned with humanistic skills, however, there was evidence that they observed a link between humanistic skills and the success of community policing programs. One police leader remarked that:

building a community partnership is an important role in community policing. Obtaining the proper communications skills to use to form a partnership with your communities will assist you in working with your communities to solve their community problems.

Another police leader argued for a focus on humanistic skills because, at its core, community policing:

is [a] collaboration between the police and the community to identify and solve community problems. COP is an expanded outlook on crime control and prevention that recognizes that crime is not a problem that the police can solve alone, but requires mutual accountability between the police and the community.

Leaders in local government and NGOs, however, had somewhat different perceptions than police leaders of the main focus of a community policing institute. About two-thirds of leaders in local government and NGOs reported that an institute should focus on improving the humanistic skills of officers and teaching them ways to involve community leaders and residents in community policing programs. One local government leader recommended that police receive "practical exposure to theory and skills related to interpersonal communication between officers and members of the community." One NGO leader stated that police should "learn about different ethnic groups in your community and their cultural beliefs. Do they view issues differently?"

The theme in responses is that once police officers are better trained in humanistic skills, they will be better able to create partnerships with community leaders and residents. Concerning the creation of these partnerships, many respondents argued that police need to be trained to engage in "assessment of the community to meet its needs" and must seek "better communication with minority groups in the area in order to create a better living environment." One local government leader argued that community policing:

should stress the importance of the police-community link. Relationships with the various facets within the community must be established. These relationships don't just happen, they must be initiated by self-motivated officers.

Finally, another local government respondent suggested that training in humanistic skills and community partnerships may help create a "change in officers' attitude away from chasing 'bad guys' . . . to becoming incorporated into the community as true 'public servants'." This analysis of one qualitative aspect of the study appears to display the same pattern observed in the quantitative analyses. Overall, police leaders appear to have very different perceptions of key community policing issues than leaders in local governments and NGOs.

DISCUSSION AND CONCLUSION

According to nearly all estimates, community policing programs, or at least the rhetoric thereof, appear to be pervasive in local law enforcement agencies nationwide. In the survey of southeastern U.S. cities, familiarity with community policing was indeed ubiquitous within law enforcement. Community policing, in its most general form, requires police to develop working relationships with the residents and leaders of the communities they serve.

In particular, police agencies are encouraged to develop partnerships with local governmental and non-governmental organizations to develop and implement community policing programs that reflect the interests of all.

Agencies are also encouraged to seek to augment relationships with minority residents with whom they often have a history of tension and even conflict. If these goals of the community policing movement are in fact being realized, then I would expect perceptual differences between police and local leaders on these issues to be minimal. Yet in this survey, community leaders in government and especially NGOs were much less familiar with the concept of community policing and perceived community policing as being utilized to a much lesser extent in their communities than did law enforcement officials. Moreover, many local government and NGO leaders were simply unable to render any assessment of the extent to which community policing is being used in their communities. Respondents in the three groups also reported very different perceptions of the most pressing police training needs for their local policing agencies, and reported very different perceptions of police-minority relations in their communities.

The interpretation of the findings from the analysis of my five key variables certainly warrants further discussion. Concerning my familiarity with community policing and extent of usage of community policing measures, it was found that 85 percent of law enforcement leaders report being very familiar with community policing and over half say that they use it extensively in their communities. However, significantly lower percentages of local government and NGO leaders report familiarity with community policing and knowledge of its use in their communities. It is suggested that differences in perceptions across the three groups may be due to a failure of policing agencies to make contacts with community and NGO leaders to educate and involve them in community policing initiatives. At the root of those failures may be a continued reliance by police leaders on the traditional professional-paramilitary model of policing.

There is, however, an alternative interpretation. The differences in perceptions of community policing across the three groups could indicate a lack of actual development and implementation of programs in local communities. If community policing does exist more in rhetoric than in actual programs as many suggest (Kraska & Kappeler, 1997; Lyons, 1999; Maguire, 1997), then it is understandable that police leaders would report high levels of familiarity and use of community policing, while local government and NGO leaders would report much different perceptions. Both interpretations have merit, but regardless of which interpretation is more valid, the implication for the community policing movement is certainly not encouraging and actually confirms what many criminal justice academicians have been suggesting for some time. Police agencies appear to either be failing to make contacts and involve community leaders in their community policing programs, or to be failing to develop and implement community policing programs in the first instance.

Community policing also emphasizes the need for humanistic skills which are necessary for creating partnerships with community leaders and residents. Chief among these humanistic skills are communications skills, dealing with ethical issues, conflict resolution, and the ability to operate in a culturally diverse milieu. The survey data suggest that leaders in local governments and NGOs, regardless of their familiarity with the term "community policing," believe that police need more training in these areas. Police leaders, on the other hand, tend to favor technical skills such as using the Internet, computerized mapping, and crime analysis software over the humanistic skills that seem to characterize the philosophy of community policing. Although police do recognize the importance of second languages, this could also be interpreted as a technical skill needed for police to more effectively do their jobs in certain settings.

These results seem to suggest that despite the ubiquitous nature of community policing rhetoric, police leaders still appear to be most influenced by the traditional professional-paramilitary value system in which technical skills are afforded greater import than humanistic skills (Kraska & Kappeler, 1997; Maguire, 1997). Just as Maguire (1997) reports a general failure of policing agencies to become more decentralized and less military-like in organizational structure as a result of the community policing movement, my results may indicate a failure of police agencies to change their value systems and police culture with the community policing movement. For police-minority relations, this study revealed significant disagreement among the three groups when it comes to assessing the level of trust between police and minority residents. Police leaders tend to offer more optimistic estimates of police-minority relations than do community leaders in government and NGOs. These perceptual differences across the three groups were strong even when controlling for race of respondents, thus suggesting a strong effect of respondents' structural positions.

Finally, when asked what the main focus of a training institute in community policing should be, the majority of police leaders argued that training should focus on ways to involve officers in community policing programs, and to a much lesser extent, community residents. Local government and NGO leaders, however, reported that the focus of training should be in improving the humanistic skills of officers and teaching them ways in which to create partnerships with community residents. This difference appears to provide yet another example of the degree to which police remain influenced by the traditional policing model and value system which emphasizes intra-agency concerns over inter-agency concerns.

The question now, for police leaders, is what can be done to "bridge the gap" between themselves and leaders in local governments and NGOs. The most obvious solution to the problems observed in this study is for officers to receive more training in community policing, especially in the areas of humanistic skills and building community partnerships (Kerley, forthcoming; Kerley & Scheb, 1998). The results indicate that police leaders are generally failing to communicate with local government and NGO leaders, and additional training in humanistic skills and building community partnerships is a good starting point. Such training is widely available in training institutes nationwide, including the SCOPE Institute.

By itself, more training in humanistic skills may not, however, lead to any real attitudinal or behavioral changes in the way officers do their jobs. As with any type of training, results often vary in terms of how those being trained internalize and apply the training to their everyday work. In this light, it is recommend that police leaders begin a cognitive shift in value systems away from the traditional professional-paramilitary model and toward the community policing model originally envisioned by Goldstein (1987). This shift would entail police leaders placing a greater emphasis on humanistic skills, community partnerships, and problem-solving compared to the technical and physical skills emphasized in traditional policing. The shift would also involve a greater agency-wide commitment to community policing. As Goldstein (1987) and others argue, community policing is more likely to be successful when it becomes internalized as an agency-wide philosophy, as opposed to only being located in a specific department or unit. Unfortunately, the results show little of this agency-wide commitment to community policing. Additionally, it is suggested that police leaders re-think the manifest goals and evaluation of community policing programs. Although they are based on the notion of creating police-community partnerships and stimulating community processes and community involvement in crime control, they are typically designed and evaluated only in terms of effects on crime rates and fear of crime (for further discussion, see Kerley & Benson, forthcoming). Using reductions in crime rates and fear of crime as the only criteria for evaluation, community policing programs are moderately successful at best. Instead, it can be argued that police leaders consider making increased police-community relations, creation of partnerships with community leaders and residents, and stimulation of community processes the manifest goals and evaluation variables for community policing programs. This, of course, would make reductions in crime rates and fear of crime secondary or latent goals (Kerley & Benson, forthcoming). It is recognized that, for many police leaders, these recommendations would require a major cognitive shift and would likely require significant time to accomplish. Nevertheless, it is believed that such a shift is warranted, and has the potential to help police practitioners and researchers to determine if community policing can be an effective and long-term strategy for crime prevention and control. To conclude, it should be noted that this study is not an attempt to assess the overall efficacy of the community policing movement, nor is it a program evaluation of existing community policing programs. The study does, however, provide important descriptive data on differences in perceptions of community policing among leaders in policing, local government, and non-governmental organizations in the Southeast region of the United States. Specifically, it found significant perceptual differences across the three elite groups on five key community policing variables.

It can be argued that these differing perceptions may be attributed to the insular nature of police organizations and a distinct value system that are characteristic of the traditional professional-paramilitary police organizational model. The results suggest that changes in the traditional policing model as a result of the community policing movement may not be as widespread as many have suggested (see Kraska & Kappeler, 1997; Maguire, 1997). The results also seem to suggest either a failure of police leaders to create partnerships with local government and NGO leaders or a failure to develop and implement community policing programs in local communities in the first instance. Neither interpretation can be seen as good news for police leaders, especially those claiming to be doing "community policing." It is hoped that the recommendations to police leaders for addressing the differing perceptions between themselves and leaders in local government and NGOs will be helpful, and that this study will lead to additional research regarding perceptions of community policing across community sectors.

REFERENCES

Alpert, G. P. and Dunham, R. G. (1988). *Policing multi-ethnic neighborhoods.* New York: Greenwood Press.

Bartollas, C. and Hahn, L. D. (1999). *Policing in America* (3rd ed.). Boston: Allyn and Bacon.

Bayley, D. H. (1994). *Police for the future.* New York: Oxford.

Brudney, J. and England, R. E. (1983). Toward a definition of the coproduction concept. *Public Administration Review,* Jan.–Feb., 59–65.

Buerger, M. E. (1994). The limits of community. In Dennis P. Rosenbaum (Ed.), *The challenge of community policing: Testing the promises* (pp. 270–273). London: Sage.

Cardarelli, A. P. and McDevitt, J. (1995). Toward a conceptual framework for evaluating community policing. In Peter C. Kratcoski and Duane Dukes (Eds.), *Issues in community policing* (pp. 229–242). Cincinnati: Anderson.

Carter, D. L. and Radelet, L. (1999). *The Police and the community* (6th ed.). Upper Saddle River, NJ: Prentice Hall.

Cox, S. M. (1996). *Police: practices, perspectives, and problems.* Boston: Allyn and Bacon.

Cox, S. M. and Fitzgerald, J. D. (1996). *Police in community relations* (3rd ed.). Madison, WI: Brown and Benchmark.

Crank, J. P. (1994). Watchman and community: Myth and institutionalization in policing. *Law and Society Review,* 28, 325–351.

Dantzker, M. L. (1999). The state of COP among grant recipients: Results from a national survey. Paper presented to the Southern Criminal Justice Association Annual Meeting. Chattanooga, TN.

Das, D. K. (1987). *Understanding police human relations.* London: Scarecrow Press.

Eck, J. E. and Spelman, W. (1987). Who ya gonna call? *Crime and Delinquency,* 33, 31–52.

Eck, J. E. and Rosenbaum, D. P. (1994). The new police order: Effectiveness, equity, and efficiency in community policing. In Dennis P. Rosenbaum (Ed.), *The challenge of community policing: Testing the promises* (pp. 3–23). London: Sage.

Fielding, N. G. (1995). *Community policing.* Oxford: Clarendon Press.

Freidmann, R. R. (1992). *Community policing: comparative perspectives and prospects.* New York: St. Martin's Press.

Friedman, W. (1994). The community role in community policing. In Dennis P. Rosenbaum (Ed.), *The challenge of community policing: Testing the promises* (pp. 263–269). London: Sage.

Gaines, L. K., Kappeler, V. E., and Vaughn, J. B. (1999). *Policing in America.* (3rd ed.). Cincinnati: Anderson.

Goldstein, H. (1987). Toward community-oriented policing: potential, basic requirements, and threshold questions. *Crime and Delinquency,* 33, 6–30.

Goldstein, H. (1990). *Problem-oriented policing.* Philadelphia: Temple University Press.

Greene, J. R., Bergman, W. T., and McLaughlin, E. J. (1994). Implementing community policing: Cultural and structural change in police organizations. In Dennis P. Rosenbaum (Ed.), *The challenge of community policing: Testing the promises* (pp. 92–109). London: Sage.

Greene, J. R., and Mastrofski, S. D. (1988). *Community policing: Rhetoric or reality?* New York: Praeger.

Grinc, R. M. (1994). 'Angels in marble': problems in stimulating community involvement in community policing. *Crime and Delinquency,* 40, 437–468.

Guyot, D. (1991). *Policing as though people matter.* Philadelphia: Temple University Press.

Kelling, G. L. (1987). Acquiring a taste for order: The community and police. *Crime and Delinquency,* 33, 90–102.

Kelling, G. L. and Coles, C. M. (1996). *Fixing broken windows: Restoring order and reducing crime in our communities.* New York: Free Press.

Kelling, G. L. and Moore, M. H. (1988). From political to reform to community: The evolving strategy of police. In Jack R. Greene and Stephen D. Mastrofski (Eds.), *Community policing: Rhetoric or reality?* New York: Praeger.

Kerley, K. R. (Forthcoming). Measuring effectiveness in community policing: Evidence from a survey of the Southeast region. *Community Policing Exchange*

Kerley, K. R. and Benson, M. L. (Forthcoming). Does community-oriented policing help build stronger communities? *Police Quarterly*

Kerley, K. R. and Scheb II, J. M. (1998). Law enforcement leaders tell researchers what they think they need to make community policing work. *Community Policing Exchange,* 23, 4.

Kraska, P. B. and Kappeler, V. E. (1997). Militarizing American police: The rise and normalization of paramilitary units. *Social Problems,* 44, 1–18.

Kratcoski, P. C. and Dukes, D. (1995). Perspectives on community policing. In Peter C. Kratcoski and Duane Dukes (Eds.), *Issues in community policing* (pp. 5–20). Cincinnati: Anderson.

Lyons, W. (1999). *The politics of community policing: Rearranging the power to punish.* Ann Arbor, MI: University of Michigan Press.

Maguire, E. R. (1997). Structural change in large municipal police organizations during the community policing era. *Justice Quarterly,* 14, 547–576.

McEwen, T. (1995). National assessment program: 1994 survey results. *National Institute of Justice Research in Brief* (May) Washington, DC: U.S. Department of Justice.

Moore, M. H. and Kelling, G. L. (1983). 'To serve and protect': Learning from police history. *Public Interest,* 70, 49–65.

Moore, M. H. (1994). Research synthesis and policy implications. In Dennis P. Rosenbaum (Ed.), *The challenge of community policing: Testing the promises* (pp. 285–299). London: Sage.

More, H. W. (1998). *Special topics in policing.* (2nd ed.). Cincinnati: Anderson.

Oliver, W. M. (1998). *Community-oriented policing: A systematic approach to policing.* Upper Saddle River, NJ: Sage.

Reed, W. E. (1999). *The politics of community policing: The case of Seattle.* New York: Garland.

Roberg, R. R. (1994). Can today's police organizations effectively implement community policing? In Dennis P. Rosenbaum (Ed.), *The challenge of community policing: testing the promises* (pp. 249–257). London: Sage.

Roberg, R. R. and Kuykendall, J. (1993). *Police and society.* Belmont, CA: Wadsworth.

Rosenbaum, D. P. (1987). The theory and research behind neighborhood watch: Is it a sound fear and crime reduction strategy? *Crime and Delinquency,* 33, 103–134.

Rosenbaum, D. P. (1988). Community crime prevention: A review and synthesis of the literature. *Justice Quarterly,* 5, 323–395.

Rosenbaum, D. P. (1994). An inside look at community policing reform: Definitions, organizational changes, and evaluation findings. *Crime and Delinquency,* 40, 299–314.

Sadd, S. and Grinc, R. M. (1994). Innovative neighborhood oriented policing: An evaluation of community policing programs in eight cities. In Dennis P. Rosenbaum (Ed.), *The challenge of community policing: Testing the promises* (pp. 27–52). London: Sage.

Skogan, W. G. and Hartnett, S. M. (1997). *Community policing: Chicago style.* New York: Oxford University Press.

Skogan, W. G. (1994). The impact of community policing on neighborhood residents: A cross-site analysis. In Dennis P. Rosenbaum (Ed.), *The challenge of community policing: testing the promises* (pp. 167–181). London: Sage.

Skolnick, J. H. and Bayley, D. H. (1986). *The new blue line: Police innovation in six American cities.* New York: Free Press.

Skolnick, J. H. and Fyfe, J. J. (1993). *Above the law: Police and the excessive use of force.* New York: Free Press.

Thurman, Q. C. (1995). Community policing: The police as a community resource? In Paul Adams and Kristine Nelson (Eds.), *Reinventing Human Services: Community- and Family-Centered Practice* New York: Aldine De Gruyter.

Thurman, Q. C. and Reisig, M. D. (1996). Community-oriented research in an era of community-oriented policing. *American Behavioral Scientist,* 39, 570–586.

Trojanowicz, R. C. (1994). The future of community policing. In Dennis P. Rosenbaum (Ed.), *The challenge of community policing: Testing the promises* (pp. 258–262). London: Sage.

Trojanowicz, R. C. and Bucqueroux, B. (1998). *Community policing: How to get started.* (2nd ed.). Cincinnati: Anderson.

Williams, B. N. (1998). *Citizen perspectives on community policing.* New York: SUNY Press.

Wycoff, M. A. (1994). Community policing in Madison: An analysis of implementation and impact. In Dennis P. Rosenbaum (Ed.), *The challenge of community policing: Testing the promises* (pp. 167–181). London: Sage.

7

Community-Oriented Policing: Assessing a Police Saturation Operation[1]

Thomas B. Priest and Deborah Brown Carter

❖

An increasing number of police departments have implemented programs described as "community-oriented" policing (Grinc, 1994). Yet, considerable diversity exists in the programs labeled "community-oriented" policing. Goldstein (1987) described elements common to most versions of community-oriented policing: "Most common . . . are the involvement of the community in getting the police job done; the permanent assignment of police officers to a neighborhood in order to cultivate better relationships; the setting of police priorities based on the specific needs and desires of the community; and the meeting of these needs by the allocation of police resources and personnel otherwise assigned to responding to calls for police assistance" (p. 7).

Compared to traditional policing, community-oriented policing involves an increase in interaction between citizens and police (Eck and Spelman, 1987; Goldstein, 1987, 1990; Skogan and Hartnett, 1997; Wycoff, 1988). Police are more accessible and visible to citizens. Increased police visibility, it is assumed, will reduce the public's fear of crime (Manning, 1984, 1988; Riechers and Roberg, 1990). Proponents also claim that community-oriented policing will ameliorate "quality-of-life" problems in neighborhoods (McElroy, Cosgrove, and Sadd, 1993; Skogan and Hartnett, 1997; Wilson and Kelling, 1982). Proponents add that

[1]The research reported here was partially supported by a grant from the Charlotte-Mecklenburg Police Department. We wish to thank Officer Vicki Bisbikis, Mrs. Carolyn Carr, Deputy Chief Deacon Jones, Chief Dennis Nowicki, Officer Monica Nguyen, and Sergeant Bob Prather of CMPD for their assistance.

111

amelioration of quality-of-life problems may have some impact upon the amount of conventional street crime in neighborhoods (McElroy, Cosgrove, and Sadd, 1993).

According to Oliver (1998), one component of community-oriented policing is "strategic" policing, in which police increase their enforcement of laws bearing on a specific problem. Oliver (1998) described three methods in strategic policing of a targeted area or problem: (a) "directed patrol," (b) "aggressive patrol," and (c) "saturation patrol." Of the three, saturation patrol involves the largest drain on police resources and greatest show of force. More specifically, saturation patrol generally involves a collection of officers, often from various agencies, shifts, or tactical units, who, in uniform, saturate a designated area for days or even weeks. After an initial period in which police establish their presence in an area with multiple arrests, investigative stops, or traffic stops, they then remain in the area, in force, for an additional period. The goal of a saturation operation is to temporarily displace or eliminate a problem from a designated area (Oliver, 1998). Saturation patrol is most closely associated with drug "crackdowns" (Kinlock, 1994; Sherman, 1990a, 1990b; Zimmer, 1990; also see Skogan, 1994), but supposedly is effective for both criminal and order maintenance issues (Oliver, 1998; Schnelle, Kirchner, Casey, Uselton, and McNees, 1977; Campbell and Ross, 1968). The effects of saturation patrol upon crime and order maintenance problems, however, have not been well researched.

This chapter describes a saturation operation conducted in the Remount Road-West Boulevard area of Charlotte, North Carolina in September of 1997. Approximately one week after the operation concluded, officers of the Adam Service Area of the Charlotte-Mecklenburg Police Department (CMPD) discussed with the authors a research project to assess the effects of this operation upon crime in the area. Some of the results of that research project are described as follows.

SATURATION OPERATION

The Remount Road-West Boulevard area is a predominantly African American residential area, located about one mile southwest of the central business district. Interstate 77 forms the eastern boundary of the area, while four-lane Wilkinson Boulevard (U.S. 74) forms the northern boundary. The area is roughly triangular in shape, slightly more than one mile long on each side. West Boulevard is a four-lane street that nearly bisects this triangular area. Remount Road also is four lanes and crosses West Boulevard near the center of the triangle. Almost all of the small number of businesses in the area are near the intersection of West and Remount. Most residences in the area are single-family dwellings, although four apartment complexes also are present. The majority of apartments in two of the complexes have been boarded up.

A high volume of traffic moves through the Remount Road-West Boulevard area. Both Remount and West serve as exits from Interstate 77. Further, West Boulevard connects the edge of the central business district to the southwestern part of the city, including the airport. Traffic moves quickly along West Boulevard; traffic lights are more than one-half mile apart in the area. Traffic also moves quickly on Remount Road, but traffic lights are more closely spaced, at least between the interstate exit and West Boulevard. West Boulevard generally is considered more dangerous than Remount Road.

Both residents and business owners and managers long have complained about speeding and other traffic problems in the Remount Road-West Boulevard area. Traffic fatalities and hit and run accidents are common. Further, residents and business people have been concerned with crime, disorder, and the physical deterioration of the area. Local neighborhood associations relayed these complaints and concerns to the CMPD via a community police officer (CPO). Largely in response to neighborhood complaints and concerns, the CMPD decided to initiate a saturation operation in the area.

The saturation operation involved the coordinated action of officers from a number of law enforcement agencies and units. These included the Highway Interdiction and Traffic Safety (H.I.T.S.) Unit of the CMPD, the Adam Service Area Street Crimes Unit of the CMPD, the Alcohol Law Enforcement Division of the North Carolina Department of Alcohol and Public Safety, and the Mecklenburg County Sheriff's Department. Approximately thirty officers, agents, and deputies were involved. The operation largely occurred during the second, or 4:00 to 11:00 P.M. work-shift, given some concern with speeding during evening rush hour.

The H.I.T.S. Unit primarily was concerned with speeding and other traffic violations. The Street Crimes Unit largely was concerned with non-traffic offenses. Agents from the Alcohol Law Enforcement Division checked for liquor law violations at area bars and lounges. Sheriff's deputies parked vehicles beside West Boulevard near the southern edge of the area, while they supervised inmates performing community service (trash pickup). The number of official vehicles in the area was approximately ten times the usual number. The number of traffic arrests was more than ten times the usual number.

The saturation operation centered on a shopping-center parking lot on one corner of the intersection of West Boulevard and Remount Road. When officers or agents apprehended offenders, the offender was brought to the shopping-center parking lot and formally arrested. Formal arrests were highly visible in all directions. Note, however, that formal arrests probably were more visible to business owners and managers than to most residents of the area.

In the week after the saturation operation, officers of the Adam Service Area of the CMPD discussed with the authors a research project to assess the impact of the saturation operation upon the Remount Road-West Boulevard area. In particular, did residents or business people perceive any decrease in quality-of-life problems, in speeding through the area, or in crime following the saturation operation? Similarly, what did longitudinal data compiled and tabulated for the Uniform Crime Report (UCR) indicate? A survey of residents and business people was planned in an attempt to answer the first question; a questionnaire was developed by the authors and officers of the Adam Service Area. Further, data compiled and tabulated by the Strategic Planning and Crime Analysis Unit of the CMPD for the UCR would be used in an attempt to answer the second question.

Method

A survey of both residences and businesses in the West Boulevard-Remount Road area was conducted between October 16, 1997 and November 3, 1997. Every third residence in the area was sampled. The sample included 274 residences. Those living at 44, or 16.1 percent of these residences, chose not to participate in the survey. No response was received at another 74, or 27.0 percent of residences, even though interviewers returned as often as six times. Language problems, large dogs, or other problems accounted for another 21, or 7.7 percent of residences. Altogether, 135 or 49.2 percent of the residences sampled were surveyed. At each, one adult resident eighteen years of age or older was interviewed.

An attempt was made to survey the owners or managers of all businesses in the area. The area is primarily residential; there are few businesses. Further, because of refusals and language problems, owners or managers of just 17, or 85.0 percent, of the 20 businesses in the area were surveyed. In what follows, greater emphasis is placed on the survey of residents.

Trained student interviewers, all of whom were African American, asked adult residents and business people questions included on a twenty-six-item fixed-response questionnaire. Among the more important questions on the questionnaire were pairs of questions that focused on "quality-of-life" issues. About midway through the questionnaire, each respondent was asked: (a) "Do young people 'hang out' on the corner?," (b) "Do you see people drinking on the street in this neighborhood?," (c) "Are there prostitutes who walk the streets in this neighborhood?," and (d) "Are there drug dealers who sell drugs on the street in the neighborhood?" Responses to each question were "yes," "no," or "don't know." These four questions were intended to measure whether the respondent was aware of possible quality-of-life problems in the neighborhood. After each of these questions, the respondent then was asked a paired follow-up question: (a) "Have you noticed fewer youngsters 'hanging out' in the past few weeks?" (b) "Have you noticed fewer people drinking on the streets in the past month?" (c) "Have you noticed fewer of them [prostitutes] in the past month or so?" and (d) "Are there fewer drug dealers around than a few weeks ago?" Responses were again "yes," "no," and "don't know." The follow-up questions were intended to measure whether respondents perceived recent decreases in possible quality-of-life problems in the area. In addition to these four follow-up questions, the questionnaire also included two other questions about possible recent changes in the neighborhood. One question asked "Are there fewer people speeding through the neighborhood than a month ago?" Another asked "Have you noticed a decrease in crime in this area in the last few weeks?" Responses to these latter two questions also were "yes," "no," and "don't know." Altogether, the survey included six questions regarding possible recent changes in the area.

The questionnaire also included some standard demographic questions. All respondents were asked questions about race/ethnicity, gender, and age. Residents also were asked about length of residence in the neighborhood, whether there were children younger than eighteen years of age living in the residence, whether the residence was owned or rented, and whether the respondent was an active member of the neighborhood association. Business people were asked how long they had been in the neighborhood and whether they were active members of the neighborhood association.

The questionnaire included a number of questions about safety and the police. Most important for present purposes were two questions near the end of the questionnaire, which asked respondents whether they were aware of the police saturation operation. The first asked: "Were you aware that police were stopping and arresting people at the intersection of Remount Road and West Boulevard for traffic violations nearly a month ago?" The other, which followed, asked: "Were you aware that police were stopping and arresting people for other offenses at the same time?" Responses to both were again "yes," "no," and "don't know."

Our second type of data consisted of reported incident statistics for the Remount Road-West Boulevard area for the period from June 30, 1997 to November 9, 1997. This period includes the week of the saturation operation (September 1 to 7), as well as nine weeks before the operation (June 30 to August 31) and nine weeks after the operation (September 8 to November 9). Reported incident statistics were compiled by the Strategic Planning and Crime Analysis Unit of the CMPD and tabulated following the UCR code breakdown. Data were matched to the Remount Road-West Boulevard area via Geographic In-formation Systems (GIS) programs. Additionally, reported incident statistics were obtained for the Reid Park neighborhood of Charlotte. Reid Park is a small, predominantly African American neighborhood, further along West Boulevard toward the airport. The eastern edge of the Reid Park neighborhood is one-half mile from the western border of the Remount Road-West Boulevard area; open space, an elementary school, a large public housing proj-ect, and a library separate the two. Most families in Reid Park own their own homes. Any displacement or diffusion from the Remount Road-West Boulevard area to the Reid Park neighborhood should be minimal. Reported incident statistics for the Reid Park neighbor-hood will be compared to reported incident statistics from the Remount Road-West Boule-vard area. Although arrest statistics for the Remount Road-West Boulevard area and for Reid Park also were available, we believe reported incident statistics are a better indicator of crime and disorder in an area.

Neither the Remount Road-West Boulevard area nor the Reid Park neighborhood is very large geographically. The number of reported incidents in each area in the period from June 30, 1997 to November 9, 1997 is fairly small, whether measured per day or per week. Given these small numbers, in what follows we simply compare the raw count of reported incidents in each area for the nine weeks before the saturation operation to the raw count of reported incidents for the nine weeks after the operation (Quinet and Nunn, 1998). Simi-larly, we examine the average number of incidents per week for the nine weeks before and nine weeks after the operation.

The saturation operation was in part a traffic operation. Unfortunately, longitudinal data on traffic incidents and arrests in the area were not available; we are not able to assess directly whether the saturation operation had any effect upon traffic in the area.

Results

Among 134 residents of the Remount Road-West Boulevard area for whom data were avail-able, 95.5 percent were African American, 0.7 percent were white, 1.5 percent were Asian, 0.7 percent were Hispanic, and 1.5 percent were of some other race or ethnicity. Among the 17 business people surveyed, 64.7 percent were African American, 23.5 percent were Asian, and 11.8 percent were Hispanic. Some 52.6 percent of the residents surveyed were male, while 76.5 percent of the business people surveyed were male. The mean age of res-idents was 42.0 years, while the mean age of the business people was 40.2 years. The resi-dents had lived in the neighborhood an average 22.0 years; the business people had been in the neighborhood an average 31.9 years. Some 35.8 percent of residents owned their own homes; 54.5 percent had children under 18 in the home. Some 18.2 percent of residents and 28.6 percent of the business people said that they were active members of the neighborhood association. In general, both the residents and the business people appeared to have a high level of commitment to the Remount Road-West Boulevard area.

Residents generally were aware of "quality-of-life" problems in the area. Among 134 residents who gave responses, for example, 67.9 percent indicated that young people hung out on the corner. Similarly, 49.3 percent indicated that they had seen people drinking on the street in the neighborhood. Some 41.8 percent indicated that prostitutes walked the streets in the neighborhood. A similar 41.0 percent indicated that drug dealers sold drugs on the street in the neighborhood. Business people also were aware of quality-of-life problems. Among

TABLE 1   Responses to Questions Asking about Recent Changes

	Responses			
Question	% yes	% no	% dk	N
Residents:				
Fewer hanging out?	45.3	39.3	15.4	117
Fewer drinking?	31.8	44.5	23.6	110
Fewer prostitutes?	28.6	33.7	37.8	98
Fewer drug dealers?	18.4	36.9	44.7	103
Fewer speeding?	31.8	58.3	9.8	132
Decrease in crime	29.1	52.2	18.7	134
Business people:				
Fewer hanging out?	25.0	58.3	16.7	12
Fewer drinking?	23.5	58.8	17.6	17
Fewer prostitutes?	29.4	47.1	23.5	17
Fewer drug dealers?	31.3	37.5	31.3	16
Fewer speeding?	37.5	37.5	25.0	16
Decrease in crime?	29.4	52.9	17.6	17

17 business people who gave responses, 64.7 percent indicated that young people hung out on the corner. Some 70.6 percent of business people indicated they had seen people drinking on the street in the neighborhood. Some 64.7 percent indicated that prostitutes walked the streets. Further, 64.7 percent indicated that drug dealers sold drugs on the street. Business people often were more aware of quality-of-life issues than residents.

As previously indicated, residents and business people also were asked about possible recent decreases in quality-of-life problems in the area. They also were asked about a possible decrease in the number of people speeding through their neighborhood and a possible decrease in crime in the area. Table 1 presents the responses of residents and business people to queries about possible recent decreases. Perhaps most important, this table demonstrates that sizable proportions of both residents and business people indicated that there had been recent decreases in each of the four quality-of-life problems, in speeding, and in crime. For example, of 117 residents who gave a response, 45.3 percent indicated that they had noticed fewer youngsters "hanging out" in the past few weeks. Similarly, of 12 business people who gave a response, 25.0 percent indicated that they had noticed fewer youngsters hanging out in the past few weeks. The proportions of residents and business people indicating decreases in other quality-of-life problems, in the number of people speeding through neighborhoods, and in crime in the area were fairly similar to these. The smallest proportion (18.4 percent) was among residents who indicated a decrease in drug dealers selling on the street. In sum, however, many residents and business people perceived

TABLE 2   Awareness of the Police Saturation Operation and Perceptions of Recent Decreases

A. Aware police stopped and arrested for traffic violations?	Fewer hanging out? % yes	Fewer drinking? % yes	Fewer prostitutes? % yes	Fewer dealers? % yes	Fewer speeding? % yes	Decrease in crime? % yes
Yes	55.8	42.1	28.2	28.2	37.8	39.1
No	41.2	23.4	26.5	10.5*	35.0	23.3*
N =	(116)	(109)	(97)	(102)	(131)	(133)
B. Aware police stopped and arrested for other offenses?						
Yes	51.7	52.0	37.5	30.8	28.1	43.8
No	47.5	22.0**	23.3	14.9**	39.4	20.9*
N =	(115)	(107)	(95)	(101)	(129)	(131)

*Difference in proportions significant at .05 level.
**Difference in proportions significant at .01 level.

recent decreases in quality-of-life problems, in the number of people speeding, and in crime in the area.

Residents and business people also were asked about the police saturation operation which occurred approximately one month before the survey. Substantial proportions of both residents and business people indicated they were aware of the operation. More specifically, 34.3 percent of 134 residents and 41.2 percent of 17 business people indicated that they were aware that police were stopping and arresting people at the intersection of Remount Road and West Boulevard for traffic violations nearly a month previous. Similarly, 24.2 percent of 132 residents and 41.2 percent of 17 business people indicated that they were aware that police were stopping and arresting for other offenses at that same time. Although these proportions are quite substantial, we expected somewhat larger proportions, given the high visibility of the saturation operation. The smaller than expected proportions may, in part, reflect problems of recall.

Were those who were aware of the police saturation operation more likely to indicate that there were recent decreases in each of the four quality-of-life problems, in the number of people speeding through the neighborhood, and in crime? Table 2 examines the relationship between awareness of the police saturation operation and perceptions of recent decreases among residents only. (The Ns for area business people were so small as to be meaningless; results for business people are not presented here). Panel A examines the relationship between awareness that police were stopping and arresting for traffic violations and perception of recent decreases. This panel indicates that those who were aware that police were stopping and arresting for traffic offenses approximately one month before were more likely to indicate that there had been recent decreases in quality-of-life problems, in speeding, and in crime in the area. Differences in proportions sometimes were statistically significant. Awareness of the police saturation operation was related to perception of recent decreases. Yet, more important, this panel also indicates that substantial proportions of residents who were *not* aware of the police saturation operation also indicated there had been recent decreases. The perception that there had been recent decreases in quality-of-life problems, in speeding, and in crime in the area was not limited just to those who were aware of the police saturation operation.

Panel B further examines the relationship between awareness of the police saturation operation and the perception that there had been recent decreases in quality-of-life problems, in speeding, and in crime in the area. Panel B examines the relationship between awareness that police were stopping and arresting for other, non-traffic offenses and perception of recent decreases. Results are fairly similar to those in Panel A. This panel indicates that those who were aware that police were stopping and arresting for other offenses approximately one month before were more likely to indicate that there had been recent decreases in quality-of-life problems and in crime in the area. Differences in proportions sometimes were significant. Those who were aware that police were stopping and arresting for other offenses were not, however, more likely to indicate that there had been decreases in the number of people speeding through the neighborhood. Awareness of the police saturation operation was, in general, related to the perception of recent decreases, but not always. More important, substantial proportions of residents who were not aware of the saturation operation indicated that there had been recent decreases. Once again, the perception that there had been recent decreases in the four quality-of-life problems, in speeding, and in crime in the area was not limited just to those who were aware of the saturation operation.

Substantial proportions of both residents and business people in the Remount Road-West Boulevard area perceived decreases in quality-of-life problems, in the number of people speeding through the neighborhood, and in crime in the area in the period after the police saturation operation. What do incident statistics indicate?

REPORTED INCIDENTS

As previously indicated, the number of reported incidents in the Remount Road-West Boulevard area in the period from June 30, 1997 to November 9, 1997 was fairly small. The number in the Reid Park neighborhood in the same period also was quite small. Table 3 presents the raw count of reported incidents in each area in the nine week period before the saturation operation and the nine week period after the saturation operation. As indicated in Table 3, the total number of reported incidents in the Remount Road-West Boulevard area was greater in the nine weeks before the saturation operation than in the nine weeks after the operation. More specifically, the total number of reported incidents declined some 11.2 percent between the pre-saturation operation period and the post-saturation operation period. This decline suggests that crime decreased in the Remount Road-West Boulevard area in the period after the saturation operation. In comparison, the total number of reported in-

TABLE 3   Raw Counts of Reported Incidents in the Remount Road-West Boulevard Area and the Reid Park Area Before and After the Saturation Operation

Reported Incident	Pre-saturation Operation	Post-saturation Operation	Pre-saturation Operation	Post-saturation Operation
Homicide	0	1	0	0
Robbery	3	2	0	0
Rape	1	0	0	0
Assault (a)	43	38	20	14
Burglary	11	26	2	5
Larceny/theft (b)	31	19	5	8
Auto theft	14	7	1	3
Arson	0	1	0	0
Vandalism	16	7	8	6
Other property offense (c)	2	4	0	0
Disorderly conduct	1	0	0	0
Sex offense	0	3	1	0
Offense against family	2	1	1	0
Traffic fatality	0	1	0	0
Hit and run	5	5	2	1
Violation state/local	14	11	3	8
Sudden death	1	0	0	0
Missing person	5	7	0	2
Missing/lost property	1	1	0	0
Other non-offense	2	1	1	0
Total	152	135	45	47

Legend: (a) Includes both aggravated and non-aggravated assault
(b) Includes larceny/theft under $50 to larceny/theft over $200
(c) Includes forgery, fraud, and embezzlement

cidents in the Reid Park neighborhood was almost the same in the nine weeks before the saturation operation and the nine weeks after the operation. There was little change between the pre-saturation operation period and the post-saturation operation period. This lack of change suggests that crime in Reid Park remained at about the same level before and after the saturation operation. Altogether, the raw counts of reported incidents presented in Table 3 suggest that the police saturation operation had some effect upon crime in the Remount Road-West Boulevard area.

Yet, a few categories of incidents included in Table 3, such as sudden death, missing person, missing/lost property, and other non-offense, are not necessarily crime-related. When these categories of reported incidents are excluded from analysis, so that only crime-related categories remain, the number of reported incidents in the Remount Road-West Boulevard area still was greater in the nine weeks before the saturation operation than in the nine weeks after the operation. The number of clearly crime-related incidents declined 12.5 percent between the pre-saturation operation period and the post-saturation operation period. Alternately, when categories of incidents are excluded, so that only crime-related categories remain, the number of reported incidents in the Reid Park neighborhood was exactly the same in the nine weeks before the saturation operation and nine weeks after the operation. These results again suggest that the saturation operation had some effect upon crime in the Remount Road-West Boulevard area in the period after the saturation operation.

Some specific categories of incidents included in Table 3 are relevant to the perceptions of residents and business people in the Remount Road-West Boulevard area. The number of reported incidents in the area involving sex offenses, for example, was greater in the nine weeks after the saturation operation than in the nine weeks before the operation. This result seems to conflict with the perception of many residents and business people that fewer prostitutes were walking the streets in the area in the period after the saturation operation. Similarly, the number of hit-and-run incidents in the area was the same in the nine weeks before the saturation operation as in the nine weeks after the operation, while the only traffic fatality occurred in the nine weeks after the operation. These results seem to conflict with the perception of many residents and business people that fewer people were speeding through their neighborhood in the previous month. Thus, while the total number of reported incidents in the Remount Road-West boulevard area generally supports the perception of many residents and business people that crime decreased in the area after the saturation operation, the number in specific categories sometimes conflicts with the perceptions of many residents and business people that certain types of crimes decreased.

Another way to investigate the possible effects of the saturation operation upon crime and disorder in the Remount Road-West Boulevard area is to examine the average weekly number of reported incidents both before and after the saturation operation. Means for the Remount Road-West Boulevard area and for the Reid Park neighborhood are presented in Table 4. Although the F-ratio presupposes a random sample, which is not the case with these data, we also present F-ratios to suggest the relative magnitude of differences between means. As indicated, in the Remount Road-West Boulevard area, the weekly average for all types of incidents declined from 16.89 in the nine weeks before the saturation operation to 15.00 in the nine weeks after the operation. This is a decline of 11.2 percent. In comparison, in the Reid Park neighborhood, the weekly average for all types of incidents increased from 5.00 in the nine weeks before the saturation operation to 5.22 in the nine weeks after the operation. In neither case was the F-ratio statistically significant. Similarly, the weekly average for violent incidents in the Remount Road-West Boulevard area declined from 5.22 in the nine weeks before the operation to 4.55 in the nine weeks after the operation. The weekly average for violent incidents in the Reid Park neighborhood declined from 2.22 in the nine weeks before the operation to 1.56 in the nine weeks after the operation. Again, neither difference was statistically significant. The weekly average for property incidents in the Remount Road-West Boulevard area declined from 8.33 in the weeks before the operation to 7.22 in the weeks after the operation. The weekly average for property incidents in the Reid Park neighborhood increased from 1.77 in the weeks before the operation to 2.44 in the weeks after the operation. These differences, again, were not statistically significant. The weekly average for other incidents in the Remount Road-West Boulevard area barely

TABLE 4 Mean Number (std. dev. in parentheses) of Reported Incidents per Week for the Remount Road-West Boulevard Area and for the Reid Park Area

| Incident Type | Remount Road-West Boulevard Area | | | Reid Park Area | | |
	Pre-saturation Operation	Post-saturation Operation	F-ratio	Pre-saturation Operation	Post-saturation Operation	F-ratio
All	16.89 (4.62) N = 9	15.00 (4.33) N = 9	.801	5.00 (2.96) N = 9	5.22 (2.68) N = 9	.028
Violent	5.22 (2.05) N = 9	4.55 (2.04) N = 9	.401	2.22 (1.99) N = 9	1.56 (1.33) N = 9	.699
Property	8.33 (3.97) N = 9	7.22 (2.05) N = 9	.557	1.77 (1.09) N = 9	2.44 (1.24) N = 9	1.469
Other	3.33 (2.00) N = 9	3.22 (1.79) N = 9	.015	1.00 (1.32) N = 9	1.22 (1.48) N = 9	.113

*F-ratio significant at .05 level.

declined at all, from 3.33 in the weeks before the saturation operation to 3.22 in the weeks after the operation. The weekly average for other incidents increased slightly in the Reid Park neighborhood, from 1.00 in the weeks before the operation to 1.22 in the weeks after the operation. These differences, again, were not significant. In sum, while the weekly average for all types of incidents, violent incidents, property incidents, and other types of incidents each declined in the Remount Road-West Boulevard area after the saturation operation, the declines were small; none was statistically significant. In comparison, in the Reid Park neighborhood, the weekly average for all types of incidents, property incidents, and other incidents increased after the saturation operation, while the weekly average for violent incidents decreased after the operation. Differences were small, however, and were not statistically significant.

SUMMARY

Largely in response to neighborhood complaints and concerns, a police saturation operation was conducted between September 1, 1997 and September 7, 1997 in the Remount Road-West Boulevard area of Charlotte, North Carolina. The operation focused upon both (a) speeding and traffic problems, and (b) crime and "quality-of-life" issues in the area. We attempted to assess the impact of this operation upon the area. We surveyed residents and business people in the area about one month after the operation, and obtained longitudinal reported incident statistics for the Remount Road-West Boulevard area and, for comparison, the Reid Park neighborhood of Charlotte from the Charlotte-Mecklenburg Police Department. Comparable longitudinal traffic statistics were not available. Perhaps most important, both survey data and reported incident statistics suggested that crime decreased in the Remount Road-West Boulevard area in the period after the saturation operation. The saturation operation appeared to have at least a modest effect upon crime in the area.

Yet, survey data and reported incident statistics sometimes were contradictory. While many residents and business people stated, for example, that prostitution decreased in the area in the period after the saturation operation, reported incident statistics indicated that sex offenses increased after the operation. Similarly, while many residents and business people stated that speeding decreased in the area in the period after the operation, hit and run incidents increased and a traffic fatality occurred after the operation. The perceptions of residents and business people were not completely congruent with official statistics.

We were asked to assess the impact of the police saturation operation upon the Remount Road-West Boulevard area approximately one week after the operation concluded. Ideally, researchers would have greater control in deciding the site and timing of research and the research design than was the case in this instance. Nevertheless, the major finding of our research—that the saturation operation had at least a modest effect upon crime in the area—seems reasonable and generally consistent with some previous research (Sherman, 1990b, p. 17; Zimmer, 1990, p. 60). Further, both survey data and official statistics suggest this result. The responses of many neighborhood residents and business people, as well as reported incident statistics for the area, suggested that some decrease in crime occurred after the saturation operation.

As previously indicated, the saturation operation described here focused upon both speeding and traffic problems and crime and "quality-of-life" issues. Typically, a saturation operation focuses on just one problem in an area, such as speeding (Campbell and Ross, 1968) or drug sales (Kinlock, 1994; Sherman, 1990a, 1990b; Zimmer, 1990). Yet, our results suggest that even a less narrowly focused operation may have some effect upon crime in an area. Apparently, the show of force represented by a saturation operation has at least some modest deterrent or displacement effects upon crime in an area. Some potential offenders apparently react to the unusual number of police officers in the area either by "thinking twice" before committing crime or by leaving the area.

Recent analyses of police saturation operations generally have focused on drug "crackdowns" (Kinlock, 1994; Sherman, 1990a, 1990b; Zimmer, 1990; see also Skogan, 1994). In contrast, the saturation operation described in this paper focused on speeding and other traffic problems and on crime and "quality-of-life" issues. Additional research on the effects of saturation operations, other than drug crackdowns, is necessary.

DISCUSSION

The results of our survey of the Remount Road-West Boulevard area were presented to a meeting of the command staff of the CMPD in April of 1998. Several members of the Adam Service Area Street Crimes Unit who had participated in the saturation operation and helped to develop the questionnaire used in our survey also were present at this meeting. When our survey results were presented, several officers asked about possible seasonality—was it possible that residents and business people noticed fewer young people "hanging out," fewer people drinking, fewer prostitutes on the streets, and fewer drug dealers around after the saturation operation simply because the fall weather was becoming colder and wetter, rather than because of the saturation operation itself? At the time of our presentation, we were not in possession of reported incident statistics for either the Remount Road-West Boulevard area or the Reid Park neighborhood. Seasonality seemed a reasonable and very possible explanation for our survey results. Further, more than one resident of the Remount Road-West Boulevard area had suggested to student interviewers that they had noticed fewer young people hanging out, fewer people drinking, fewer prostitutes, etc., but added that this was probably because of the colder fall weather. At the urging of then Chief Dennis Nowicki of CMPD, we obtained reported incident statistics first for the Remount Road-West Boulevard area, and later for the Reid Park neighborhood. Reported incident statistics for the Reid Park neighborhood provide the strongest argument against seasonality as an explanation of our results. In Reid Park, reported incidents increased slightly, rather than decreased, in the weeks after the saturation operation. This increase strongly suggests that seasonality is not a satisfactory explanation for our survey results, nor for the decline in reported incidents in the Remount Road-West Boulevard area in the weeks after the saturation operation.

Professor Thomas Priest can be reached at tpriest@jcsu.edu

Professor Deborah Brown Carter can be reached at dbcarter@jcsu.edu

REFERENCES

Campbell, D. T. and Ross, H. L. (1968). The Connecticut crackdown on speeding: Time-series data in quasi-experimental analysis. *Law and Society Review* 3, 33–53.

Eck, J. E. and Spelman, W. (1987). Who ya gonna call? The police as problem-busters. *Crime and Delinquency* 33(1), 31–52.

Goldstein, H. (1987). Toward community-oriented policing: Potential, basic requirements, and threshold questions. *Crime and Delinquency* 33(1), 6–30.

Goldstein, H. (1990). *Problem-oriented policing*. NY: McGraw-Hill.

Grinc, R. M. (1994). 'Angels in marble': Problems in stimulating community involvement in community policing. *Crime and Delinquency* 40, 437–468.

Kinlock, T. W. (1994). Problem-oriented data collection: Toward improved evaluation of police drug crackdowns. *American Journal of Police* 13, 59–94.

Manning, P. K. (1984). Community policing. *American Journal of Police* 3, 205–227.

Manning, P. K. (1988). Community policing as a drama of control. In J. R. Greene and S. D. Mastrofski, (Eds.) *Community policing: Rhetoric or reality* (pp. 27–45). NY: Praeger.

McElroy, J. E., Cosgrove, C. A., and Sadd, S. (1993). *Community policing: The CPOP in New York.* Newbury Park, CA: Sage.

Oliver, W. (1998). *Community-oriented policing*. Upper Saddle River, NJ: Prentice Hall.

Quinet, K. D. and Nunn, S. (1998). Illuminating crime: The impact of street lighting on calls for police service. *Evaluation Review* 22, 751–779.

Riechers, L. M., and Roberg, R. R. (1990). Community policing: A critical review of underlying assumptions. *Journal of Police Science and Administration* 17, 105–114.

Schnelle, J. F., Kirchner, R. E., Jr., Casey, J. D., Uselton, P. H., Jr., and McNees, M. P. (1977). Patrol evaluation research: A multiple-baseline analysis of saturation police patrolling during day and night hours. *Journal of Applied Behavior Analysis* 10, 33–40.

Sherman, L. W. (1990a). Police crackdowns. *National Institute of Justice Reports.* March-April.

Sherman, L. W. (1990b). Police crackdowns: Initial and residual deterrence. In M. Tonry and N. Morris, (Eds.) *Crime and justice: A review of research* (pp. 1–48). Chicago, IL: Chicago 12.

Skogan, W. G. (1994). The impact of community policing on neighborhood residents: A cross-site analysis. In D. Rosenbaum, (Ed.) *The challenge of community policing: Testing the premises* (pp. 167–181) Thousand Oaks, CA: Sage.

Skogan, W. G. and Hartnett, S. M. (1997). *Community policing, Chicago style.* NY: Oxford.

Wilson, J. Q., and Kelling, G. L. (1982). Broken windows. *The Atlantic Monthly* 249: 29–38.

Wycoff, M. A. (1988). The benefits of community policing: Evidence and conjecture. In J. R. Greene and S. D. Mastrofski, (Eds.) *Community policing: Rhetoric or reality* (pp. 103–120). NY: Praeger.

Zimmer, L. (1990). Proactive policing against street-level drug trafficking. *American Journal of Police* 9, 43–74.

8

Youth Crime Watch of America: A Youth-Led Movement

Gerald A. Rudoff and Ellen G. Cohn

❖

Over the few years, a number of violent incidents in public schools throughout the United States have seriously jeopardized the safety and security of our children in one of the few places where they are believed to be safe. One of these events was the school shootings at Columbine High in Littleton, Colorado, which left sixteen people, including one teacher, dead. Within weeks of this shooting, a large number of schools around the United States were closed because of rumors and threats of more violence (*Miami Herald,* 1999a). Exactly one month after the Littleton event, a shooting at Heritage High School in Conyers, Georgia left six students wounded (*Miami Herald,* 1999b).

During an April 23, 1999 speech in response to the Littleton shooting President Clinton stated:

> This week's tragedy reminds us again that one act of violence is one too many. We must do more to keep guns out of the hands of children; to help our young people express their anger and alienation with words, not weapons; to prevent violence from shattering the peace of our schoolyards.

Our society is now beginning to question the safety of our children and their ability to learn in an environment that has always been believed to be immune from social violence (Mudglin, 1999). Schools have always been considered a safe haven where the learning process could proceed in an environment of mutual respect and trust and without fear of violence, intimidation, or harm. As the national debate continues at all levels of government, with many and varied attempts to define the problem and apportion blame, society may have lost sight of its basic promise or contract to our youth: to provide a safe and secure environment of learning in our schools within which our children can prepare for their futures.

Connelly (1999, p. 1) has pointed out that an important element in dealing with the problem of juvenile crime is collaboration. As a result, some communities have "expand[ed] community policing strategies to focus on juvenile crime and violence issues." One of the first attempts to create a collaborative community-based response to juvenile crime in the schools and in the community was the Youth Crime Watch (YCWA). This program first appeared in the 1970s when the concept of youth participation in crime watch and crime prevention programs both in the community and in the schools first began to develop. Youth Crime Watch programs are now in use throughout the country and are designed to enable the students themselves to create within their schools that safe haven from violence. In response to the school shootings in Littleton, the Executive Director of the YCWA stated that:

> Although there is no one answer to the problem . . . no guaranteed solution for school shootings . . . it is clear that communication between students, teachers, and school administrators is essential in preventing school shootings and other crimes. Y Because Youth Crime Watch of America emphasizes peer reporting and student-adult communication, it offers a basic way to help prevent these tragedies. (Modglin, 1999, p. 1)

This chapter examines the theoretical bases of youth crime watch programs, including the concepts of modeling and risk-focused prevention and will review the history, goals, and activities of the YCWA.

THE THEORETICAL BASES OF JUVENILE CRIME PREVENTION: SOCIAL LEARNING THEORY

In the 1960s, while studying to be a social psychologist, Rudoff studied a condition or diagnosis involving juvenile delinquents that was known as adolescent situational behavior. Simply stated, this concept suggested that adolescents act out in accordance with immediate environmental influences or stimuli, frequently in a negative way. This relates to police work because, if an individual is in a particular situation or environment and is presented with a given action, his or her reaction will often be predictable. Therefore, many police discretionary decisions are based on immediate situational and environmental factors and the possible expected effect they will have on the participants in each specific situation. The type of police action may determine whether the adolescent responds in a positive or negative manner.

As a young juvenile probation officer just out of college, Rudoff regularly dealt with male and female adolescents who had no sense of self-worth or direction. He frequently attributed this to the general lack of positive role models in their lives. After studying Albert Bandura's (1969, 1973, 1986) theories relating to modeling, Rudoff became convinced that the presence of a positive role model was a vital and necessary ingredient in the lives of young people if they were to succeed in becoming responsible adults. Bandura's social learning theory suggests that children imitate the behavior of others through a process of observation and modeling. Although Rudoff was unable to apply this theory to his work as a probation officer, it significantly influenced his later career.

In the late 1960s, Rudoff left the field of probation to attend graduate school and eventually became a police officer with the Miami-Dade Police Department (then known as the "Public Safety Department"). At that time, the concept of a police-community partnership in crime prevention was virtually unknown. The typical procedure was for the police to unilaterally decide what the needs of a community were and then work to address those needs without any input or involvement from the community members themselves. This led to confusion, concern, and resentment on the part of citizens in the community, particularly juveniles. As Rudoff observed this process in various neighborhoods, he became increasingly convinced of the need for prevention and intervention programs specifically targeting and involving young people.

Additionally, at that time Metro-Dade Police Department Director E. Wilson Purdy, considered to be one of the early law enforcement reformers of his time, was encouraging the department to move from the then-popular public relations mode of policing to a focus on community relations and an understanding of the needs and desires of each community. Purdy had formerly served as the Commissioner of the Pennsylvania State Police and, while there, "saw the need for professionalization of law enforcement but . . . also realized a need for the development of a leadership program in police community relations." (Rudoff, p. 9) He continued this emphasis when he moved to Miami and "helped to lay the groundwork and foundation for what has emerged today as full grown partnerships between the police and the communities they serve" (p. 9).

In 1977, Rudoff was assigned to the Community Relations Bureau (now known as the Community Affairs Bureau) and began working with a local junior high school to combat the problem of vandalism on school grounds. Other junior high schools in the area were experiencing similar problems and Rudoff wanted to develop a prevention program that would apply to all the schools at once. Remembering Bandura's social learning theory, he hypothesized that a program begun in one school might spread to the others through the process of observation and imitation. He also felt that the only way to prevent vandalism on a long-term basis was to involve the students themselves in the prevention process.

To test this, Rudoff tested a vandalism prevention program in one target junior high school in the county. Within the target school, students' awareness of the problem of vandalism was heightened, they were made aware of the cost to the school (e.g., paying maintenance workers, cost materials to repair or repaint portions of the school, etc.), and were encouraged to help the school reduce the losses incurred. The students were given the opportunity to take pride in their school and to feel a sense of ownership so that they were less inclined to commit acts of vandalism and at the same time were more willing to stop others from damaging the school. Interest levels were maintained by features such as a bulletin board in the school and daily announcements concerning the progress of the program. The bulletin board illustrated the changes in costs to the school from vandalism; as vandalism decreased, students were able to see the cost savings achieved by their school from their own efforts. In addition, the school promised to host a pizza party and "sock hop" out of the savings, further motivating the students to participate in the anti-vandalism drive.

The program was then spread to other "feeder" schools with vandalism problems, using the basic premise developed by Bandura. Bandura's social learning theory (1986) involves four steps: attention, retention, reproduction, and motivation. Students in the feeder schools had their attention drawn to the program in the target school; they were made aware of the problem of vandalism in their own schools and shown what was being done about it by students in a nearby institution. Through multiple presentations and reminders of the problem (such as bulletin boards and announcements), they retained their awareness of the information. They were then encouraged to reproduce the behavior of the students in the target school and attempt to reduce vandalism in their own home schools. The motivation for their participation was a contest: The feeder school that demonstrated the most significant drop in vandalism was promised a pizza party and sock hop, paid for by the school out of the money they saved through the reduction in vandalism. In actuality, all the schools were given parties as a result of their success.

RISK-FOCUSED PREVENTION

In the early 1990s, Rudoff became aware of a concept called risk-focused prevention (Hawkins, Catalano, and Miller, 1992). Hawkins, like Rudoff, began his career as a juvenile probation officer. However, Hawkins went on to more formal academic pursuits while Rudoff, largely motivated by the Vietnam War, moved into law enforcement. Hawkins (1995) felt that "prevention is more effective and less costly than treatment after the fact" (p. 10). He suggested using the public health model to "[identify] the factors that put young people at risk for violence in order to reduce or eliminate these factors and strengthen the protective factors that buffer the effects of exposure to risk" (p. 11). According to Hawkins, risk-focused prevention involves identifying both the risk factors, which have a negative impact on juveniles, and the protective factors, which may help reduce the juvenile's exposure to risk.

Protective factors are positive elements which work to reduce the effect of the negative risk factors on the juvenile. Hawkins (1995) identified three categories of protective factors. The first relates to the individual characteristics of the juvenile: juveniles who have a positive social orientation, a good self-image, and a positive disposition are more likely to be protected from negative risk factors. Other individual characteristics include intelligence, gender, and temperament.

The second protective factor is social bonding; Hawkins emphasized the importance of juveniles maintaining positive relationships with family members, teachers, and other significant adults and friends as a mechanism for reducing the child's risk of behavior problems.

Finally, the third factor involves healthy beliefs in the juvenile's ability to succeed in school and to avoid crime and drugs, and the establishment of clear rules, standards, and expectations which govern the juvenile's behavior. If a child's parents have high expectations for the child's achievement and success, the child is less likely to drop out of school, become involved in delinquent behavior, or use alcohol or drugs. Similarly, in the vandalism prevention program discussed above, the school teachers and administrator had clear positive expectations of the students in the school: to reduce vandalism. The students responded to these expectations and school vandalism decreased precipitously.

Hawkins also identified a variety of risk factors associated with communities, families, schools, and peer groups. There are five community or environmental risk factors that Hawkins suggested will increase the likelihood that a juvenile will become involved in crime and violence. The first is the availability of guns: The easier the access to firearms, the more likely the juvenile will become involved in violent crime. For example, the youth involved in the school shooting in Conyers, Georgia, grew up around guns, was taken hunting from a very young age, and had easy access to his grandfather's collection of firearms. The second environmental risk factor is the presence of community norms and attitudes that favor criminal behavior among adults and juveniles. Hawkins suggested that young people need to be taught not only the difference between right and wrong, but also what society considers to be ethical and moral behavior. If a juvenile is in an environment which encourages unethical and/or immoral behavior, the likelihood of delinquency increases. A third risk factor is violence in the media; Hawkins (1995) stated that "exposure to media violence . . . teaches violent problem-solving strategies and appears to alter children's attitudes and sensitivity to violence" (p. 12). Today's proliferation of violent television programs, movies, and video games, the violence reported by the news media, and the violent internet sites to which children have access all expose juveniles to a significant amount of violence on a daily basis. While parents may be able to shield children from violent movies and video games, they cannot prevent youth from all the violence portrayed by the media in daily news broadcasts. Nor is it possible to successfully limit children's access to violent Web sites.

The fourth factor is community disorganization. Wilson and Kelling's (1982) "broken windows" theory supports this and also points out that communities in which there is limited involvement, organization, or attachment have higher rates of crime and delinquency. For example, when Rudoff visited Sao Paulo, Brazil, he found that those areas of the city in which graffiti was allowed to proliferate also showed other signs of vandalism and disrepair, including broken windows, damaged roofs, garbage and litter in the streets and on the sidewalks, and the increased presence of the homeless, alcoholics, and drug users.

Finally, the fifth environmental factor is poverty or low economic status; juveniles who live in extremely lower-class communities are more likely to develop behavior problems and to become involved in delinquency, crime, and violence. Researchers in Chicago's Project on Human Development (Sampson, Raudenbush, & Earls, 1998) have found that neighborhood cohesion or collective efficacy (a sense of mutual trust and a willingness to work together to intervene on behalf of a common good) plays a very important role in lowering crime rates even in poor neighborhoods (DeWitt, 1992).

There are also three risk factors associated with the family. The first is poor parenting and family management, which is characterized by parents who lack good parenting skills (for example, they may fail to provide clear standards and guidelines for the child's behavior or may punish the child inconsistently). The presence of dysfunctional parents increases the likelihood of dysfunction and potential delinquency on the part of the children in the family. Haggerty, Kosterman, and Catalano (1999, p. 1) argued, "Effective parent training has been shown to help parents avoid specific parenting practices that increase the risk for adolescent problem behaviors." The second is the presence of family conflict between parents or among parents and children. For example, research that shows that abused children are more likely to become violent and/or abusive.[1] Widom (1992) argued that children who were abused or neglected were 40 percent more likely to become delinquent or to engage in adult criminal behavior. The third risk factor is parental attitudes and behaviors which favor involvement in criminal and violent behaviors. Essentially, Hawkins's theory is consistent with a recent proposal by Samenow (1999), who concluded that while parents may not directly cause children to be antisocial, delinquent, or criminal, they may unknowingly encourage rather than inhibit such behaviors.

---

[1]See, e.g., DeWitt, 1992; National Committee for Prevention of Child Abuse, 1986; Widom, 1989.

Hawkins (1995) identified two school-based risk factors. The first is early-onset anti-social behavior patterns (aggressive behavior, hyperactivity, isolation, withdrawal, etc.) According to Hawkins, children who manifest such behaviors prior to the third grade are at a greater risk for violence in adolescence. A second factor is poor academic performance in school, which also increases the likelihood that the juvenile will become involved in violence and crime. This suggests that we can identify, as early as the third grade, which children may be at risk for delinquency, violence, and crime. Therefore, it is possible that crime prevention programs begun by the third grade might have significant impact upon the future of these children.

Finally, Hawkins states that there are potential risk factors within the individual juvenile and his or her peer group. First, juveniles who associate with peers who are involved in delinquency and crime are provided with negative role models and are more likely to become involved in delinquency themselves, regardless of the presence or absence of other risk factors within the family environment. Individuals who either lack positive role models on which to base their behavior patterns or who are closely attached to negative role models tend to exhibit increased levels of crime. In addition, Hawkins has also pointed out that youth who have not been provided with the proper foundations for good decision making, and who have not learned peer-resistance strategies, are more likely to be influenced by negative peers. This lends support to Bandura's modeling theory; juveniles who associate with delinquent peers may model their own behavior on that of these peers. In the vandalism prevention program Rudoff conducted, this risk factor was reversed by providing students at the feeder schools with positive role models (the students at the target school) on which to base their behavior.

Secondly, there may be inherent personality characteristics, such as sensation seeking, lack of impulse control, and low self-esteem, which increase the juvenile's risk of delinquency. These may be compounded by a lack of behavior training, which may assist youth in resisting the lure of delinquent behavior. Children who have a negative self-image (i.e., who do not have a strong positive believe in themselves and what they are able to accomplish), and who are denied access to programs which provide them with the ability to achieve within their potential and to receive the necessary support and encouragement to enhance their self-worth, are more likely to be attracted by delinquency and crime.

Since its development, the concept of risk-focused prevention has been applied to a variety of juvenile crime prevention and treatment programs throughout the United States. For example, Seattle's Preparing for the Drug Free Years (PDFY) program focuses on providing parents with the skills to prevent their children from becoming involved with substance abuse by both emphasizing protective factors and reducing risk factors (Haggerty et al., 1999). The remainder of this chapter examines a youth program which incorporates the principles of modeling and risk-focused prevention to prevent crime and delinquency in schools throughout the United States and abroad.

YOUTH CRIME WATCH OF AMERICA

The History of Youth Crime Watch Programs

One national program that attempts to apply the principles of risk-focused prevention is the Youth Crime Watch of America, Inc. (YCWA). YCWA is a non-profit organization that establishes youth crime watch programs throughout the United States and in other countries. YCWA originated in Miami, Florida, in 1986 and has three primary goals:

- to provide crime-free, drug-free, and violence-free environments for healthy learning and living;
- to instill positive values, foster good citizenship, and build self-confidence in youth while instilling a sense of personal responsibility and accountability; and
- to enable youth to become a resource for preventing drug use and other crimes in their schools and neighborhoods.

YCWA was first developed as an attempt to replicate nationally the activities and effectiveness of a local program, the Youth Crime Watch of Miami-Dade County, which formally began in 1979. Miami-Dade County's Youth Crime Watch program began as an outgrowth of the adult Neighborhood Crime Watch. Adults involved in neighborhood crime watch programs began to realize that the youth living in the neighborhood frequently knew more about what was going on in the community and in the schools than did the adults. However, at that time, a mentality on the part of both police and citizens that did not strongly encourage citizen participation in crime-prevention activities, combined with the complexities involved in merging adult and juvenile participation in the neighborhood watch, made a joint adult-juvenile neighborhood watch program difficult to organize and administer.

During this period, Rudoff was involved with the Miami-Dade County Public School System on the anti-vandalism project described above. Through this project, Rudoff found that long-term success in crime prevention within the schools could only occur with the involvement of the students themselves. As a part of the anti-vandalism initiative, and as an attempt to harness the energy and knowledge of the youth, and apply it to the school environment, Rudoff and his team created a school-based version of the adult neighborhood watch program. This was the beginning of the Youth Crime Watch of Miami-Dade County.

Not unexpectedly, the idea of a school-based crime watch program was not uniformly welcomed. According to Good (1999, personal communication), Director of the Citizens' Crime Watch of Dade County, the biggest barrier to the development of the program came from school principals, who had a number of objections to the formation of a youth crime watch. While there was little objection to the vandalism-prevention program Rudoff had developed, this was a formalized youth crime prevention program that did not focus merely on one specific issue (e.g., vandalism) but on the problems of crime and disorder throughout the school system and which emphasized the concept of youth-led programs to solve these problems. First of all, many school principals felt that the students would be unwilling to participate in the program, because they could be labeled as a "snitch" or "narc." The principals were also concerned that students would be required to participate in crime watch activities and meetings during the school day, thereby taking time away from their educational activities. Finally, many principals did not want to admit even tacitly that there was a crime problem in the schools; they felt that if they even considered implementing the program, parents would become concerned or even fearful about crime in the schools (Jones, 1999).

At the same time, the greatest support for a youth-based crime watch program came from the police. Under then Director E. Wilson Purdy's leadership, the Miami-Dade Police Department eventually provided the necessary initiative and support to ensure the survival of the youth crime watch program. Rudoff, along with Betty Ann Good, the director of the

Citizens' Crime Watch of Dade County (the adult neighborhood watch), persuaded the Dade County Superintendent of Schools to test the program in one school. The principal of North Miami Beach (NMB) Senior High School was reasonably receptive to the concept and the Law Enforcement Assistance Administration provided the funds to develop a handbook for student participants. Participation in the program was voluntary; this applied not only to the students involved in the program but also to the teachers and police officers who served as adult advisors. According to Good (1999, personal communication), students found the program especially attractive because they realized that they could organize their own crime watch groups and plan their own events and activities. In other words, while the adults acted in an advisory capacity, the students ran the program.

After the success of the youth crime watch in NMB Senior High, the program was expanded to other high schools in the county. A board of directors composed of police officers, educators, and corporate members was formed, with all members volunteering their time to the program. Director Good attributes much of the program's success to the dedication of the adult counselors (teachers and police officers), the support of the parents, and the energy and expertise of the board members, as well as of course to the students themselves.

Beginning in the early 1980s, the Youth Crime Watch of Miami-Dade County sponsored an annual county-wide conference focusing on youth-related crime prevention issues. Eventually, participation was expanded to include representatives from around the state of Florida. In 1985, the National Crime Prevention Council (NCPC) was invited to send a speaker, Terry Modglin, to address the conference. As a result of Modglin's visit, a proposal was made that the NCPC and the Youth Crime Watch of Miami-Dade County jointly sponsor the first National Youth Crime Prevention Conference. In 1986, the Youth Crime Watch of America, a national organization, was formally incorporated and has held a national conference every year since 1987. The founding director of YCWA was Betty Ann Good; the current director is Terry Modglin.

YCWA Today

YCWA has been recognized by Presidents Reagan, Bush, and Clinton, and has received a large number of national honors and awards, including being named a U.S. Department of Education Exemplary Program of Excellence. Today, YCWA has programs in over five-hundred sites in sixteen states and in Guam, with many more currently under development. YCWA relies primarily on government grants and private donations from individuals and corporate sponsors to continue providing programming. As the necessary funding becomes available, YCWA plans to expand into additional states within the United States and abroad. Despite the benefits that YCWA brings to schools, the only school district that currently provides a significant amount of funding to support YCWA programming is Miami-Dade County, in Florida. No other school district participating in YCWA provides a comparable level of funds to support these program activities. However, in late 1999, Congress and President Clinton endorsed a request to provide $1 million of funding to YCWA and the Department of Education earmarked an additional $500,000. YCWA is proposing to use the funds to facilitate national expansion.

Today, society encourages the participation of youth in crime prevention activities throughout the community, rather than limiting their involvement to the school setting. YCWA provides students and teachers with the tools and guidance needed to start and sustain a youth crime watch in their own school or neighborhood. The YCWA emphasizes a "watch out, help out" commitment, which encourages youth not only to look for problems within their school and community, but to become actively involved in solving those problems. A youth crime watch program, motivated by the principle of good citizenship, enables students to take an active role in addressing the violence, drug, and crime problems that exist in their communities and neighborhoods. Youth and youth advisors trained in YCWA methods currently run youth crime watch programs in elementary, middle, and high schools, neighborhoods, public housing sites, recreational centers, and parks. The program is able to function in these diverse locations due to its flexibility and its age-appropriate programming. YCWA has enabled participants to greatly reduce crime, violence, and drug use in their environments. For example, after the formation of a youth crime watch program in 1994, Leto High School in Tampa, Florida, reported a 72 percent drop in crime. In 1995, Carol City High School in Miami, FL reported a 45 percent decrease in student crime after beginning its youth crime watch (Jones, 1999).

YCWA Activities and Events

Through local youth crime watch programs, YCWA sponsors and encourages a wide variety of activities. Every youth crime watch program includes at least some of the following components:

- Providing drug, crime, gun, and violence awareness and prevention education
- Facilitating communication between police and youth
- Creating anonymous crime reporting systems
- Establishing youth patrols
- Creating a mentoring program and teaching mediation skills
- Teaching school bus safety
- Co-sponsoring training programs at the National Youth Crime Prevention Conference
- Providing conflict resolution training
- Creating action plans
- Organizing leadership retreats for youth and youth advisors
- Providing on-site training of youth and youth advisors, as well as regional training for youth advisors
- Cultivating positive youth/police relations
- Establishing community networks and partnerships all over the world
- Planning events and activities throughout the year

One of the most important events for youth crime watch members is the annual National Youth Crime Prevention Conference, which is jointly organized by the YCWA and the National Crime Prevention Council (with their mascot, McGruff the Crime Dog and the "Take a Bite Out of Crime" campaign). This event, a four-day anti-crime training conference for both youth and adults, helps give youth the power to make both their schools and their communities a safer place. Youth are involved in the development of the conference agenda and in the organization of the conference itself, and are exposed to a variety of national leaders in the field of crime prevention. Both youth and adults attend programs designed to educate them about the prevention of violence, crime and drug use, with the goal of developing crime-prevention partnerships between youth and adults. In 1999, almost 2,000 youth and adults from the U.S. and abroad attended the conference to learn new and innovative crime prevention strategies. Youth and youth advisors attend training sessions that enable them to further implement YCWA programs in their schools and communities.

YCWA Honors, Awards, and Benefits

Another important aspect of YCWA is honoring the individuals who work to keep schools and communities free of crime, drugs, and violence. At each National Youth Crime Prevention Conference, YCWA recognizes more than seventy-five individuals around the world with the following awards:

- Law Enforcement Officer of the Year
- Advisor of the Year
- Student of the Year
- The Casey Award (named after the YCWA mascot, Casey the Crime Watching Cat), in the following categories:
  - Youth volunteer
  - Adult volunteer
  - Education
  - Law enforcement
  - Legislative
  - State/national/international
  - YCWA alumni

For example, at the 12th Annual National Crime Prevention Conference in March, 1999, Officer Martin Shorkey, of the Hallandale Beach, Florida, Police Department, was the recipient of the Law Enforcement Achievement Award. Officer Shorkey was the first advisor to successfully institute a youth crime watch program in a public park.

Other benefits of YCWA membership include monthly updates and quarterly newsletters that inform members of upcoming training sessions, special events, conference activities and speakers, new resource materials, and current news from YCWA chapters. To assist youth and adult advisors in initiating and maintaining a local program, YCWA has developed a special "Start Up Kit." This kit contains a variety of materials including an operating manual to help adult advisors implement a program, youth handbooks written by students and containing a step-by-step plan to start a youth-led youth crime watch program, YCWA t-shirts and posters, a copy of the training video "Getting Started With the Six Steps for Establishing a YCWA Program," and manuals targeting the specific type of program (high school, elementary school, or community).

The YCWA also has developed an extensive resource library that contains a wide variety of support materials, including operations manuals, youth handbooks, model YCWA varsity patrol programs, YCWA mentoring activities handbooks, community-based YCWA program handbooks, a book profiling many of the YCWA programs, and video and audio tape programs. YCWA also provides technical assistance, assistance in the dissemination of materials, help in building community alliances, program certification, conference scholarships, and many other forms of assistance to local programs.

CONCLUSION

Clearly one of the key elements in the solution to combating youth-related violence, crime, and drugs in both the schools and the communities is the youth themselves. Society must realize that it can no longer look the other way and hope these problems will just disappear; they are many and varied, and often are an integral part of how we live our lives. We as a society cannot raise children in a vacuum; they must be taught to understand the effects of violence, drugs, and crime on their lives and learn that they must work together to reinforce positive influences that will help them avoid further violence in our schools and communities. Until youth-related issues become a social priority, youth crime and violence will continue to exist as serious social problems and concerns, with no positive movement toward successful solutions.

As we progress in the twenty-first century, it is necessary to change both our conceptualization of and our approach to issues of youth-based violence. Rather than the old view that the glass is half empty and all youth are "at risk" and subject to failure and crime, we suggest that instead we must view the glass as half full and see all children as being "at promise" for a safe and productive life that will allow each to succeed to his or her own extent.

In addition, the law enforcement community must reexamine how it interacts not only with youth but with all segments of society. As society moves into a new era of "modern age" of policing, it is essential that police consider the continual changes society is undergoing; the police must avoid espousing a particular style of policing merely because that concern currently is in vogue.

Whether the police emphasize traditional styles of policing or prefer community-oriented policing programs, they must balance institutional vision with the needs and desires of all members of the community. As communities and police work towards collaborative problem solving of community issues, they must seek solutions that satisfy everyone. As a result, police-community collaboration programs such as the YCWA are creating the concept of "solution-oriented" policing.

Further information on the Youth Crime Watch of America can be obtained by contacting the YCWA at the Miami office, 9300 South Dadeland Blvd, Suite #100, Miami, Florida, 33156; 305-670-2409, at the Washington, D.C. office: 212-466-3322, or via e-mail at: ycwa@ycwa.org. The YCWA is found on the internet at www.ycwa.org.

REFERENCES

Bandura, A. (1969). *Principles of behavior modification.* New York: Holt, Rinehart & Winston.
——— (1971). *Social learning theory.* New York: General Learning Press.
——— (1986). *Social foundations of thought and action.* Upper Saddle River, New Jersey: Prentice Hall.
Clinton, W. (1999). Remarks by the President on School Safety. Washington, D.C.: The White House Office of the Press Secretary, April 23.

Connelly, H. (1999). Youth-focused community policing: Establishing partnerships for addressing juvenile crime and victimization. *Community Policing Exchange* 6, 24, January/February, p. 1.

DeWitt, C. B. (1992). *The cycle of violence.* Washington, D.C.: National Institute of Justice.

Good, B. A. (1999). Personal communication.

Haggerty, K., Kosterman, R., Catalano, R. F., and Hawkins, J. D. (1999). *Preparing for the drug free years.* OJJDP Juvenile Justice Bulletin, July.

Hawkins, J. D. (1995). Controlling crime before it happens: Risk-focused prevention. *NIJ Journal,* 299, August, pp. 10–18.

Hawkins, J. D., Catalano, R. F., and Miller, J. M. (1992). Risk and protective factors for alcohol and other drug problems in adolescence and early childhood: Implications for substance abuse prevention. *Psychological Bulletin,* 112, pp. 64–105.

Jones, V. (1999). *Youth crime watch of America.* OJJDP Youth in Action Fact Sheet #2. January.

Modglin, T. (1999). Youth Crime Watch of America responds to the Colorado school shooting. *YCWA Media Alert,* April 21.

Miami Herald (1999a, May 1). Threats of violence close half-dozen schools around nation. Miami Herald. p. 3.

——- (1999b, May 21). Georgia teen held after school attack. *Miami Herald.* p. 1.

Rudoff, G. A. (2000). Community diversity in a crime watch environment. *Secure Our Streets* 1, 1, pp. 6–16.

Samenow, S. E. (1999). *Before it's too late: Why some kids get into trouble—And what parents can do about it.* New York: Times Books.

Sampson, R. J., Raudenbush, S. W., and Earls, F. (1998). *Neighborhood collective efficacy: Does it help reduce violence?* Washington, D.C.: National Institute of Justice.

Widom, C. S. (1989). Child abuse, neglect and violent criminal behavior. *Criminology* 27, pp. 251–271.

——- (1992). The cycle of violence. *National Institute of Justice Research in Brief.* October.

Wilson, J. Q., and Kelling, G. L. (1982). Broken windows. *Atlantic Monthly,* March, pp. 29–38.

9

From Polarization to Partnerships: Realigning the Investigative Function to Serve Neighborhood Needs Rather than the Bureaucracy's Behest

The Change Experience of the Madison, Wisconsin Police Department

Michael F. Masterson

❖

Community policing initiatives change the way typical police officers do business. While there is a large amount of literature on the relationship between police officers and community policing, there is little about the new role of investigators in a community policing initiative. This chapter examines the changing role of investigators to accommodate community policing initiatives and hopes to aid detectives to better understand their new role within a community policing philosophy. Confronting and challenging the status quo of any organization is guaranteed to generate a storm of emotional debate, controversy and discord. Testifying to that effect was the North American Free Trade Agreement (NAFTA), national health care, mandatory seat belt use, gun control, the college football bowl coalition, and of course, even among policing, the effectiveness of community policing. These new initiatives are centered in a common philosophy that impacts a department-wide commitment to proactive strategies rather than incident driven strategies. Much to the surprise of most investigators, department wide includes their unit, too. I have witnessed when the new role the investigative function has in community policing to detectives the discussion will immediately intensify.

There were two studies conducted long after the Madison Police Department implemented their organizational changes that would have been helpful if they were available several years ago. The most extensive research was conducted by the Police Executive Research Forum as part of a National Institute of Justice grant on "Investigations in the Community Policing Context" (Wycoff and Cosgrove, 1999). Those writers surveyed police and sheriff's agencies serving populations of fifty thousand or more and having at least one-hundred sworn personnel. Their report described various innovative approaches to the structural and functional aspects of selected departments' investigative processes. The authors discovered that rapid change among investigators moving toward a community policing philosophy to be complex and difficult task (Wycoff and Cosgrove, 1999).

Another study of criminal investigations currently underway by Horvath, Lee, and Meesig (1999) at Michigan State University includes the participation of 3,128 law enforcement agencies. The research goal is to develop a better understanding of the criminal investigation process because of its impact on our social and judicial systems. The writers created a Web site (www.ciol.org) where summaries of past/ongoing research are available; bulletin boards exist to exchange information and ideas on the investigative process; and funding resources identified for those interested in further research. The introduction of an electronic forum for practitioners and academicians to provide and exchange contemporaneous information from many disciplines has the exciting potential to expedite changes on how we police our ever-changing communities.

Our problem at the Madison Police Department (MPD) was that when we implemented major organizational change, none of the above was available. For the most part, emphasis on the investigative function and its contribution to those goals was largely ignored. Was it a deliberate avoidance because some felt that the resistance of a deeply ingrained culture that tended to be among investigators and the intolerance to change by vociferous, fiercely independent, and highly talented individuals? Who knows? One certainty seemed to exist: Investigators can no longer afford to perpetuate the "Lone Ranger syndrome" characterized by turf wars, finger pointing, and an attitude of "that's not my job." Investigators could no longer expect to read two separate books if they wished to learn about community policing and detectives. Times change and so must investigators. What worked ten, twenty years ago may no longer be the best way of working in the twenty-first century.

Many of the inherited managerial practices and structures of investigators were prime examples of just-in-case and just-because reasoning commonly perpetuated by excuses like "we've always done it that way" (Masterson, 1992). Investigators don't drive the same squad cars or carry the same firearms as they had when they started their careers. Why then, would they be extraordinarily protective of traditional assumptions on the best ways to lead and organize their units in advance of a community policing initiative? This logic reminds me of the message inherent in "The Calf Path," by Sam Walter Foss.

> One day through the Primeval wood,
> A calf walked home, as good calves should,
> But made a trail all bent askew,
> A crooked trail as all calves do. . .

The next few verses described how over the years and centuries the trail became a path, then a lane, then a road, street and finally a highway. It concludes:

A moral lesson this might teach,
Were I ordained and called to preach;
For men are prone to go it blind
Along the calf-paths of the mind;
And work away from sun to sun
To do what other men have done.
They follow in the beaten track,
And out and in, forth and back,
And still their devious course pursue
To keep the path that others do.

This engaging poem conveys an important lesson in understanding why investigative units are slow to change. Changing a profession steeped in tradition such as a Detective Bureau is an arduous task because time honored policing traditions are a powerful force. Our legacies were revered therefore seldom questioned until a court or commission mandated change. It can't wait for another time or someone else. We are entering an era of unprecedented change. Time is of the essence. Our current organizational designs are marginal, at best, in guiding our response to the types and severity of violent crime and social disorder we are experiencing in our neighborhoods and continue to isolate us from the citizens we serve. Consistent with this idea, the Community Policing Consortium (CPC, 1995) argues that:

Violent crime rates are soaring (are not controlled yet). Inner cities continue to deteriorate. Suburbs, once havens from harsh realities of urban decay, can no longer claim that privilege. And citizens in many areas of the country are increasingly frustrated and in many cases alienated from the police. (p. 1)

Investigative units must look for better ways to organize its workplace; to protect and serve; and to restore working partnerships with communities. One suggestion is that investigative units:

Do not follow where the path may lead. Go instead where there is no path and leave a trail.

About eight years ago, an article in *Reader's Digest* that chronicled the career of a New Orleans Police Officer named Jacklean Davis (Michelmore, 1992). As a young police officer patrolling the housing projects, she saw the bodies of teenage shooting victims and listened to their mothers weep. Then she watched homicide detectives arrive in three-hundred-dollar suits. "Any witnesses?" they asked perfunctorily (Michelmore, 1992, p. 182).

Fortunately, Ms. Davis recognized the polarization between the police and the people who lived in the neighborhoods affected by crime. The design of most present-day investigative structures encourages a continued separation and isolation from the people who need our services the most. It is seen symbolically through our clothing, but also in our indifference, intolerance and arrogance, manifesting itself through expressions like "we're the police and you're not." When promoted to detective, Davis changed the paradigm. She worked directly with neighborhood residents gaining their trust and confidence along with an exemplary clearance record for solving serious crimes. She achieved this distinction by personally changing how investigative business was done. She successfully challenged the status quo. Should we, too, think about redesigning the organizational model for policing? It is time that we concentrate on the needs of the people we serve, like Detective Davis, instead of on the needs of the bureaucracy?

HISTORY

Those who managed before us in the investigative units created the current specialization of investigations. It was a necessary part of our professional evolution, argues Geller (1991, p. 133). He adds that:

> As part of their department-wide reform efforts, police chiefs sought to change the focus of investigative work from offenders to cases. Under this approach to investigations, supervisors assigned detectives specific crimes, or cases, to investigate. Thus, supervisors could more easily control the work of detectives. They could also measure detective performance statistically, through clearance rates. Control over workloads and the ability to measure performance, when combined with department-wide efforts to break the hold of political machines on the police force, helped supervisors control what detectives did.

Most large police agencies had adopted this model or a variation of it, including the Madison Police Department.[1] At the time of its inception, it may have been necessary to organize the workplace this way. Change, by no means, constitutes an indictment of those who have led the investigative function before us. That was then—this is now. This particular investigative model, which emphasizes investigative specialty above all else, may no longer be the best way to prevent, investigate or solve crime in the contemporary police mission which emphasizes working with neighborhood residents to address problems, maintain safety and improve their quality of life.

Internally, it's much the same story. Although we talked about the need to maintain the integrity of investigative specialties for numerous reasons such as teamwork, exchange of information, and consistency of practice, it rarely happens. Case loads varied according to section and time of year. Everyone saw these variations. As leaders, we continued to hear about the lack of productivity by some. Depending on who you talk to, someone else included virtually all of us at one time or another.

To keep busy, many detectives work on issues that have little relationship to their principal assignment. Despite specialization, detectives would voluntarily respond to the traditional "big one," the high-profile case, oftentimes abandoning what they were working on. Special units are inclined to serve special people. The result was, we focused on issues important to us or the special interests of a select few, but perhaps not particularly important to the livability of the neighborhood.

---

[1]See the Madison Police Department at their Web site: http://www.ci.madison.wi.us/police Also, the Madison Police Department serves approximately 200,000 residents with 366 sworn officers and 74 civilian personnel.

Veteran detective leaders realized the creation of special relationships and units that have developed for example with the District Attorney's Office, Financial Institutions, victim support groups, credit card companies, auto insurance companies, and so on. We perpetuated the existing bureaucracy by being subordinate to the system rather than concentrating on neighborhood problems and serving the needs of the people we were originally created to represent. We could go so far as to suggest that some of us were dutifully serving a partner rather than a customer.

One of the goals of community policing was to change the line of decision-making processes from top down to across the Detective Bureau (Goldstein, 1993, and personal communication). But how? In 1986 the consensus was that a major realignment in the investigative area to address neighborhood problems was needed. Madison Police Department leaders believed this could be accomplished by realigning the existing organizational model. Our first major hurdle therefore was that each Section with the Detective Bureau was highly specialized.

Within the detective bureau, one captain was at the top of hierarchy and commanded seven Sections: Person Crimes, Property Crime, Metro Vice/Narcotics, Criminal Intelligence, Youth Aid, Sensitive Crimes, and White Collar/Forgery/Fraud/Courts. Each section had one lieutenant except Criminal Intelligence Section and there were a number of detectives in each Section and either a clerk typist or report typist. Directives flowed from top down in all matters.

After making the decision to alter our chain of command and integrate our Sections within the department there was a review of the limited data and information available from other Detective Bureaus across the country who successfully transformed their Bureau. After a lot of research it became clear that relatively few of those models reviewed offered a template that was readily transferable to the Madison Police Department and a model that could provide immediate results. Despite those findings, it was decided that the MPD didn't have time to "reinvent the wheel" and produce a uniquely labeled Madison's own, but instead turned to our colleagues elsewhere for working examples.

Taking a lead from the detective bureau at the Houston PD, we recognized that in order for integration to occur within the detective bureau at the Madison PD, a consensus should be reached by all individuals impacted by the change as to how reorganization could be accomplished. Part of that realization suggested that if we reorganized and those decisions came from top down, without a substantial catalyst or a consensus from most of the detectives, the chances were that most of those detectives would revert to their traditional chain of command and remain isolated, legitimized through turf battles and other rationalizations that could develop. Detective resistance was something that would take more time to overcome. On the other hand, we realized that every model was unique unto itself or put another way, one size did not fit all. Those thoughts were consistent with Carlson (1993) who added that:

> While it is important to study other agencies and learn from the experts in the field, one must be mindful not to adopt, without modification, programs or strategies solely because they have been successful in other communities. The demographics of a community, its crime problems, workloads and staffing, along with offender and victimization patterns must be considered when tailoring an approach for an agency. (p. 23)

OUR THOUGHTS AND OUR PLAN

Research in the private sector lead by a Sloan Management Study found that service team-work is important because people in service organizations typically depend on one another. Same-story holds true for detectives. The need for teamwork is particularly evident in policing where the co-dependency of police officers and detectives working together, exchanging information and sharing skills and expertise influences the quality of investigations and problem solving.

TEAMS: TALKING THE TALK

The interrelatedness of the various functions performed by the principal parties cannot be overlooked or denied. These responsibilities were neither separate nor likely to be congruous all the time. Officers and detectives routinely relied upon each other and that dependence was magnified if physically placed in the same environment. The importance of organizational design to accomplish these goals cannot be overstated. Working together in teams required physically occupying the same space. Through spatial positioning we would be able to overcome functional isolation and increase communication. This hypothesis was tested, evaluated and evidence was brought to bear on Madison showing that there were more frequent and positive contacts between officers and detectives and greater reported involvement of officers in follow-up investigations. The synergy of working together in a de-centralized, team based model provided an increased sense of cooperation, increased frequency and satisfaction in contacts between officers and detectives. This thought was consistent with Wycoff and Skogan (1993) who added that this cooperation would produce increased officer participation in investigations, too.

Looking at this in terms of burden of proof however, required additional explanation. In legal jargon, we have more than a preponderance of evidence but less than a standard of beyond a reasonable doubt to support changing our organizational models to integrate investigative services into our community policing philosophy. For those who frequently relied on the higher standard of evidence (i.e., detectives) there were reservations in accepting those findings. This was not a panacea that would solve all crime or will it correct society's ills. Nor was integration into a community policing philosophy of department-wide proactive driven organization, a quick fix especially for detectives. We needed more than proof.

We realized that innovation in policing service could not be achieved within a short period of time. Genuine, sustainable change takes time (Zhao, 1996). Thus, we began to understand the difficulty of expecting significant resistance in the process of pursuing organizational change. Any unreasonably high expectations set forth would only serve to hinder the process of change.

The inference of the research findings created the optimism that we were headed in the right direction and there were greater gains to be realized. Personnel were invited to work in team relationships to solve internal problems and conduct criminal investigations learned, in this way, to work with citizens in team relationships to solve neighborhood problems. However, we realized that the Madison PD detectives could never create organizational structures based on teams linked to neighborhoods until we broke down the stronghold of the classical model of vertical and horizontal specialized units serving the bureaucracy's behest. The latter breeds a pervasive attitude of "that's not my job."

Breaking down barriers between organizational units would be a decisive victory toward integration of each section and our bureau. One of the points from the Public Service by City of Madison Employees suggested that we had to work together as a team to foresee customer needs and service delivery problems. Of course, change would not simply happen because we said it should happen. The need to redesign our organizations was occurring because we were incongruous with the precepts that underlie community policing, the principles of contemporary leadership and the needs of our communities. Maybe more proof wouldn't be that important.

Meetings were held, information was passed both ways, discussions pursued, decisions were made, unmade and remade. During those meetings it became clear that top management's role was that of a facilitator as opposed to a dictator. It became our task to help guide the detectives to decisions that best served the mission of the Bureau, the department, and the communities. A decentralized team model aligned to serve designated neighborhoods was created. We used some of Creech's (1994) notions to guide us. He argued that "the focus, sense of purpose, agility and responsiveness the team arrangement offers simply can't be matched by other structural approaches" (Creech, 1994, p. 14). Companies discovered that fact after realizing that organizing by functions creates separation, not integration.

Reorganizing into teams is no small task as Air Force General Bill Creech (1994) experienced with the Tactical Air Command in 1982. He called them "vertical functional silos." Creech made changes by decentralizing into smaller teams centered on their primary mission—the aircraft. He succeeded.

It rarely happens in the public sector, but the powerful pull of tradition has made it extremely rare in policing. Cincinnati, Ohio, and Rochester, New York, provided us with valuable research on organizational models that included detectives and officers working together. For instance, among the changes instituted in the Rochester Police Department that could have created the improvements were:

- improving the quality of initial investigations by patrol officers,
- decentralizing detectives to neighborhood teams, and
- using case screening extensively ("Local government," 1991).

The research did not produce definitive answers therefore others were not anxious to follow. Nearly two decades later in 1986, former Madison Police Chief David Couper, resurrected this old idea by creating the Experimental Police District, a neighborhood-based, decentralized team model that included the detective bureau. In 1991, this model was replicated throughout the department. Each of Madison's five district teams includes the full range of police services from neighborhood and patrol officers to detectives and supervisors.

RESTRUCTURING OTHER DETECTIVE DIVISIONS

Houston, Texas, recognized the same need along with learning just how difficult it is to introduce organizational change in similar experimentation at their Westside Command Station. Their leaders were among the first to realize that changing organizational structure isn't purely for a cosmetic administrative purpose but more importantly for organizational and managerial efficiency.

The Philadelphia Police Department in an unprecedented reorganization eight years ago (1992) decentralized its Juvenile Division to district stations. Department leaders believed that decentralized investigative functions were customer-focused, proactive, autonomous and accountable. Decentralization enabled investigators to more readily provide localized and holistic service that was individually and internally rewarding, effective against crime, cost-efficient and satisfying to the public (Smith, 1994).

In June 1997, Chief Larry Soulsby of the DC Metropolitan Police Department reassigned two thirds of the department's 120 homicide investigators to work in the city's seven districts ("Can community policing solve murder crisis?" 1997, p. 1). The Santa Ana Police Department created the Developmental Policing District (DPD) where the full range of policing services, patrol, investigations and traffic were managed in a decentralized area through a community-based, problem-oriented policing strategy. For example, Carlson (1993) argues that:

> The assigning of investigators to district rather than crime-specific responsibility has several potential benefits for the Santa Ana Police Department and for the community. This type of structure is consistent with and supports the Patrol Division's community policing and district commander concepts. It will enhance an investigator's knowledge of the community and communication with field officers—two critical factors in identifying community problems and solving crime. (p. 23)

Incidentally, the issues regarding detective interaction with neighborhood/district police officers is a theme currently being examined by our colleagues abroad, too. The Danish Police Service with nearly ten percent of its eight thousand uniformed police officers deployed in small "area beats" is examining coordination and teamwork among its service providers including detectives (Bro, 1994). They discovered nearly ten years after implementing community policing that:

> it is a toilsome task to establish, and especially to maintain, coordination between area beat officers, district relief, the CID, and specialists departments and community policing resources are not always utilized adequately as support for investigations. Whenever that happens, however, it provides excellent results. (p. 11)

They were researching organizational designs in regard to teamwork, decentralizing investigations and targeting active criminals in their area. Even in less densely populated municipalities such Greenville, SC where the Sheriff's Office and community police officers are assigned to the Street Crimes Unit (burglary, robbery, narcotics) for supervision and direction, arrests and cases were cleared in these areas in record time since the restructuring. The North Miami Beach, Florida, PD reported that team policing such as command officers, community patrol officers, detectives, sergeants, and police officers working together, has permitted the provision of department wide, proactive police services to the community. Within months of its implementation, the benefits of team policing became visible and include increased police-community interaction, increased departmental communication, fewer repeat calls for service and increased customer satisfaction (Berger, Mertes, and Graham, 1994).

The Spokane, Washington Police Department assigned a police officer and detective to a small geographic area in early 1992. They've slowly expanded that concept to three locations where neighborhood resource officer teams up with a detective (neighborhood investigative resource officer). Future plans include designating twelve resource officers working in smaller neighborhoods. They make it work despite having one of the lowest ratio's of police officers per residents of any city in the nation.

Canadian police leaders in Edmonton, Alberta (pop. 600,000) are thinking the same as their counterparts in Madison where there have been nearly identical changes to organizational design. Edmonton created "beat officers" in the mid-1980s while Madison prefers to call them neighborhood officers. In 1993, Edmonton decentralized most of its investigative function to district teams as did Madison.

These departments demonstrate that it's not how many detectives they have in relationship to the case loads, it's how they used those detectives that counts. Placing many more police officers on the street may be appealing rhetoric to the public and the politicians, but, if they are used in traditional ways it will produce highly visible arrests that are effects of more complex social, economic and environmental causes. Yet more arrests do not necessarily impact the root causes of crime. Police cannot afford to engage in the bumper sticker slogans and five-second sound bites that do little to solve chronic problems. It's underlying neighborhood problems that can effect crime control and ultimately public safety issues. The fact is that for every youth we arrest off the neighborhood street corner for selling a rock of crack, there are twenty-five more waiting to take his spot. Unfortunately, more detectives used in traditional ways will simply generate more arrests, a call for building bigger prisons and a gloomier outlook of crime and violence in society. We will never resort to the untenable position of turning our back on violent crime and the disorder leading to it. Those who break these laws will be arrested. It must be that way, *always*.

Nonetheless, the tough law and order approach is not mutually exclusive with softer efforts of helping people residing in economically disadvantaged neighborhoods to gain employment, become healthier, receive better training and education, increase their safety and improve the physical environment. If we don't intercede there will always be an endless procession of young people to replace them. The inextricable link among housing, crime, employment, education and poverty makes it virtually impossible to segregate a single issue as a solution for complex social problems. Community policing affords us the best of both worlds and detectives have an important contribution to offer, reactive, coactive, and proactive. The design of many of our current organizational models makes that difficult to happen.

For instance, detectives and patrol officers traditionally have had parallel responsibilities within our organization. This distinct organizational separation manifests itself through different offices, separate briefings, door locks at entrances to the detective office that won't accommodate department keys issued to police officers, and much, much more that is inherently latent but readily apparent to most insiders. We, as managers of big investigative divisions, have had tremendous difficulty in managing "the white spaces" that exist between segregated branches of our departments not to mention coordinating the functional units of the investigative area. A station commander of a large Midwest city, (pop. 500,000 +) told me this story. Officers had just taken four juveniles into custody on burglary charges and requested a detective to interview them to determine possible involvement in other crimes. Only a small wall separated his office from the detective's desk but he had to telephone the detective commander at a centralized location to obtain permission to use the detective to conduct the interview. True story and unfortunately all too common in policing today. This thought lends itself well to Creech's (1994) perspective of "Vertical Functional Silos" implying that police units and sections seldom interact with each other. Sadly, we see competition for budgets, personnel, vehicles, and equipment, etc. often promoting the parochial interests of separate units. Unfortunately, neighborhood concerns and problems become secondary to our preoccupation with fulfilling internal needs and wants.

That may explain why leaders haven't focused on the community's problems. Not by choice, our attention has been on internal operating problems which are compounded by the way we organize our agencies. Despite what we have learned about the benefits of working together, the design of today's typical police organization is the antithesis of teamwork (Krauss, 1994). Organizational structure does indeed influence behavior. We have created a structure whose parts have become deliberately indifferent to each other. That design, in turn, creates other barriers that may partially explain why very few organizations have been willing to scrutinize their current structures. The power and standing of criminal investigators (detectives) may also frustrate attempts to change police culture and organization, as their status is derived from their ability to solve cases, rather than prevent crime (Oritz & Peterson, 1994). This is a not new issue. We've heard the message before but have been hesitant to act.

> Detectives' perception of their job will remain my job is to solve crime until they are removed from the group that reinforces that perception. Their goals will remain the same until their professional territory is redefined. Their professional territories, if the detectives are to adopt and understand the ideals of community policing, should be defined segments of the community. . . They have to be encouraged to work closely within neighborhood policing units. Thus, the valuable intelligence that detectives gain through crime investigation can be fed back into the patrol operation. . . The essential change, whatever the prevailing circumstances, is that the detectives' professional territory has to be extended some considerable distance beyond the instances of reported crime. The detectives may end up looking more like district investigators than members of an elite, and separate unit. (Sparrow, 1987, 7)

We, as managers, have the power to alter that situation. We made a decision to abandon the separate, divisive and competing interests of patrol, traffic, and detectives by creating a new paradigm emphasizing partnerships, both inside and outside of our police organization. The model the Detective Bureau of the Madison PD selected was to decentralize most of the organization, including detectives, to serve specific geographic areas. This model incorporates the full range of police services yet provides for specialization where necessary and appropriate (i.e., Narcotics and Gang Task Force, court detective, etc.). Other variations we considered included decentralizing operations by function (patrol, detectives, etc.) but retain separate command responsibilities (i.e., Detective, Captain) and designating liaison functions within existing structures to create cross functional reporting relationships with other operational components. The problem we saw with both options was the lack of clear management responsibility for responding to neighborhood concerns and creating partnership networks to solve problems. Of course, the chart looked great but implementing it would be another huge task.

In Madison, we decided to expand our semi-decentralized model, to include detectives who were assigned first where people live and work and secondly on the type of crime committed. We aligned the organization, including the investigative function, based first on "turf" then on "time" (of day), shifts, and investigative specialty. We eliminated bureaus and divisions replacing them with geographic teams led by a captain and two lieutenants. Although we frequently talk about the need for teamwork, it is for the most part, the exception rather than the rule. It has become hollow rhetoric. According to a recent United States Chamber of Commerce survey less than 5 percent of companies organize by teams (Ghoshal & Bartlett, 1995). Approximately one out of every four American businesses uses a form of teams and then it's reserved for small numbers of their workforce. The lesson to be learned is shared from Houston, Texas and their early experiment with neighborhood oriented policing:

> Attention should be placed on having personnel work together in an environment characterized by a willingness to share knowledge, experiences and skills so that citizen needs and expectations can be more effectively addressed. To accomplish this, there must be a unification of effort on behalf of the patrol officer and the investigators commensurate with a mutual expectation of shared accountability for the services rendered to the public. (Ottmeier and Bleck, 1990, p. 74)

CHANGE IS ALWAYS EASIER SAID THAN DONE

Although we realized the tremendous potential of teamwork involving officers and detectives, recent national research conducted through the National Institute of Justice indicates only 10 percent of all departments have physically decentralized investigations (Wycoff, 1995). For municipal police agencies with 100+ personnel identifying themselves as implementing community policing for one year or longer that percentage nearly doubles and it triples for sheriff's agencies having 100 or more members. We have been slow to realize the importance of this message but it is gradually gaining attention. There is a growing interest in physically decentralizing the investigative function but it will likely take five to seven years to realize the full benefits. These thoughts are consistent with Dennis J. Stevens's (2001) current findings derived from case studies of many departments across the United States. In a thought, time is required to weed out the old and bring in the new.

INTERNAL DYNAMICS OF CHANGE

Perhaps even more compelling then recognizing a need for change is an understanding of how to introduce and guide the process so the desired results are attained. It's not easy in any organization but in policing it can be especially tough. Why? Cultures with a tendency for arrogance, inward focus and bureaucracy are characteristics that undermine an organization's ability to adapt to change (Kotter & Heskett, 1992). Recognizing the need and actually doing it are totally different tasks. Here's what we knew in some cases, and learned the hard way in others.

- Ideally, the proposed changes should be part of the department's strategic plan to demonstrate the commitment. By all means, don't attach a personal identity to the planned change. This will prevent the attacks from becoming too personal.

- Labels tend to stick indefinitely so don't give the change a cute acronym. History assured us slogans only become ammunition for the latent creativity of those who vehemently disagree. Avoid the lessons learned from C.O.P.E. (Cops on Pension Early) and NOP (Nobody on Patrol).
- Don't be impulsive. Avoid springing surprises by presenting a well-defined plan. There was no stealth implementation as we were forthright with our plans and dedicated the necessary time to do it right.
- Structure the process so the plan receives plenty of input. "Much of the resistance to change springs from the universal need to have a sense of control over one's surroundings and one's destiny. You've probably taken pleasure in rearranging your home at times—redecorating, moving furniture around, putting up different pictures. What a different feeling if you lived in a regime where some government employees might unexpectedly arrive one day to redecorate and rearrange your home in a style dictated by the official master plan" (Hutton, 1994, p. 84). Ask those affected by the decision to participate in developing the best model. We discovered through dialogue, detectives willingness to clarify new expectations and sort out what they were hearing and what it really meant to them.
- Introduce an orderly process, be cautious not to make it go too quickly. Be patient. Keep in mind that it's not just management's timetable but others affected by the change too.
- Support those promoting change but be careful not to do it at the expense of others. Be cautious to avoid exacerbating the polarization of opinions. Don't divert valuable time in trying to fight the cynics but don't totally ignore them either.
- Use every opportunity available to help people understand the change process and how it will affect them. Changers always see the potential outcomes differently than the changes.
- Employees need constant reassurance their leaders will continue to care about them after the change. It helps fulfill their basic need of belonging then and later.
- Effective change leaders must have a high tolerance for ambiguity. Don't expect the original blueprint outlined on paper to be the final outcome. It helps to possess the big picture view of the organization by explaining how processes interrelate to form one cohesive team.
- Maintain a healthy sense of humor; keep a balance of quiet determination and a firm resolve; and, have fun. This was one lesson we learned as we went along that should be on board before starting.

Given the controversial nature of a change of this magnitude, convincing all parties having a proprietary interest in this decision, that indeed it was a better way to do business was not easy. There were as many personal agendas as there were members of the organization. We didn't believe it could be accomplished through orders. Unfortunately, too many chiefs who have issued edicts like "it's this way or the highway" have often times found themselves on the latter because of tenacious, organized internal resistance. It wasn't achieved by manipulating employees since we knew they would vigorously resist being changed. It was only accomplished through education and by providing information that lessens the uncertainty. Changing how people think ultimately changes the way people behave. It was not so much the announced change but the fear of its unknown ancillary consequences. Detectives wanted to know if, and how the change would:

- increase workload?
- lessen ability to perform their job in a quality manner?
- mean they have been doing their jobs poorly?
- reduce opportunities for overtime?
- change the people they would work with and for?
- create a new job just as challenging?
- there be sufficient work in their specialization in a smaller geographical area ?
- they be competent to handle other types of investigations outside of their specialty?

Despite these lingering doubts, it was decided that it couldn't wait until a major crisis forced the Madison PD to change. The stakes were too high and we risked the potential loss of confidence in the police by the people we serve. In our most recent change experience with detectives, the ability to guide change and maximize the opportunities for success and sustain the momentum largely depended on a process of doing the right things.

THE FOUR RIGHTS

Prior to implementing the new organizational structure of the Madison Police Department, leaders identified four critical issues relating to reasons, method, persons, and responses. They are not sequential, so we didn't place too much emphasis on the listed order. We believed they are essential ingredients for orderly and successfully guiding an entrenched culture toward a preferred future and would be helpful for other leaders serious about initiating and guiding a similar change process.

The Right Reasons

We believed it wasn't fair to our personnel, suppliers, and/or customers (citizens) to continually vacillate between styles, and pointed out that our last change, specializing detectives, occurred in 1963. We believed the proposed model was key to becoming a learning organization.

This learning method involved detectives teaching patrol officers and less experienced detectives the most effective investigative techniques; creating an environment for dialogue; enhancing the ability to learn from the experience and best practices of others; developing a capacity to transfer knowledge and information quickly, efficiently, and accurately throughout the workplace. For example, we didn't assign multiple person crimes detectives to a serious case any more. That way effectively precludes "newer" detectives from important on-the-job training. In the new model, one of the district's person crimes detectives was the primary investigator who was assisted by the other detectives working in the district, regardless of their specialty. Actually, the former system of specialized units created conflict and dissension on the best ways to handle a case. As a manager myself, one way to describe the former method was to liken it to coaching a group of all-stars each having the best way to play their position. Our new model, while retaining investigative specialties, was also very utilitarian allowing lieutenants to assign cases outside of specialties when special needs of their neighborhoods arise. The work gets done, and we don't hear "that's not my job." Detectives working in a smaller geographic district, versus citywide responsibility, have a unique opportunity to work with the same officers to:

- improve the quality of initial reports by providing feedback to investigating officers (we lessen the potential number of officers routing reports to a particular detective from 180 citywide to approximately thirty to forty within a district).
- review reports on a daily basis to become familiar with environmental causes of crime and become knowledgeable of individuals committing crimes, their associates, vehicles, access to weapons, etc.
- share information and expertise with neighborhood and district officers at daily briefings and, more importantly, other times because they work in the same physical environment.
- become more adaptive by being in a better position to read rapidly changing neighborhood environments and respond quickly to newly identified needs and problems.
- identify and discuss problems and strategies to resolve them.
- develop reliable sources of information and relationships based on mutual trust and respect. We needed to establish communication links with neighborhood residents since they know what's going on in terms of criminal behavior. A lot of people who might be reluctant to call a big organization with information might confide in a police officer or detective they know (and trust) in their neighborhood.
- aggressively seek out fugitives wanted on warrant and suspects of crime where there is probable cause to arrest.
- through daily personal contact, guide sergeants on how to do a better job of supervising crime scenes, conduct initial criminal investigations and coordinate follow-up with detectives.
- create integrated training sessions that have a system perspective involving supervisors, detectives and officers versus the rank specific component training we've been comfortable in holding. Integrated training allows all members to gain a better understanding of the entire process, clarification of responsibilities, investigative needs and reporting requirements to ensure a quality investigation.
- remove violent offenders likely to be involved in multiple offenses by increasing the likelihood of identification and arrest.
- develop trust, respect and a sense of teamwork.

It would have been an interesting experiment to survey detectives prior to creating this decentralized model asking them to list as many people known to them who are believed to be involved in current criminal behavior by name, alias, address, associates, vehicles, etc. We should have asked detectives to identify neighborhood-based probation officers or name five high-risk offenders living in their area who are considered most likely to be recidivists or to identify a neighborhood association president or three major property owners/managers in the area they serve and how to contact them. Intuitively, we believed the quantity and quality of the information held by decentralized detectives was superior to those held by detectives working in a classical, centralized model.

The Right Methods

We introduced the realignment of the investigative area by memo. We scheduled a series of five, sometimes intense, meetings to openly discuss the proposed changes. Expect controversy in whatever forum you choose to present the plan to employees. There were a few employees who insisted on tenaciously protecting the status quo. Leaders need to channel their energy productively so it doesn't become destructive. A written plan or a meeting agenda became the prospectus in helping to sell the idea and break down initial resistance. A crucial first step was to personally go to employees as their leader to represent the department's position. Why?

First, it sent the message that you, backed by the chief and management team, were willing to defend what other managers believed was best for the community and organization.

Second, if we hadn't scheduled meetings to discuss the potential impact of the change, we were certain detectives would have done it anyway at the organization's equivalent of existing information superhighways like the coffee shop, in hallways and other places without an invitation for us to participate in the discussions. Rumor and innuendo have a way of taking on a life of their own.

Third, we avoided blaming those who don't immediately embrace the planned change. They were not whiners or naysayers. They are good workers with legitimate questions. Their early fears were often exaggerated and eventually disappeared over time. We were aware some members would be enthusiastic, a few petulant, but most cautiously reserved. This was a defining moment for leadership credibility and personal integrity along with winning support for the proposed change. People closely watched how co-workers, however incorrigible they would be, were treated.

Fourth, it was an opportunity for others involved or affected to provide input into the decentralized model. It would have been an egregious injustice to force a new organizational design on the investigative section without open discussion of advantages, disadvantages, benefits and costs. While we unquestionably heard most excuses imaginable as to why it wouldn't work, there were good points presented as well. It wouldn't have served any legitimate purpose to engage the most rancorous resistors. That reciprocal behavior tends to become destructive, especially if there is any hint of "blame" being expressed or implied as a reason for change. Consensus will never be reached unless there is ample opportunity for everyone to voice their opinions, and put their issues out on the table. We expected rigorous debate and found it healthy. This finding is consistent with Johnson and Johnson (1991) who add that:

> rational argumentation includes generating ideas, collecting and organizing relevant information, using inductive and deductive logic, and making tentative conclusions based on current understanding. Rational argumentation requires that participants keep an open mind, changing their conclusions and positions when others are persuasive and convincing in their presentation of rationale, proof, and logical reasoning. The abilities to gather, organize and present information to challenge and disagree, and to engage in reason logically are essential for the constructive management of controversies. (p. 282)

Fifth, we were not reluctant to share our fears about taking on this new challenge. While we conceded there would be minor bugs inherent in the new design, we also assured our employees there were no fatal flaws that would seriously jeopardize our operations or reputations. We left no doubt that plunging the organization into the abyss was not an acceptable risk. Those types of gambles were not ours to unilaterally make.

As expected, debate was vigorous with many of the detectives. Their concerns centered on the uncertainty of the operational aspects of the new organizational structure. After all, the majority of the detectives had become quite familiar and comfortable with our current centralized structure of specialized investigation units. Daily activities were routinized. They were accustomed to doing a certain task, at a certain time, in a certain way, and with certain people. Any deviation from those practices would surely interrupt set routines and likely create uncertainty. We lessened the unreasonable doubt and uncomfortableness by confidently explaining exactly how new systems would work and by answering all questions in writing explaining how they would impact them personally. This thought finds congruence with Hammer and Stanton (1995), who argue that:

> New people working in new ways also need to be organized differently. The traditional emphasis on hierarchical, functional departments is replaced by an emphasis on process teams. These changes lead to a ripple effect as career paths, manager roles, interpersonal arrangements and value systems all undergo profound transformations in order to support a very different way of working. (p. 118)

With patience we gradually gained support. Several senior detectives actually spoke in favor of selected aspects of the model contradicting exaggerated statements being voiced by other colleagues. Nearly all detectives made convincing arguments as to why we shouldn't adopt an investigative model based solely on generalists. Our managers agreed that everyone shouldn't be expected to know a little about each investigative function with an expectation of delivering the highest quality service. We recognized each special investigative function, (PC—Person Crimes, FC—Financial Crimes, SC—Sensitive Crimes, YAS—Youth Aid Services, etc.) had a percentage (perhaps 15 to 20 percent maximum) of what we referred to as critical work. Critical work was defined as "those investigations requiring the experience of a detective who had both contemporary training and expertise in a particular field."

In person crimes investigations, for instance, it included homicides, life-threatening stabbing or officer-involved shooting. In Madison, we averaged two homicides in each of the last five years and officer-involved shootings were slightly increasing with the department experiencing one incident every two years. For Sensitive Crimes it's a stranger/ violent sexual assault or the physical abuse of a child. Madison rarely saw serial types of crimes being committed citywide. In 1992, for instance, 92 percent of sexual assault victims knew their assailant (Ring, 1993). We worked extremely well in solving the "big ones" after they happened. Policing shouldn't be organized based on the occasional big one or to work on crimes after they have been committed. Everyone literally dropped what they were doing to help. This fact didn't diminish the seriousness of the offense but required a second look at how we assigned those cases. We didn't do nearly as well in coordinating our daily work, particularly on crimes we considered of lesser significance not to mention totally neglecting crimes important to the neighborhood. We took that exact attitude with open market drug sales reported to us. What happened when we knew for certain that the same individuals were committing multiple types of crimes in the vicinity where they live? This model represented a compromise on the continuum between the extremes of specialization and generalization. It may not just be for cities having a limited crime problem. To the contrary, it may have a greater impact in cities where there is higher crime, especially if internal relationships can be built and sustained that emphasize a closer relationships with neighborhoods. This thought is consistent with those who argue that:

> In large cities, decentralization of most detectives makes more sense than the alternative. A few crimes may be investigated by central detective units. But there are enough crimes to keep each area's locally assigned detectives productively occupied; most crimes do not require esoteric skills for their investigation; and most offenders operate within a relatively local area. Thus decentralization should be the rule, not the exception. ("Local government," p. 156)

There will always be a need to call on special skills. It will be too costly to train everyone for everything. The overwhelming majority of our cases, however, require sound basic investigative skills which most detectives possess and are capable of performing in a quality manner. A primary reliance on specialties creates battleships and tugboats. It's standard "cop-speak" among detectives that battleships investigate high-profile crimes and attract media attention while the tugboats handle the majority of the day to day crimes without the notoriety. We should not be in the business of creating investigative stature.

Unfortunately, strict specialization exacerbates those differences by establishing uniqueness. Organizations should never intentionally emphasize lateral differences that drive the wedges of isolation, power and separation deeper and wider.

In our meetings, detectives pointed out that our former Experimental Police District shouldn't be allowed to operate independently from the remainder of the department. We heard this said for both investigative and primary services. We responded by designating minimum staffing levels for each district and a system whereby a district detective was responsible for handling an investigation if it occurred in their area regardless if another detective with that specialty was working elsewhere in the city. Of course, other detectives may assist and offer their expertise. Geographic teams do not mean creating small worlds unto themselves. We wanted to avoid the arbitrary displacement of people and reinforce our stated goals of encouraging detectives to become intimately familiar with a specific area. Detectives don't solve cases through office discussions. They clear most cases by information received through officers, other criminals and citizens. One veteran investigator conceded, "getting out on the streets and talking to people is the only way crimes get solved" (Heitzkey, 1994, p. 6). Yes, we need to be high-tech oriented with Automatic Finger Print Identification Systems and Mobile Data Terminals, etc., but we must remain high touch as well by cultivating those relationships with the people most familiar with the neighborhood and knowledgeable of the people committing the crimes. This thought is reinforced by Heymann (1995) who suggests that:

> Hiring additional police and increasing punishments are not necessarily the most promising ways to increase deterrence. The weakness of police operating without local cooperation is that criminals will make sure they are not seen by patrols, but by the people who live in a neighborhood do often know who is doing what. If dangerous neighborhoods can become communities committed to making the neighborhood truly livable, the community may repudiate those who practice violence. This creates both community pressure as a powerful incentive and an increased willingness to cooperate with law enforcement. Getting this cooperation is a major goal of community policing as it addresses violence. (p. 10–11)

We believed detectives had a pivotal role in contributing to this goal. The intensive development of relationships with neighborhood officers, patrol officers, detectives, public health nurses, county social workers, neighborhood employment counselors, private security, building inspectors, state probation officers and residents holds immense potential to stop the vicious cycle of people resorting to committing crimes and to produce more clearances than our most elaborate machines will ever be capable of telling us. We must never lose sight of this fact. To achieve greater effectiveness we need to become part of our neighborhoods. It can't be done as outsiders, even if we are equipped with the fanciest gadgets. The last three decades have proven that.

We didn't neglect to frequently and publicly communicate both department and personal appreciation to employees. It was important to give them feedback on their input regardless of whether or not it was positive or constructive. This written "thank you" was distributed to all in the October 13, 1992, *Detective Team Newsletter.*

> I want to thank each of you for your willingness to provide both positive and constructive feedback on the 1993 Detective Team model. Although we may not be in total agreement with the proposal, I learned new details of issues that are important to you and critical to the success of the plan. I depend on you and you on me. What we are able to accomplish each year is a direct result of your support and understanding of what it takes not only to operate this department, but to provide the best police services we can, improving both personally and organizationally. I have not forgotten that commitment. You may also be sure I remain most grateful for the quality of work you so generously give which enables our department to carry on that mission.

Police employees, particularly detectives, have demonstrated they are anything but reticent about expressing their views ranging from critiquing other's personal investigative style to case workload. As a general rule, we didn't hear filtered feedback. If they didn't like it, they said so. We heard from a limited few on the need for perfect planning before we initiated a change of this magnitude. As the saying goes "it's resistance masquerading as morality" or the expectation that we plan things to perfection (and death) thus avoiding the actual implementation. That's how the status quo is perpetuated. We didn't believe we could wait until we found ourselves in a crisis to initiate this change. Regrettably, today's prevailing attitude is exactly that. We conveniently avoid the issue entirely until faced with a major crisis we are forced to confront.

Why do we procrastinate in making change in our profession? Basically, for three reasons. First, avoidance. That is, the required changes were painful, and rather than face up to them and inflict the losses, executives sought to avoid the reality of the need to make changes (Stephens and Moore, 1991, p. 10).

Second, impotence. Police executives have seen the necessity for change but are powerless to convince subordinates that change is important. The realities may have been there for a long time, but widely and deliberately ignored by the organization because their implications were far too threatening (Stephens and Moore, 1991).

Third, exhaustion. Although police administrators are committed to change in principle, some lack the driving commitment necessary to effect it. Some may even be consumed by the complexity of running a police agency leaving them little time for innovation. These thoughts are consistent with Ortiz and Peterson (1994) who also add that active resistance from officers can further complicate the process of implementing change. The chief's role as sponsor and champion of change is important but he or she cannot be expected to guide this massive effort alone. We learned the effort far exceeds the capabilities of a single individual acting independently of others and it takes more time than most think it does. For instance, Sparrow (1988) advises that:

> Altering an organizational philosophy is bound to take considerable time. Another analogy may be helpful: the greater momentum of a shop, the longer it takes to turn. One comforting observation is that a huge ship can nevertheless be turned by a small rudder. It just takes time, and it requires the rudder to be set steadfastly for the turn throughout the whole turning period. It is worth pointing out, also that there will be constant turbulence around a rudder when it is turning the ship and no turbulence at all when it is not. This analogy teaches us something if the office of the chief executive is seen as the rudder responsible for turning the whole organization. The lessons are simple. First, the bigger the organization, the longer it will take to change. Second, throughout the period of change the office of the chief executive is going to be surrounded by turbulence, like it or not. It will require personal leadership of considerable strength and perseverance. (p. 4)

The Right Persons

Traditionally, the most senior captain has been assigned to lead Investigative Services in our department. Over the last twenty years, three of my four predecessors have retired in that capacity (or shortly thereafter). Police leaders serious about redesigning their investigative area may want to avoid placing those about to retire in such a significant position if you are contemplating a structural (read cultural) change. At this stage in their careers, they may be more inclined to maintaining relationships than on focussing on the emotionally draining issue of organizational design. It was crucial to choose a leader who had a positive attitude and the perseverance to guide change while simultaneously maintaining a healthy personal perspective. Fact is, the most visible factor that distinguishes major cultural changes that succeed from those that fail is competent leadership (Kotter & Heskett, 1992). There should be key managers in various levels of the organization (cascading sponsorship) who play an active and unified role in the change process, if change is to be successful (Goldstein, 1993).

Just as we learned about the crucial need to involve the first-line supervisors (sergeants) in adopting community policing with police officers, we found a comparable need to include the first-line detective supervisor (lieutenants) in leading change in the investigative area. It was not only desirable, but mandatory for successful change to gain their active participation. Initially, the lieutenants were skeptical about realigning the structure they knew and operated in for more than fifteen years.

We paid attention to their needs, responded to their questions, solicited their active involvement and gave them ownership in developing the new model. We were aware of Senge's (1990) conclusion that mid-level police managers and line supervisors become frustrated when top managers do not spend the time in explaining the importance and relevance of organizational change and their new role in the new organization. Therefore, once we discussed the specifics and expected benefits of change and resolved the issue on whether or not change would take place, the lieutenants actively participated in developing specific operational guidelines. Our experience was that communicating the need for compliance removed any bad faith about the change and it helped them to make choices since it furthered their participation.

Specifically, the lieutenants recommended their own responsibility and authority for daily operations while the captain concentrated on administrative duties. With the elimination of specialized investigative units, they strongly believed the captain should become the department's representative on the numerous committees they had previously served on (i.e., Child Protection Coalition, Domestic Violence Task Force, Sensitive Crimes Commission, etc.). Their recommendations were particularly relevant when we considered the policy-making aspects of these interagency groups. The key point to remember is that inclusion and involvement of the detective lieutenants was critical to successfully realigning the investigative function in our department. Without their active participation and support any attempt to change the culture would most surely have been suppressed.

Why did we need to involve others beyond command staff? We have highly educated, extremely talented men and women who wanted to actively participate in the running of the organization. Detectives are no exception. A simple task of assigning cars, revising annual call numbers or ordering light packages for unmarked vehicles often times generated a considerable amount of informal debate and rhetorical comment. But equipping vehicles to satisfy the individual preferences of two detectives sharing the same vehicle is entirely different than gaining total agreement on creating a new organizational design. It was not surprising to learn that in our department (as I'm sure yours) there were as many different personal views on the best ways to solve problems, manage investigations and organize the work place as there are employees. Since views are often varied, it is an ever increasing challenge for leaders to build consensus on one universally acceptable way while avoiding the risk of polarizing those who were excited about the change and those who were not. It was a task which, often times, failed to meet everyone's needs. It can be an extremely stressful experience for managers. Generally, we found the weaker the argument on substantive issues, the stronger and more pretentious the words and tactics necessary to challenge the changers.

A change of this magnitude prompted some to openly express their derision. If you have any doubt as to how thick your body armor is, you're likely to discover it now. As the visible change champion, I was faced with an anonymous source contacting the media insisting the changes being made were the result of over-active personal ambitions.

Our findings were consistent with Block (1993), who argued that top leadership was an absolute requirement when an agency tries to turn a new process design concept into a reality. It is at that point that change affect personnel directly. "When change bites people, they bite back" (p. 70). Top management must communicate change and solicit input from the beginning, not necessarily to overcome resistance, but to preempt it, we learned.

Instead of letting emotions dominate the issue or openly condemning the outspoken critics who went to the media I chose to use the forum of the *Detective Team Newsletter* to express a carefully prepared response. There was an intentional and noticeable refrain from finger pointing at those who internally and externally promote cynicism because other employees were watching closely on how we treated their co-workers, however implacable they would be.

> I have not suppressed contrairian views on how we should organize. The expression of everyone's view is healthy, to a point. The negative impact is that when comments are made in a public forum, such as newspapers, a degree of doubt on operational effectiveness is raised in the community. An issue is raised about the quality of police operations and our ability to solve crime and maintain order. Although this creates a temporary distraction from other responsibilities, I believe it is important to take the time to respond to all inquiries on the topic. My preference would be to entirely avoid the debate. I don't know why the Police Department should be any different than other private or public institutions in this community,

which are subject to continual debate, controversy and IMPROVEMENT. It's become part of Madison's culture for those who live and work here.

Despite this growl, a hallmark of our detective team had been their unquestionable dedication and loyalty. Attack them collectively for the outspoken actions of an unidentified source and we risked alienating all of them. This could be a planned, deliberate action to divert attention from the real issue. Attack a person's credibility and open up a new front. We can't take it personally. Most importantly, we can not let limited internal dissension turn into endless self flagellation. There were limits to having a say and a big difference in holding a popular vote which led me to the last right.

The Right Responses

We were repeatedly questioned on why the department was undertaking this change "when it's not broken" and "why aren't you listening to me." People confused the opportunity to provide input with what they interpreted as a final and binding say-so. Because we didn't do exactly what they said didn't mean were any less quality leaders. Our employees have a right to be justifiably resentful only when we don't seek their input. Police organizations do not operate as democracies. Majority opinions cannot rule. We could not afford to hold a popular vote on difficult issues. Leaders have responsibilities to perform that are quite different than detectives and officers who deliver services directly to the customers. If we truly believe this is the future organizational direction, we need to make that intention clear and unambiguous. One of the most liberal champions on employee empowerment agreed with management reserving the right to make this decision confirms this thought (Gurwitt, 1995) and added that:

> If as bosses we are convinced that we should structure the unit in multi-functional teams, or around customers, or geographic areas, a whole piece of the manufacturing process, business units as opposed to organizing by functions—then we should present this determination as a given to our unit. It is bosses' wider view of the whole system and the environment that gives them a special voice in determining structure. (p. 45)

Here's an example of how that message was conveyed in the October 5, 1992, *Detective Team Newsletter:*

> I won't mislead you by saying you have a vote that will determine the outcome of this proposal. Leaders have to stand for something. My job is to align our daily work with our vision and mission. I see this organization as having committed itself to a single direction. While some will argue this direction is physical decentralization, I maintain it is becoming more responsive to neighborhood needs. Physical decentralization is just one component of the strategy to get there. I have not concealed my belief on the direction the department should be headed. I have actively contributed to the design of that model starting with the creation of neighborhood officers nearly ten years ago. My job is to align our work unit with organizational goals, however unexciting they may be to some. I can assure you with some degree of certainty, we do not intend to abandon the vision which includes a primary focus on organizing and working with neighborhoods on lessening crime and social disorder. Many of us believe this can best be accomplished by geographic responsibility or what the British call patch policing. (p. 2)

As leaders of change, it's unlikely that any of us expected to be showered with appreciation and gratitude. We relied on the support of other managers and those excited about the prospects of creating a better way. We overcame the temptation to give in to the resistance and those nagging self-conscious questions like is this really worth it? Leadership efforts to improve the quality of police services might not be fully appreciated by others. For instance, Senge (1990) argued that anyone who had tried to change the way government works has had similar thoughts. Indeed, ingratitude is one of the milder responses that change provokes. Whatever label given to change, Senge added, productivity, quality, reinvention, benchmarking—a leader's ability to reform government ultimately lay in how successfully s/he wooed others to the idea that it needs to be done.

We knew that forcing change upon the agency through coercion would be quicker, but that method results in gaining simple obedience of employees. Coercion wins compliant obedience, but we preferred to win their hearts and minds too. We wouldn't gain acceptance for these changes by citing a need for reform that only management could deliver. We were constantly reminded of this important change tenet through writers such as Ghoshal and Bartlett (1995) who say that:

> The leaders who fare best are those who continually see themselves as designers not crusaders. Many of the best intention efforts to foster new learning disciplines flounder because those leading the charge forget the first rule of learning: people learn what they need to learn, not what someone else thinks they need to learn. (p. 94)

Our focus proved to be fairly simple. It's revolved around the way we organized people to work together. As leaders we set the tone. The Madison Police Department emphasized teamwork as one of its primary leadership principles. How we organized the workplace said something about the fundamentals we believed in and what the organization represented. More importantly, our ability to initiate, guide and sustain change increased the likelihood of success. In a relatively brief period of time, others began to discover the way it should be, ultimately becomes the way it is. That's how cultures (calf paths) are changed.

MOVING RHETORIC TO REALITY: IMPLEMENTATION

Seven years have now passed since the Madison Police Department made significant changes to incorporate the investigative function into its command structure. In 1994, the issue was still unsettled as several veteran detectives appealed to a new police chief to turn back the clock and allow detectives to revert to the old model of having a separate bureau. The new chief of police, himself a former community police officer in a large urban department, came from an organization that already had decentralized its investigative function. As a result of the appeal however, he asked a committee of detectives and managers (Detective Issues Team) to identify issues critical to providing effective criminal investigations.

In early 1997, a Detective Function Team was created to offer recommendations to the chief on the appropriateness of various investigative models developed as the result of input developed from the group above. Prior to developing operational models, the chief asked department leaders to provide a strategic vision and direction on how the investigative function would be incorporated in our community policing model.

The Department's Management Team identified a number of attributes that were "must haves" in any recommendation to reconfigure how we managed the detective function. Those attributes were:

- Improve service delivery;
- Provide a contact/resource person to form relationships with individuals and organizations wanting information;
- Support citywide communication and coordination; facilitate communication and interaction among districts;
- Provide for efficient case management;
- Facilitate problem identification and analysis, community policing and respond to needs with solutions;
- Support patrol and detective needs; be facilitative of two way communication;
- Enable daily interaction between/among detectives, patrol officers, neighborhood officers and others;
- Establish clear chain of command for detectives;
- Provide for district accountability with management authority for investigative function;
- Enhance teamwork;
- Support the overall decentralization efforts of the department.

The Detective Function Team developed three models consistent with the mandatory criteria developed by department leaders, many of whom were commanding officers who had realized, through experience, the value of having detectives as part of their district teams. The outcome is a preferred model we have operated under for the last seven years and can best be described as each of the five district's having a lieutenant of detectives who is responsible for reviewing, assigning, and managing all cases occurring within that geographic area. For the last three years, they also have a liaison responsibility for a specific crime specialty, i.e., person, sensitive, financial, youth, and arson/auto theft crimes.

Much of the entrenched resistance to the original model and its improved successors has now abated. There are probably many reasons and I can only speculate as to how much they have influenced this outcome. First, the Madison Police Department experienced a massive cultural shift as it has lost over one-third of its detectives to normal retirement over the last four years. The new detectives are a group of younger officers raised on community policing and problem-solving philosophies. Second, detectives who were originally skeptical about the changes have now begun to experience them firsthand and found that the environment was not so bad after all. A simple but excellent example is parking for detective's unmarked squads. Parking is scarce for department vehicles at the central city work location. We've outgrown our internal workspace and street, basement and ramp parking is severely limited; consequently, detectives face the threat of a parking ticket almost daily. Third, nothing has changed affecting overtime compensation and other benefits. Fourth, the department has made huge advances in technology that provides investigators with needed information at decentralized work sites. Finally, detective lieutenants have a cross-functional responsibility for a specialty crime. For instance, the north district lieutenant is responsible for a geographic area but is also the "facilitator" for the financial crimes detectives citywide insuring that training needs are met and information is routinely exchanged among investigators and financial institutions.

CONCLUSION

In the spirit in which this paper was written, I hope police leaders everywhere will continue to examine the design and effectiveness of their existing organizational structures as they relate to:

- preventing and solving crime,
- lessening the conditions underlying neighborhood disorder,
- building teamwork and communication,
- delivering quality police services, and
- reducing fear and gaining the trust and cooperation of neighborhood residents.

Hopefully, it will sustain the thoughtful discussion underway by innovators in our profession on the different ways to organize the work place to protect and serve communities. It is hoped that by sharing our experiences, others can be guided from those experiences and produce a new organizational structure that best suits their department and community needs.

Too often we live by the old maxim, if it isn't broke, don't fix it. Policing isn't broke, and many of us have provided excellent police services, however, change is necessary since the face of crime has changed and it seems that our resources have also changed—they've become scare. Frankly, standing still is no longer an option in policing or for that matter any organization that provides a public service. Traditional leaders of outstanding organizations in the private sector and in policing have waited until it was too late. To avoid crisis, police leaders need to think of a continuous improvement. Ford Motor Company did not rest on their laurels by having the best-selling car in America, the Taurus. Despite its enormous popularity, its engineers are constantly redesigning the vehicle to meet the future needs and expectations of potential buyers. We need a similar introspection on our policing model. It's easy to understand how a process, law, product, service, etc., becomes the status quo. "Yesterday's winning formula ossifies into today's conventional wisdom before petrifying into tomorrow's tablets of stones." Policing has far too many tablets of stones.

In the complex world of policing, we need now, more than ever, leaders who are not afraid to question business as usual and not unwilling to seek creative and effective answers. Along the way we can not be dissuaded by excuses like "we've always done it that way." Our challenge as caretakers is to protect and serve communities to the best of our abilities making them safer (than we found them) for our children and future generations. As stewards of the profession, we are obligated to leave our successors with well run, efficient and effective organizations. That's what police leadership encompasses today and will undoubtedly require in the future too.

The Madison PD Detective Bureau has avoided the popular euphemisms of reinventing and reengineering throughout or organizational change. Realigning, simply means to make new groupings. In policing, we have a solid foundation, i.e. patrol officers, neighborhood officers, detectives, etc., and we can't afford to lose a single one of them. We need to realign those functions to serve our neighborhoods. There is an urgent need for leaders who can create a shared vision and then obtain the support of co-workers in aligning their organizations to fully support its attainment. There is an equally important and concurrent task of building consensus with other government, business and community leaders on the best ways to work together in meeting these goals. These are the essential acts of leadership. Our task will be made easier by the inclusion, not exclusion of detectives to help facilitate change. I have learned firsthand the most important lesson and *final right* of change and it was best articulated by Newton in this quote, "If I have seen further, it is because I stood on the shoulders of giants."

Captain Masterson can be reached at mmasterson@ci.madison.wi.us

Commanding Officer—Detective Team and Dane County Narcotics and Gang Task Force [1991–1995] and Personnel and Training Team [1996–1999]. Currently he is the Commander of the North Police District of Madison, Wisconsin.

REFERENCES

Berger, W. B., Mertes, L., and Graham, A. (1994, May). C.O.P.—A blueprint for police-community partnerships. *The Police Chief,* 30–35.

Block, P. (1993). *Stewardship, choosing service over self.* San Francisco: Berrett-Koehler Publishers.

Bro, J. (1994, October). *Community policing—An international perspective.* London: IPEC.

"Can community policing solve murder crisis?" (1997, June 16). *Legal Times.*

Carlson, B. R. (1993, June). Redefining investigations . . . a detective's role in a community-oriented police department. *California Peace Officer.*

Community Policing Consortium. (1995, March). *Community policing strategies offer promise of improved public service.* Washington, D.C.: Community Policing Exchange.

Creech, B. (1994). *The five pillars of TQM.* New York: Truman Talley Books.

Geller, W. A. (1991). *Local government police management.* Washington, D.C.: International City Management Association.

Ghoshal, S. and Bartlett, C. A. (1995, January). Changing the role of top management: Beyond structure to processes. *Harvard Business Review.*

Goldstein, H. (1993). *The new policing: Confronting complexity.* Madison, WI: The University of Wisconsin Press.

Gurwitt, R. (1995, January). Creating a constituency for change. *Governing,* 7–8.

Hammer, M. & Stanton, S. A. (1995). *The reengineering revolution.* NY: Harper Business.

Heitzkey, V. (1994, July 16). Cracking the case. *The Capital Times,* 3.

Heymann, P. (1995, March). *A serious law enforcement program to deal with violence.* Paper presented at UW Law School Lecture Series, Madison, WI.

Horvath, F., Lee, Y. H., & Meesig, R. T. (1999, November). *Police policies and practices in the criminal investigation process: A national survey.* Presented at the 1999 American Society of Criminology, Toronto, Canada.

Hutton, D. W. (1994). *The change agent's handbook: A survival guide for quality improvement champions.* Milwaukee, WI: ASQC Quality Press.

Johnson D. W. and Johnson, F. P. (1991). *Joining together: Group theory and group skills.* Needham Heights, MA: Allyn and Bacon.

Kotter, J. P. & Heskett, J. L. (1992). *Corporate culture and performance.* New York: The Free Press.

Krauss, C. (1994, July 28). New York City Precinct Reengineering Team: Major changes recommended in New York City Police Department. *New York Times.*

"Local government police management." (1991). Washington, D.C.: ICMA.

Masterson, M. (1992, Autumn) Are TQM and community policing inextricably related? You don't plant seed corn on a parking lot pavement!, *The Express,* Canadian Police Association, Ottawa, Canada.

Michelmore, P. (1992, November). From outcast to supercop. *Readers Digest.* Pleasantville, NY: Time.

Oettmeier, T. N. and Bleck, W. H. (1990). *Integrating investigative operations through neighborhood oriented policing.* Houston, TX: Houston Police Department.

Ortiz, R. L. and Peterson, M. (1994, August). Police culture: A roadblock to change in law enforcement. *The Police Chief.*

Ring, K. J. (1993, August). Rape in Madison: An investigative report. *Madison Magazine,* 43–44.

Senge, P. N. (1990). *The fifth discipline: The art and practice of the learning organization.* New York: Doubleday Publishing.

Smith, W. J. (1994, March). Community policing for investigators. *Law Enforcement News,* 5–7.

Sparrow, M. K. (1988). *Implementing community policing.* Washington, D.C.: NIJ Perspectives on Policing.

Stephens, D. W. and Moore, M. H. (1991). *Beyond command and control. The strategic management of police departments.* Washington, D.C.: Police Executive Research Forum.

Stevens, D. J. (2001). *Case studies in community policing.* Upper Saddle River, NJ: Prentice Hall.

Wycoff, M. A. (1995). *Community policing strategies.* Washington D.C.: National Institute of Justice.

Wycoff M. A. and Skogan, W. K. (1993, December). *Community policing in Madison: Quality from the inside-out.* Washington, D.C.: National Institute of Justice.

Wycoff, M. A. and Cosgrove, C. (1999). *Investigations in the community policing context.* Washington, D.C.: Police Executive Research Forum.

Zhao, J. (1996). *Why police organizations change: A study of community-oriented policing.* Washington, D.C.: Police Executive Research Foundation.

10

Community Policing
and Police Leadership

Dennis J. Stevens

❖

Certainly, it has been advanced that there is an important distinction between the self image of the police and the day to day reality of routine policing (Goldstein, 1977; Walker, 1984). The emphasis on crime control is and has been largely a matter of what the police say they are doing about crime (Walker, 1984). Some writers imply the police also manipulate community policing efforts in order to advance professional and political autonomy (Manning, 1997; Walker, 1984). The police have their critics, some of whom suggest that the authority of both top management and middle management are affected by a host of regulations and obstructions advanced by politicians, community leaders, and organizational leaders in both public and private sectors (McNamara, 1967; Stevens, 2001, 1999c, 1998a). Also, surveys report a vast number of Americans hold a low opinion concerning decisions made by the police.[1] Even when a police agency engages in a justified critical response employing technical initiatives to further public safety, community members reject that deployment and imply the police are reckless (Landry, 1998; Stevens, 1999a, 1998a, 1998b). Yet, the American public has a litigious nature and bring civil suits against police departments and police personnel at all levels in record numbers often influencing day-to-day, serve and protect decisions (Stevens, 2000). One assumption held by this researcher is that professional leadership skills can enhance public perception of the police and help bring the police closer to their organizational mission.

---

[1]For an indepth look at national studies concerning the police see Sourcebook of criminal justice statistics of 1998 (1999).

There are changes in the philosophical mandates of police agencies across the country, and many of those changes challenge the way police organizations are managed (Bayley, 1998; Carter and Radelet, 1999). One of the primary changes concerning police service is development, implementation, and maintenance of a community policing philosophy. Police managers can no longer take comfort in the traditional response of a punishment centered organizational bureaucracy accentuated through a reactive policy because in part of a due process revolution—the people in a democratic society want and will be heard.[2] Police leaders, especially police middle managers, have few prerogatives about organizational change and are encouraged to welcome it and to see it as continuum in order to fulfill community policing initiatives (Kelling and Coles, 1996). Managers at all levels develop a mindset to see creative opportunities and different ways to deliver police services (Nowicki, 1998). It is a matter of toughness and a matter of decisiveness in making difficult choices or changes that must be made for the health of the department and the well-being of the community (BJA, 1994; PERF, 1996). Appropriately empowering rank-and-file officers and community members, enabling them to mutually solve community problems, might be a laborious task within a paramilitary hierarchy of command organization. Yet, it is a task that must be accomplished if community policing strategies are to bring the community closer to social order expectations. Therefore, decentralization might be one of the few options available to move the organization closer to its mission through quality service (Carter and Radelet, 1999). Furthermore, decisions about patrol deployment, technical and use of force limits, and police disciplinary prerogatives might be decisions that require input from many sources contrary to traditional methods of control (Cardarelli, McDevitt, and Baum, 1998).

While there is a prescribed process of resolving violator challenges including due process remedies, the philosophy of the twenty-first century for police service emphasizes that action be taken by police managers as that of a facilitator as opposed to that of an enforcer as seen in traditional police organizations (DuBois and Hartnett, in press; Stevens, 2001). Thus, discovering what is being experienced by rank-and-file officers and by community members is vital, and those experiences must be articulated to everyone concerned in order to improve the quality of police service (Trojanowicz and Carter, 1988). Regardless of the accolades by public servants to this contemporary philosophy, evolutionary methods of sharing command is a method of doing business that is both inevitable in a democratic society and required to accommodate the changing demographics and expectations of American society (Trojanowicz and Carter, 1988).

The primary question seems to relate to police service models, which depend on the managerial skill level of police supervisors. Are they professionally prepared to meet the organizational change expected of them to better serve their constituents? That is, supervisors must be visionary to the extent that they have a mental picture of where the department is going, and they must be able to describe that vision to others in order for everyone to be headed in the same direction (Carter and Radelet, 1999). Lastly, police leaders should be morally, ethically, and legally guided by an inner strength that speaks of their integrity to the individuals

---

[2]For an indepth look at the changes in police management see Bureau of Justice Assistance [BJA] (1994), Kelling and Coles (1996), Stevens (2001). For a look at occupational change among the police see Van Maanen (1974).

who report to them and the individuals whom they serve exemplifying levels of commitment in today's climate of uncertainty (Moore, 1998). To bring evidence to these concerns, ninety-seven police executives who hold the command rank of lieutenant and above, from eighteen police agencies across the United States were asked about their managerial practices.

COMMUNITY POLICING

Community policing is an outreach by the police to the community. The purpose of this outreach is to promote a partnership with the community to enhance public safety, reduce the fear of crime, and to improve the quality of life (Skogan, Hartnett, DuBois, Comey, Kaiser, and Lovig, 1999; Stevens, 2001). At the core of this relationship lay problem-solving strategies linked to social problems that might lend themselves to eventual crime (Goldstein, 1977, 1990). Therefore, the priorities of community policing include a preventive response to public order through a level of delegation of authority with community members and line officers as a response to future crime as opposed to a response after crimes have occurred (Carter and Radelet, 1999; Kelling and Coles, 1996). That is, police executives must demonstrate facilitative skills as opposed to enforcer skills should they wish to move their agency into a twenty-first-century policing model (DuBois and Hartnett, 2002).

Community policing expands the responsibility of crime control and public safety to the community at large. Through this association problems relating to social disorder are identified, prioritized, and attempts are made to resolve those problems to the mutual satisfaction of the partnership without compromising Constitutional guarantees (Stevens, 2001). To accomplish this goal, community policing becomes a department-wide change in the way police agencies do business and, of course, the way police executives manage that business.

However, a worthy concern is that there is not, and probably never will be, one best way to lead, manage, and assist any organization including a police agency in the areas of strategy, policy, performance, productivity, human relations, or implementation (Nowicki, 1998; Stupak, 1998). Borrowing from Police Chief Ramsey (2002) who is quoted in Chapter Three of this book, he says: "In a very short period of time, community policing has fundamentally changed how American police officers and executives view themselves and their respective roles in the community. Community policing has also significantly changed—and raised—public expectations of what the police can, and should do, when it comes to the old concepts of serving and protecting."

Unfortunately, police management as a distinct entity has developed less extensively when compared to other organizational management entities due to organizational variations from police department to police department and due in part to the variations of the diversity of the constituents they serve. Departments are more like little nations, clans, and tribes as opposed to rational units, mechanistic entities, or a set of scientific management processes.[3] But, there are universal characteristics that can be utilized by police supervisors to professionalize their management techniques.[4] Cox (1990) makes one suggestion that the

---

[3]For more detail on this concept see Stupak (1998).

[4]See Carter & Radelet, 1999; Harrison, 1998; Houston, 1999; Keiger, 1997; Klockars, 1985; Manning, 1997; Nowicki, 1998; Skogan, 1990; Stojkovic, Kalinich, & Klofas, 1997.

quality of police leadership should automatically improve, not because of managerial training, professionalism, or public demand but because the gap between private enterprise and public service will narrow in terms of administrative skills, technology, and fiscal responsibility. Therefore, this chapter is an exploratory examination of the leadership characteristics of police managers since agencies must rely on those executives to plan, organize, and deliver quality police service from every employee, with the support of the community, to contribute to public safety and efficiently use every resource. Leadership characteristics, it could be argued, aid in bringing about appropriate police strategies without endangering public safety or compromising the integrity of the men and the women who work hard to provide a quality lifestyle for others through good police service. It can also be argued that police managers must process proficient leadership characteristics in order to deliver contemporary quality police service.

LEADERSHIP

One definition of leadership can be defined as the process of directing and influencing the actions of others to bring a police agency closer to its objectives. This notion is consistent with writers who argue that leadership skills are typical of efficient management regardless of the service or product produced by an organization (Cox, 1990; Hatten, 1997). Leadership qualities are professional skills, characteristics, and/or a style of managing others.

Originally, it was assumed that a leader was born with leadership characteristics or traits but research has demonstrated that personal characteristics of leadership patterns can be viewed separately from an individual's personality or a situational context (Tosi, Rizzo, and Carroll, 1986). Another approach explaining leadership skills is a behavioral approach which emphasizes distribution of influence and the tasks and social behaviors of leaders. A third approach, the contingency approach, tends to emphasize multiple variables, particularly situational variables that constrain leadership. These situational variables, argue Stojkovic, Kalinich, and Klofas (1997), include characteristics of subordinates, organizational, context, and style of leadership. Understanding the complexity of community policing strategies, it appears that the contingency approach might apply more often than a behavioral perspective largely because police management operates in adversarial environment that tends to constrain police leadership more than advance it. Therefore, police leadership can be seen as a process that effectively accomplishes organizational objectives but depends on how a commander interacts with other domains of leadership outside the department and subordinates of the department (Klockars, 1985; Stojkovic, Kalinich and Klofas, 1997; Tosi, Rizzo, and Carroll, 1986).

Leadership characteristics among police supervisors is seen as crucial for commanders because they must work closely with individuals who provide police service (i.e., their own subordinates), and officers whom they have little control (i.e., local, state, and federal personnel from other law enforcement agencies) (Trojanowicz and Dixon, 1974). But unlike their police sergeants, commanders have little direct influence over the daily lives of any of those officers (Klockars, 1985). They must also work closely with community members, business and social agency executives, and civic officials who can vigorously influence police service, yet these commanders seldom possess an outcome-decision in most of the enterprises those individuals represent (Alpert and Piquero, 1998).[5] Lastly, police managers are held accountable through courts and disciplinary committees with individuals whom police service affects, and again it appears that commanders have little influence in directing courts or committees to action (Carter and Radelet, 1999).

Taking direction from manager trainers, Jim Kouzes, president of Tom Peters Group/Learning Systems, says, "If people don't believe in the messenger, they won't believe in the message" (Hatten, 1997); that is, *credibility*. How does a police commander build credibility? Kouzes prescribes an acronym—DWWSWWD (do what we say we will do). There is the rub . . . how?

In the introduction section of this work a number of leadership skills were explained in relationship to community policing trends. Most of those skills are consistent with Hatten's (1997) notion about leadership characteristics, but there were some added which best serves quality police service.[6] Those characteristics it could be argued when professionally employed would tend to motivate others, moving the department closer to its mission of crime control and a reduction of the fear of crime, and an enhancement of quality-of-life issues. This is accomplished in association with an empowered community partnership that emphasizes problem-solving prerogatives. Summarizing the above leadership characteristics from an earlier section, those key points are:

- **Organizational Change**

  Police leaders need to see change as continuum in order to fulfill community policing initiatives (Kelling and Coles, 1996).

- **Creative Ability**

  A commander must develop a mindset to see creative opportunities and different ways to deliver police services (Nowicki, 1998).

- **Toughness**

  Leaders should become decisive in making difficult choices or changes that must be made for the health of the department and the well being of the community (BJA, 1994; PERF, 1996).

- **Subordinate Trust and Public Trust**

  Empowering line officers and community members will enable them to mutually solve community problems.

---

[5]In fact, the political leadership in St. Petersburg, Florida recently invited Chimurenga Waller president of the St. Petersburg chapter of the National People's Democratic Uhuru Movement, to the Citizen Review Committee which examines decisions of the St. Petersburg Police Department. Mr. Waller and his organization are bitter critics of the St. Petersburg, Police Department. See Landry (1998) for more detail.

[6]The magazine *Management Review* conducted a study to determine the attributes that leaders will need for the year 2000. However, this researcher added three: organizational change, sharing command, and police decisions. The purpose of these additions is in keeping with community policing strategies.

- **Delegation of Responsibility**

  Fulfilling trust initiatives will be a laborious task within a paramilitary hierarchy of command organization and for that reason decentralization and delegation might be one of the few options available to move the organization closer to its mission (Carter and Radelet, 1999).

- **Police Decisions**

  Decisions about patrol deployment, technical and use of force response limits, and police disciplinary prerogatives might be decisions that require input from many sources contrary to traditional methods of control (Cardarelli, McDevitt, and Baum, 1998).

- **Taking Action**

  Leaders need to take the initiative as a facilitator as the appropriate model as opposed to traditional responses of enforcer (DuBois and Hartnett, 2001; Stevens, 2001).

- **Communication**

  Discovering what is being experienced by rank-and-file officers and by community members is key, and those experiences must be articulated to everyone concerned through in order to improve the quality of police service (Trojanowicz and Carter, 1988).

- **Sharing Command**

  Evolutionary methods of sharing command is a method of doing police business that is both inevitable in a democratic society and required to accommodate the changing demographics and expectations of American society (Trojanowicz and Carter, 1988).

- **Visionary**

  Supervisors should be able to develop a mental picture of where the department is going and be able to describe that vision to others so everyone is headed in a similar direction (Carter and Radelet, 1999).

- **Integrity**

  Leaders should show that a moral, ethical, and legal guide exists linked to an inner strength demonstrating integrity to both the individuals who report to them exemplifying trust as one indicator of a bond that exists between supervisor and officers and public.

- **Commitment**

  Leaders need to demonstrate a commitment in today's climate of uncertainty to the individuals whom they serve (Moore, 1998; Stevens, 2000). The police become facilitators with an eye on quality police service.

These items were chosen because each item seemed repetitive in the community policing literature and in the leadership literature. These few should at best give us an idea as to the readiness of police executives.

METHODOLOGY

In the spring of the year 2000, a survey was developed through trial and error to measure the leadership characteristics of police executives in numerous police agencies across the country. Once a survey reported the desired results through many pretests, it was e-mailed to twenty different police agencies personally known to the researcher as they and/or their departments were involved with the researcher in other projects. They were asked to duplicate the survey and distribute it to police supervisors who held the rank of lieutenant and above and who supervised other officers in their agency. One estimate is that there were 235 surveys originally distributed. But only 145 were returned via the U.S. Mail by the original person who duplicated the survey, distributed it, and collected it. In some cases, individual participants mailed their survey to the researcher themselves (the researcher's address was on the survey). There was a one-month deadline written on the survey, but surveys were accepted one month past the deadline (surveys continue to be received months later, but none of those were added to the data).

Of the 145 surveys received within the two-month period, 35 were completed by non-supervisory personnel, 8 by non-sworn officers, and 5 were illegible. Thus, 97 surveys were used in this study. Of those surveys, the average participant reported 17 years experience as a sworn police officer, and 10 years as a supervisor (See Table 1).[7] The average number of sworn officers under the command of all but three of the respondents ranged from 19 to 225 with an average of 95. Those 3 excluded respondents reported an average of 701 sworn officers under their command with a range of 545 to 784 officers under their command. (These totals were not included in the preceding average, but the responses from these respondents were included in the all other equations). The 97 respondents reported an average age of 44 ranging from 34 to 56. They reported an average of 15 years formal education (aside from vocational training and police academy training) with a range of from 12 to 19 (3 J.D.s, and 6 masters) years of education. Eighty-seven percent (84) of the respondents were male and 89 percent (77) were white. Eighty percent (78) of the respondents were married and 20 percent (19) were either single or divorced.

Importance of the Variables

The importance of this test is to determine which set of leadership characteristics police supervisors would expect an "excellent police leader" to demonstrate most often and to see how they would grade their own departmental community policing efforts. Are there distinctive patterns that might be reported by the participants that effect their perceptions of community policing practices? Since community policing is a department-wide philosophy, then all supervisors, it can be argued, have an impact on the community policing initiatives of a department. Therefore, it may not be a priority how these supervisors are linked to the responsibility of their departmental community policing efforts to understand how well community policing fits within their department.

---

[7]Facts not known about the participants are how many of them supervised the same officers. That is, a captain who heads a division of 100 sworn officers might have been a respondent as well as his only two lieutenants both supervising 50 sworn officers each. Also what is not known is how many of the supervisors included other personnel other than sworn officers despite the indicators that only sworn officers were to be counted.

TABLE 1   Characteristics of Sample   N = 97

	Average Number	Range/Percent*
Years of Sworn Experience	17	7–30
Years of Supervisory Experience	10	3–21
Number of Subordinates Group I*	60	6–123
Number of Subordinates Group II	701	545–784
Age	44	34–56
Education	15	12–19
Male	84	87%
Female	13	13%
White	77	89%
Black	7	7%
Other	3	3%
Married	78	80%
Single/Divorced	19	20%

*percents rounded

*There were few differences between the reported respondents in Group I versus Group II except in the number of sworn officers they supervised.

It would seem logical that there are other perspectives missing from the above list. It is hardly an exhaustive list. Also, it is not a list intended to imply that if a characteristic were missing that it was not worth pursuing. Nonetheless, it could be argued that the more often the above characteristics are practiced, the more creditable a police supervisor would appear to subordinates, colleagues, and community members as well as civic, organizational, and business leaders, and therefore, the more likely the supervisor would be a productive community policing leader. Perhaps large-scale tests with many more variables and a larger sample could be done at a later time.

Finally, a latent expectation that could be impacted through leadership techniques would be job satisfaction levels of line officers. Questions such as do managerial practices of a department permit sergeants and patrol officers room for advancement in the departmental hierarchy? Are officer grievances handled fairly? That is, leadership practices impact job satisfaction levels of officers which ultimately impact quality police service which includes community policing initiatives (Stevens, 2001, 1999a, 1999b). However, questions of these varieties, while equally important, are not part of this test. Therefore, what will be tested is that quality leadership characteristics give rise to effective community policing strategies.

Statistics

Frequency tests were run on all the data to ensure spread sheet entry accuracy. Correlation Coefficient, Regression, and ANOVA tests aided in understanding the data. Crosstabulation was used to deter relationships between some of the variables.

TABLE 2   Percent Responses of Leadership Traits*

Characteristic	Mean	5**	4	3	2	1	SD
Organizational Change	2.73	3%	21%	26%	47%	3%	.93
Creative Ability	1.78	0	0	5%	68%	27%	.52
Toughness	3.91	12%	64%	21%	0	0	.58
Trust Subordinate	3.09	4%	34%	34%	23%	5%	.97
Public Trust	3.09	4%	34%	34%	23%	5%	.97
Delegation of Responsibility	3.35	10%	36%	32%	22%	0	.94
Police Decision	3.43	8%	51%	20%	20%	2%	.97
Taking Action	4.38	42%	49%	5%	0	0	.59
Communication	2.69	3%	6%	50%	37%	3%	.77
Sharing Command	3.55	28%	25%	22%	26%	0	1.15
Visionary	2.72	0	10%	52%	38%	0	.64
Integrity	3.82	21%	41%	38%	0	0	.75
Commitment	2.93	5%	7%	66%	18%	3%	.77

*rounded
**5 5 always, 4 5 very often, 3 5 sometimes, 2 5 seldom, 1 5 never

FINDINGS

The respondents were asked how often they felt "an excellent" police leader should use each of the thirteen leadership characteristics outlined above. When the data were pooled together, distinctive, yet surprising, patterns arose. That is, 24 percent (23) of the participants reported that *organizational change* among police departments was always or very often something an excellent leader should concern himself with, while 26 percent (25) reported that sometimes an excellent leader should deal with organizational change (see Table 2). Ninety-five percent (92) of the participants reported that an excellent leader should demonstrate *creative abilities* seldom or never, while 64 percent (62) reported that excellent leaders should be *tough* and decisive very often.

Four percent (4) of the participants reported that *trust of their subordinates* should always be a characteristic of an excellent police leader, 34 percent (33) reported very often, 34 percent (33) sometimes, and 28 percent (27) reported seldom or never as their response. A mere 4 percent (4) of the participants reported that an excellent leader should always *trust the public* while 68 percent (66) reported sometimes or seldom as their response.

Forty-six percent (45) of the participants reported that *delegation of responsibility* to others should be practiced always or very often by an excellent leader, but 54 percent (52) reported that delegation should be used only sometimes or seldom. Interestingly, 59 percent (57) of the participants reported that *police decisions* (deployment, technical and use of force, and disciplinary activity) should always or very often be made by police commanders, and 40 percent (38) reported that only sometimes or seldom should commanders make those decisions alone. However, 91 percent (89) reported that excellent leaders should always or very often *take action.*

	Excellent	Above Average	Average	Below Average	Poor
TABLE 3 Community Policing Grades N = 97					
Community Policing Grade	12%	34%	25%	24%	5%

Eighty-seven percent (84) reported that *communication* among excellent leaders should be practiced sometimes or seldom. Fifty-three percent (51) of the respondents reported that excellent leaders should always or very often *share command* with other officers or individuals, and 48 percent (46) of them reported that sharing command should occur sometimes or seldom.

None of the participants reported that excellent leaders should be *visionaries* all the time, 10 percent (10) reported very often, 52 percent (50) sometimes, and 38 percent (37) reported that leaders should seldom be visionaries. Twenty-one percent (20) of the participants reported that *integrity* should always be a quality of an excellent leader, 41 percent (40) reported very often as their choice, and 38 percent (37) reported that only sometimes integrity should be a characteristic of an excellent leader. Lastly, 5 percent (5) of the participants reported that an excellent police leader should always be *committed* to public safety, the department, and the public, 7 percent (7) reported very often, 66 percent (64) reported sometimes, and 22 percent (21) reported seldom or never.

Finally, when the respondents graded their agency's community policing strategies, on a scale of 1 to 5 (with 5 representing an excellent grade and 1 representing a poor grade), distinctive, yet unanticipated patterns arose, too. That is, 13 percent (12) of the participants rated the community policing efforts of their department as excellent, 34 percent (33) rated it as above average, 25 percent (24) average, 24 percent (23) below average, and 5 percent (5) poor (see Table 3). Further computation shows that a significant correlation existed between grades in community policing efforts and the following variables: delegation, trusting other officers, public trust, dealing with organizational change, sharing command, and making police decisions.[8] However, predicting community policing scores could best be accomplished by two variables: delegation and trust of subordinates. When the participants rated the community policing efforts of their department as low, they also reported that delegation of responsibility should seldom or never represent a characteristic of an excellent leader and that the subordinates should never or seldom be trusted.[9]

---

[8]Using Spearman's Correlation Coefficients, two tailed tests, with each of these variables, they showed a .000 level of significance (except change which was .001) when computed with the community policing variable. Also in a test of regression (which might not be reliable with ordinal scores) among all of the variables, R = .824, significant at .000 with df2 at 71 and df1 at 17, and ANOVA F score at 12.326, significant at .000.

[9]Regression scores produced a R at .808 and an ANOVA F score at 88.230, significant at .000.

CONCLUSION

Based on the data, leadership among police supervisors, at least those who participated in this survey, has a long way to go relative to community policing initiatives. In most cases, the responses largely mirror leadership characteristics typical of traditional policing strategies as opposed to community policing philosophy. The results were unexpected. One implication of these results is that most police middle managers operate from an antiquated control, arrest, and command hierarchy with top-down dictates about deployment, tactical and use of force limits, and constituent conduct. Of course, it isn't plausible that one survey can produce significant data that might lend itself well to routine behavior of middle managers. But, the results speak for themselves in the sense that middle-manager characteristics of traditional policing are strongly supported throughout the reports of the participants. What might be the blame for that? A brief review of the literature shows that police officers have high burnout rate, caused in part by a lack of coping with family problems, occupational stress, little status, low public trust, and that they are likely to be involved in a civil liability suit more than any other occupation (Carter and Radelet, 1999; Dantzker and Surrette, 1996; Stevens, 2001, 1999d, 1999e). It needs to be understood that many officers often deal with violators and people who generally have a different regard about social order and compliance than most law abiding individuals among other things.

With that said, why aren't police middle managers advancing with the times? One answer comes from the idea that there needs to be a balance that supervisors work towards which often is unnoticed and unlikely in other organizations. That is, while police agencies need to address the root causes of crime through community partnerships, the problem is that if real crime is ignored, it will escalate both in intensity and in totals. Since crime is a response in most cases to living conditions, relationship expectations, and pure selfishness, most of those issues are not police business. Therefore, finding the balance between professional intervention for the purposes of prevention, crime escalation, and police responsibility is a complex task of commanders, their advisers, and policy makers. Yet, officers, virtually at every rank, cannot follow through with community problem-solving decisions if policy, regulations, and employment expectations dictate otherwise. The traditional, incident driven police organization (and policing as an institution) must alter policy, regulations, and expectations to fit within a contemporary framework of policing strategies for the twenty-first century. Just as community policing models are different in different jurisdictions and within those jurisdictions, so to are community group techniques (Stevens, 2001).

Another answer might relate to the amount of obstacles faced by police middle managers and top managers alike from political leaders who have little knowledge of policing strategies but have a great deal of input concerning the well being including unemployment of any officer (including chiefs) who might oppose a political mandate. One example comes from Camden, New Jersey, where the department failed at community policing initiatives because of both unstable political and police leadership, incisive police history, pervasive officer resistance, ramped crime, and devastating poverty (Stevens, 2001). The Camden police department's remains a paramilitary operation with the politicians making police policy and the police dictating those policies of arrest, calls, and stops as a method of measuring its success. What it came down to for Camden, was "too many chiefs of police, too many involved officials, too much poverty, too much crime, too much officer resistance, and too little professional leadership," Stevens (2001, p. 285). In fact, state government gave up on Camden when the sewers backed up and other city departments failed except the jails which were jammed, and the third mayor of the city was indicated on corruption changes. The state of New Jersey stepped in and took control of Camden the 17th of July, 2000. It is the biggest city takeover in the United States since the Great Depression.

Recommendations

Nonetheless, leadership characteristics can lend themselves well to greater levels of compliance among both the individuals located inside and outside an agency. Those characteristics relate to a style of motivating others toward the mission or goals of an agency. The process is referred to as management. Management can be defined as the process of planning, organizing, and controlling resources in order to achieve public safety through community policing initiatives. Just as police agencies are experiencing philosophical changes about police service and relationships with the community, the process in which police executives manage must also change (Carter and Radelet, 1999). One optimal approach to developing and maintaining substantial change in a police agency advancing community policing prerogatives might be to enter into deliberate, continual, and rational process of planned change. With that said, begging inquiry might be the question—motivating individuals in what way to accommodate a community policing agenda? Is there a managerial process that complements the primary components of community policing—making a commitment to quality police service through community policing and thinking in terms of preventive measures through problem-solving techniques that include empowerment and decentralization? One managerial philosophy that advances foremost quality police service and customer satisfaction is Total Quality Management (TQM), which has served private enterprises such as Ford Motor Company and some criminal justice agencies, too. Like community policing practices, much has been written about TQM recently blurring many of its meanings and worth. TQM consistent with community policing principles is a philosophy focusing on problem-solving and control. TQM like community policing was never intended as a panacea or cure-all. TQM is based on the writings of W. Edward Deming, who helped teach the concept of quality to Japanese manufacturing at the invitation of General Douglas MacArthur after the Second World War. Therefore, using Carter and Radelet (1999, p. 514) as a guide, police agencies might adapt TQM in light of its core principles which follow:

- The organization must address both internal and external customers (police personnel and residents).
- Most individual performance measures are counter-productive because they invite conflict and competition rather than cooperation. Moreover, individual performance measures do not measure customer needs; instead they focus on organizational expectations (arrest, service calls, and dollar amounts of confiscated property and contraband).
- The organization should have a constancy of purpose subscribed to by all employees and the desire to constantly improve service rather than be satisfied with what has been accomplished so far.
- Evaluations should be done on the basis of team accomplishments and comparisons.
- Emphasis should be placed on providing the best possible service the first time and not rely on inspections and reparations.

All organizational members must be goal-driven and participate in goal-attainment, not personal achievements within the organization. It is ironic that TQM appears to be a managerial tool that has strong parallels with community policing initiatives, so much so that its adoption by police agencies will only be a matter of time.

REFERENCES

Alpert, G. P. and Piquero, A. (1998). *Community policing: Contemporary readings.* Prospect Heights, IL: Waveland Press.

Bureau of Justice Assistance. (1994, August). Understanding community policing: A framework of action. NCJ 148457. Washington D.C.: Department of Justice.

Bayley, D. H. (1998). *What works in policing.* New York: Oxford Press.

Cardarelli, A. P., McDevitt, J., & Baum, K. (1998). The rhetoric and reality of community policing in small and medium sized cities and towns. *Policing: An International Journal of Police Strategies & Management, 21*(3), 397–415.

Carter, D. L. and Radelet, L. A. (1999). *The police and the community.* Upper Saddle River, NJ: Prentice Hall.

Cox, S. M. (1990). Policing into the 21st century. *Police Studies, 13*(4), 168–177.

Dantzker, M. L. and Surrette, M. A. (1996). The perceived levels of job satisfaction among police officers: A descriptive review. *The Journal of Police and Criminal Psychology, 11*(2), 7–12.

DuBois, J. and Hartnett, S. M. (2002). Making the community side of community policing work: What needs to be done. In Dennis J. Stevens (Ed.), *The Police and Community Policing* (p. 1–20). Upper Saddle River, NJ: Prentice Hall.

Goldstein, H. (1977). *Policing a free society.* Cambridge, MA: Ballinger.

Goldstein, H. (1990). *Problem-oriented policing.* New York: McGraw-Hill.

Hatten, T. S. (1997). *Small business: Entrepreneurship and beyond.* Upper Saddle River, NJ: Prentice Hall.

Harrison, S. J. (1998). Police organizational culture: Using ingrained values to build positive organizational improvement. *Public Administration and Management. An Interactive Journal, 3*(2). (online), Available: http://www.pamij.com/harrison.html

Houston, J. G. (1999). *Correctional management.* Chicago: Nelson Hall.

Keiger, D. (1997, June). Top cops hit the books. *Johns Hopkins Magazine.* (online), Available: http://www.jhu.edu/~jhumag/0697web/cops.html

Kelling, G. L. and Coles, C. M. (1996). *Fixing broken windows: Restoring order and reducing crime in our communities.* New York: The Free Press.

Klockars, C. B. (1985). *The idea of police.* Beverly Hills, CA: Sage Publications.

Landry, S. (1998, May 30). Police decry naming of Uhuru activist to panel. *St. Petersburg Times.*

Manning, P. K. (1997). *Police work: The social organization of policing.* Prospect Heights, IL: Waveland Press.

Moore, M. (1998, Winter). The pursuit of integrity. *The Law Enforcement Journal,* 36–96.

McNamara, J. H. (1967). Uncertainties in police work: The relevance of police recruits' background and training. In David J. Bordua (Ed.) *The Police: Six Sociological Essays.* New York: John Wiley & Sons, p. 163–252.

Nowicki, D. E. (1998). Mixed messages. In Geoffrey Alpert and Alex Piquero (Eds.) *Community Policing,* (pp. 265–274), Prospect Heights, IL: Waveland Press.

PERF. (1996). *Themes and variations in community policing: Case studies in community policing.* Washington, D.C.: The Police Executive Research Forum.

Ramsey, C. H. (2002). Preparing the community for community policing: The next step in advancing community policing. In Dennis J. Stevens (Ed.) *The Police and Community Policing.* Upper Saddle River, NJ: Prentice Hall.

Skogan, W. G. (1990). *Disorder and decline: Crime and the spiral of decay in American neighbor-hoods*. New York: The Free Press.

Skogan, W. G., Hartnett, S. M., DuBois, J., Comey, J. T., Kaiser, M, and Lovig, J. H. (1999). *On the beat: Police and community problem solving*. Boulder, CO: Westview Press.

Sourcebook of criminal justice statistics of 1998. (1999). Washington D.C.: US Department of Justice, U.S. Government Printing Office (online). Available: http://www.albany.edu/sourcebook/1995/pdf/t232.pdf

Stevens, D. J. (2001). *Case studies in community policing*. Upper Saddle River, NJ: Prentice Hall.

Stevens, D. J. (2000). Civil liabilities and police arrest issues. *The Police Journal, LXXIV*(6), 119–142.

Stevens, D. J. (1999a). American police resolutions and community response. *The Police Journal, LXXII*(2), 140–150.

Stevens, D. J. (1999b). Stress and the American police officer. *The Police Journal, LXXII*(3).

Stevens, D. J. (1999c). Interviews with women convicted of murder: Battered women syndrome re-visited. *International Review of Victimology*, 6(2), 117–136.

Stevens, D. J. (1999d, December) Do college educated officers provide quality police service? *Law and Order, 47*(12), 37–41.

Stevens, D. J. (1999e). Corruption among narcotic officers: A study of innocence and integrity. *Journal of Police and Criminal Psychology, 14*(2), 1–10.

Stevens, D. J. (1998a) What do law enforcement officers think about their work? *The Law Enforcement Journal, 5*(1), 60–62.

Stevens, D. J. (1998b). Urban communities and homicide: Why American blacks resort to murder. *Policing and Society, 8,* 253–267.

Stojkovic, S., Kalinich, D., and Klofas, J. (1997). *Criminal justice organizations: Administration and management*. Belmont, CA: West/Wadsworth Publishing Company.

Stupak, R. J. (1998). Symposium on organizational culture: Theory, practice, and cases. *Public Administration and Management. An Interactive Journal* (online). Available: http://www.pamij.com/stupakintro.html

Tosi, H. L., Rizzo, J. R., and Carroll, S. J. (1986). *Managing organizational behavior.* Marshfield, MA: Pitman.

Trojanowicz, R. C., and Carter, D. L. (1988). *The philosophy and role of community policing*. East Lansing: National Neighborhood Foot Patrol Center, Michigan State University.

Trojanowicz, R. C. and Dixon, S. L. (1974). *Criminal justice and the community*. Englewood Cliffs, NJ: Prentice Hall.

Van Maanen, J. (1974). Working the street. In Herbert Jacob (Ed.) *The potential for reform of criminal justice*. Thousand Oaks, CA: Sage.

Walker, S. (1984). Broken windows and fractured history: The use and misuse of history in recent police analysis. *Justice Quarterly, 1*(1), 75–90.

11

The Community
in Community Policing:

The Key to Success Is the Police and Community Partnerships

M. L. Dantzker

❖

Citizens have long been outspoken about the effectiveness of the police in controlling crime (Moore, Trojanowicz, and Kelling, 1988) and quick to criticize the handling of problems, crime-related or social-oriented, by the police (Dantzker, 1997). Police departments have been criticized for their inability to control crime and for their poor relationships with citizens. Throughout the decades, in response to these criticisms, attempts have been made to improve police response and effectiveness through a variety of innovations and reforms. In the 1970s it was team policing, in the 1980s it was patrol decentralization, and the wave of the 1990s, and upon entering the new millennium, appears to be a community-based policing most often referred to as community-oriented policing (COP) (Dantzker, 1997; 1999).

Primarily resulting from the civil unrest of the 1960s, for more than twenty years police agencies have searched for ways to improve police-community relations (Carter and Radelet, 1999; Hunter, Mayhall, and Barker 2000; Peak and Glensor, 1999; Trojanowicz, Kappeler, Gaines, and Bucqueroux, 1998). Team policing and patrol decentralization attempted to bring policing and the community closer together by providing community sectors where a variety of police services were available. Both programs had a limited impact on community relations because they failed to seek assistance and input from an important element of the community—the residents themselves (Bennett, 1998; Community Policing Consortium, 1994; Lurigio and Rosenbaum, 1997; Miller and Hess, 1994; Oliver, 1998a,b; Skogan, 1998).

In more recent times, police departments are being called upon to become more proactive and innovative in their patrol strategies (Friedmann, 1992; Sparrow, Moore, and Kennedy, 1990; Rosenbaum, 1998; Strecher, 1997; Watson, Stone, and DeLuca,1998). Furthermore, these strategies require that police not only listen to the voices of residents, but to seek out and request residents to speak of the problems with policing and crime and to assist in seeking ways to combat the growing problems; in particular, those problems that may eventually lead to crime (e.g., community disorder) (Goldstein, 1990; Lurigio and Rosenbaum, 1997; Pace, 1993). However, this is one of those requirements that has not been as readily accepted. At one point, this drive for change led one scholar to note that "a quiet revolution" (Kelling, 1988) was occurring, reshaping how policing is performed in the United States. The catalyst of the revolution has become known as community-oriented policing (COP), and it is no longer quiet but taking the country by storm.

Rectifying and remedying problems continue to be a challenge for many police departments. As noted by Brown (1989), "Like many other social institutions, American police departments are responding to rapid social change and emerging problems by rethinking their basic strategies" (p. 1). Furthermore, "regardless of how one experiences it, something is happening, and this something is an attempt to rethink and restructure the role of the police in society" (Rosenbaum, 1998, p. 3). The most current attempt to eliminate problems and restructure policing has been through projects or strategies falling under the rubric of "community policing." As noted by Trojanowicz and Bucqueroux (1994), "Community policing is being touted by some as the cure-all for the problems within and without the criminal justice system" (p. vii). According to Sparrow (1988),

> The concept of community policing envisages a police department striving for an absence of crime and disorder and concerned with, and sensitive to, the quality-of-life in the community. It perceives the community as an agent and partner in promoting security rather than as a passive audience. (p. 1)

Recent literature has noted that community policing appears to be improving the problems leading to resident criticism of the police, such as lack of citizen input, poor police-citizen interaction, and rising crime rates (Dewitt, 1992; Kennedy, 1993; Peak and Glensor, 1999; Skogan and Hartnett, 1997; Trojanowicz and Bucqueroux, 1994; Vardalis, 1992). Community policing also seems to be providing a variety of potential benefits to communities, such as an active voice in problem-solving, improved police-citizen interactions, and a better understanding of what the police are doing leading to enhanced police accountability (Community Policing in the 1990s, 1992; Community Policing Consortium, 1994; Jiao, 1998; Kratcoski and Dukes, 1995; Toch and Grant, 1991; Trojanowicz et al., 1998; Watson et al., 1998).

Because of early reports of a number of positive experiences community policing apparently has produced for both police and communities (Brodeur, 1998, Eggers and O'Leary, 1995; Jolin and Moose, 1997; Memory, 1999; Palmietto and Donahue, 1995; Rosenbaum, 1994; Wycoff, 1995) and the funding available from the federal government, an increasing number of police agencies seem to be looking toward community policing as an answer to their communities' problems.

In implementing community policing, police agencies have had to step back and seriously consider "One of the most important tenets for the success of community-oriented policing . . . " (Dantzker, 1994, p. 16), citizen involvement. To address this vital element, police agencies are attempting to establish "partnerships" with citizens. This book offers just a sampling of how the police are attempting to solidify this important aspect of community policing.

How to begin? Obviously many police agencies have to deal with the concept as to how to get the community involved. DuBois and Hartnett in Chapter One offer advice on the subject through a discussion of their observations of the Chicago Police Department's efforts, which are carried out through what is called the Chicago Alternative Policing Strategy (CAPS). In particular, their chapter focuses on how CAPS paid special attention to the community component. One of the key elements of the CAPS strategy was marketing. This was done through billboards, neighborhood meetings, flyers, and the media. It was found to be especially useful in Hispanic communities to run commercials in Spanish on the Spanish radio channels.

According to DuBois and Hartnett, it took considerable effort in some communities to get people to trust and join in the CAPS efforts. As a result of the efforts, they offer four lessons learned:

1. Community support must be won,
2. Effective community involvement depends on an organized community,
3. Training is as critical for the community as it is for the police, and
4. There is a real risk of inequitable outcomes.

In sum, DuBois and Hartnett advise that the community can be brought into the fold, but it will take time, patience, and a real effort.

An interesting observation about community policing efforts in this country is that large efforts are expended in "poor and crime-ridden areas" to the exclusion of more prominent areas. However, community policing is not just a "specific area" tool. It is for the whole city and all communities. Yet, some police agencies might find that creating partnerships in the more affluent communities more difficult because if there is low crime and a perception of limited need of the police, there may not be much impetus for citizen involvement. In Chapter Two, Chief D'Ambra tackles the issue of creating community partnerships in affluent communities. In addressing this situation, Chief D'Ambra suggests that there are nine "Phantom Menaces" that could be roadblocks to forming solid partnerships.

The first phantom menace is "Perception is fact, regardless of whether it is true or false." To counter this menace, the Chief suggests that police leaders need to recognize and identify concerns before citizens can grasp them and form what often are misperceptions. Menace two is the "parallel government" or the business as usual group (business leaders, past government officials, etc.) who "don't particularly like change, but love to whine." The action against this menace is for police leaders to find or develop some commonality with the group(s) and its/their members. Racism is the third menace. Obviously one of the more difficult roadblocks in any community is the concerns of various races and ethnicities that there is favoritism toward one and not another. The action against this menace is to establish equitability, that is, play no favorites. While menace four applies more to municipal agencies, the High Sheriff, it could be argued that county agencies may face a similar dilemma that perhaps we can call the "High Chief." In either case, what exists is another agency within the area that could be part of the community policing effort and should not be excluded. The suggestion is to invite the agency to participate.

Often perceived as a thorn in the side of policing, menace five is the media myth. The media tends to wield considerable influence over citizens and having them on your side is very important (which is supported by DuBois and Hartnett and CAPS in Chapter One). Chief D'Ambra suggests that in order to combat this menace, give the media what they need, but only what you want. The sixth menace is the rigid bureaucrat, something that many of us have had to deal with at sometime or another. The suggested action against this menace is to lead by example, be flexible and demonstrate flexibility. As with the previous menace of the high sheriff, along those same lines is the outside agency menace. Community policing cannot be done in a fish bowl and is not solely a police agency effort. There are numerous other agencies that can play important roles. Rather than ignoring or shutting them out, Chief D'Ambra advises to attempt a team effort approach in which members from other agencies take part in the activities and actions toward the establishment of community policing.

Police leaders, particularly police chiefs and sheriffs, are often invited to participate on several community boards. Menace eight is being "board to death." The chief notes that there are only so many boards that you can realistically participate on. Therefore, only serve on those you have something to offer. Finally, the last menace offered by D'Ambra is the Super Chief.

Through the first two chapters the authors support the need to get the community involved and roadblocks to this effort. In Chapter Three, Chief Ramsey takes us to the next phase, preparing the community for community policing. He starts by noting that the implementation of community policing first begins in-house. This can be accomplished through four steps: getting employees to buy-in, training, information and information technology, and advocating new tools and tactics. However, the personnel acceptance of community policing is only half the battle. To continue to advance and improve community policing requires the expansion of the community's role. To accomplish this, Chief Ramsey suggests using the same approach as you did with employees. First, get citizens to buy-in to the change. To facilitate this action requires informing citizens of what is being done, why, and how they fit in. A primary tool for this is the media (as advocated in Chapter One). Using the media to inform citizens greatly assists in getting them to eventually buy-in to community policing. The second step is to provide directly related training to citizens. Just as you do with employees, citizens need to learn what it is that is being done, how, why, and what is expected of them. Using technology and information sharing is the third step to building that partnership. When informed of what is taking place, citizens are less likely to form wrong perceptions (Chief D'Ambra's first menace). With the advent and availability of computer technology, it is much easier to make more information readily accessible to citizens. Finally, the police are not the only ones who should have new tools and tactics. Citizens can also have new tools such as court watch or citizen patrols. Ultimately, for community policing to advance, citizen partnerships are very important, and it all begins by preparing the community for the change and then welcoming, encouraging, and demanding their participation.

So what are some agencies doing to address the citizens' partnership element of community policing? In Chapter Four, Ferguson discusses the community policing initiatives undertaken in Columbia, South Carolina. The catalyst for community policing came from crime, neighborhood concerns, the role of the churches, and police leadership. Having accepted that community policing was a necessity, Ferguson advises that the first challenge for Columbia was embracing the importance of community involvement. To meet this challenge, Columbia undertook several efforts under the umbrella of the Comprehensive Communities Program (CCP), an effort that called for a variety of programmatic activities that would include: community policing, alternatives to incarceration, drug court, conflict resolution, diversion, and Boys and Girls' clubs.

The first effort would require restructuring the organization so that services could be provided more readily to all citizens. Enhancing this effort were several elements for community policing operations such as decentralization, which increased accessibility and visibility; new ways to manage calls for service, and a police homeowners' loan program. This last element led to the creation of police community mobilization officers who lived in targeted neighborhoods, purchasing homes through the loan program, and maintaining offices in same neighborhoods. Ultimately, all the efforts have aided in bringing citizens in direct relationships or partnerships with the police.

How do we know what we are doing works? The literature is becoming more abundant with evaluation research on community policing efforts. Yet, little is offered as to why it is important to evaluate what is being done. Masterson and Stevens venture into this arena in Chapter Five by looking at the value of measuring community policing performance in Madison, Wisconsin.

As noted, evaluation of community policing is no longer rare but the evaluation conducted in Madison is unique in that the survey was conducted solely by police personnel. The survey which has undergone change over several years was completed using officer-interviewers. The lessons that the Madison Police Department (MPD) taught were three-fold:

1. The MPD enhanced police decision-making practices that better served crime control issues through quality police services;
2. The MPD is only one of many participants that shape the meaning of quality police services; and
3. The MPD police personnel have greater opportunities to develop community policing initiatives and enhance some of their police skills when they conduct the research themselves.

By conducting their own survey, measuring their performance became more valuable to the officers than if an outside conducted the study and simply gave them the results. Masterson and Stevens suggest that the Madison experience can be easily duplicated by other police agencies. To assist in that they offered sixteen activities (which was not exhaustive) police agencies could use to develop neighborhood studies. Ultimately, it comes down to those being directly involved in providing and receiving services need to be involved in the creation and evaluation of said services.

In the Madison experience, the officers learned some important lessons about what they were doing. The ability of a police agency to conduct its own surveys is definitely a plus. However, there are still many agencies that rely on consultants and academics to survey and evaluate. Kerly, in Chapter Six, offers an example of a survey conducted by external personnel. What is of particular interest in this study is that it looks at the familiarity with community policing of three very important groups:local law enforcement, local government officials, and leaders in non-governmental organizations.

The tendency has been to believe that when community policing is implemented that everyone it reaches understands and is familiar with the concept. Kerley reports that this may be a fallacy that could be detrimental to the success of community policing. He reports that while the police leaders were familiar with community policing parlance and rhetoric, the members of the other groups were not. Since the members of the other two groups can play such pivotal roles in the success of community policing, especially in the area of partnership development, this finding had very negative connotations. Obviously, a police agency will want its local government and non-governmental people at the same levels of knowledge as the police personnel. Further, Kerly reports that all three groups reported very different perceptions of training needs and police minority relations. The results from this study put to question just how well informed those outside of the police agencies really are about community policing. As it has been established throughout the first five chapters of this text, community involvement is a key component to a successful community policing effort. Therefore, informing all interested parties is a must.

Perceptions tend to play an important part of everything that we do. As previously noted, it is usually for different groups to have differing perceptions of the same event, situation, or concept. Even when perceptions may not be based on reality, if they are positive, then we seldom have a problem with them. Therefore, conducting surveys of citizens for their perceptions of how well something is working is becoming more common among community policing practices. In Chapter Seven, Priest and Carter share the results of a survey that assessed a police saturation operation in Charlotte, North Carolina.

To address speeding and traffic problems, crime, and quality-of-life issues for a given area in Charlotte, a saturation operation was conducted. Shortly after the completion of the operation a survey was conducted of citizens and business people in the given area. The survey's results indicated that substantial proportions of both residents and business people perceived that a decrease in quality of life problems, speeding, and crime had occurred. Interestingly enough, statistics available for the area for some of the related activities didn't necessarily support the positive perceptions. However, it has been well documented that if people feel safer and believe less crime has occurred, then they will have a more positive outlook toward the police and will be more willing to get involved with the police.

It seems that a majority of the community policing literature examining the community component focuses on the adult population. However, there is a secondary population of considerable importance to the success of community policing, children. Although little research has been offered that includes youth involvement in community policing, national efforts are underway that include the youth in a community policing approach. One such effort was addressed by Rudoff and Cohn in Chapter Eight in which they discuss the development of the Youth Crime Watch of America (YCWA).

The YCWA began as a local effort in 1979 when one of the authors (Rudoff) was working with the Miami-Dade police department. The attempt was to improve youth and police relations by getting the youth involved in bettering their schools. Rudoff formulated this idea using Bandura's social learning theory and starting the program in one high school, which eventually spread to many other schools in Dade County. Because this program, which encourages youth to develop an "ownership" mentality was so successful, it became a national organization in 1986 and has continued since then to include youth in the community policing movement nationally, perhaps a very important aspect of successful community policing efforts.

Throughout the first eight chapters, the primary focus has been on those efforts to get the community involved in community policing. Chapter Nine takes us back to police efforts to get police personnel more involved in the community policing effort, in particular the investigative function. In this chapter, Masterson discusses the importance of moving investigations to the neighborhoods as with other services. This is because early efforts found that while patrol operations were being divided out to the "neighborhood level," investigations tended to remain centrally located. Time has found that for the police to be more successful in their community policing efforts, investigations must be decentralized. Although it is not an easy task, Masterson discusses just how it can be done and that it revolves around the ability to address four elements. The first element is "reasons," that is, why the change is necessary. Police leaders must be able to provide legitimate explanations as to why this change must take place. The second element is the "method." The police leader must be able to fully describe how the change would occur so that everyone is clear on what to expect. The third element is "persons." Masterson notes the importance of having the right people lead the change and that the proper personnel are assigned accordingly. Finally, Masterson advises that responses, responding to why changing with legitimate answers and not just "because" will go a long way toward assisting in a smooth decentralization of the investigative functions.

Finally, the last element that this text examines is perhaps the most important of all for a successful community policing partnership effort, police leadership. The lack of good police leadership will lead to unsuccessful community policing efforts (Dantzker, 1999). The question is, what makes a good leader or manager? In Chapter Ten Stevens describes the results of a study of police executives about their managerial practices. In the study, the respondents were asked to identify their practices from several characteristics that were viewed as a mix of "traditional" and "community policing" characteristics. Stevens advises that the data suggest police leaders indicated having characteristics more familiar with the traditional approaches to leadership than those that may be more pertinent to a community policing need. Stevens suggests that police leaders heading a movement toward community policing should move toward a Total Quality Management (TQM) approach.

In closing, there is no doubt that community policing is a major mode of operation today. Paramount to its success is having everyone affected by this change, police and non-police personnel, on board. Of particular importance is the development and solidification of the police and community in partnerships that will enhance and advance community policing. This text has offered just a small portion of how it can and why it should be done.

REFERENCES

Bennett, T. (1998). Police and public involvement in the delivery of community policing. In J. P. Brodeur (Ed.), *How to recognize good policing: Problems and issues,* pp. 107–122. Thousand Oaks, CA: Sage Publishing Company.

Brodeur, J. (Ed.) (1998). *How to recognize good policing: Problems and Issues.* Thousand Oaks, CA: Sage Publishing Company.

Brown, L. P. (1989). Community policing: A practical guide for police officials. NIJ, *Perspectives on Policing,* September (12), 42–49.

Carter, D. L. and Radelet, L. A. (1999). *The police and the community,* 6th ed. Upper Saddle River, NJ: Prentice-Hall Publishing Company.

Community policing in the 1990's. (1992). *NIJ Journal,* August (225), 1–8.

Community Policing Consortium (1994). *Understanding community policing: A framework for action.* Washington, D.C.: U.S. Department of Justice.

Dantzker, M. L. (1994). The future of municipal law enforcement is community-oriented policing: Suggestions for implementation. *Texas Police Journal, 42*(4), 15–17; and *Alternative Visions* (Reprinted), August, 3A–4A.

Dantzker, M. L. (1997). Job satisfaction and community policing: A preview of future research? *Police Chief, 64*(10), 97–99.

Dantzker, M. L. (1999). *Police organization and management: Yesterday, today and tomorrow.* Newton, MA: Butterworth-Heinemann.

Dewitt, C. B. (1992). Community policing in Seattle: A model partnership between citizens and police. NIJ, *Research in Brief,* August.

Eggers, W. D. and O'Leary, J. (1995). The beat generation: Community policing at its best. *Policy Review,* 74, 4–12.

Friedmann, R. R. (1992). *Community Policing: Comparative perspectives and prospect.* NY: St. Martin's Press.

Goldstein, H. (1990). *Problem-oriented policing.* New York: McGraw-Hill.

Hunter, R. D., Mayhall, P. D., and Barker, T. (2000). *Police-community relations and the administration of justice,* 5th ed. Upper Saddle River, NJ: Prentice-Hall Publishing Company.

Jiao, A. Y. (1998). Community policing in the eye of the beholder: Perceptions of the community-oriented model. In M. L. Dantzker, A. J. Lurigio, M. J. Seng, and J. M. Sinacore, *Practical applications for criminal justice statistics,* pp. 169–193. Woburn, MA: Butterworth-Heinemann.

Jolin, A. and Moose, C. A. (1997). Evaluating a domestic violence program in a community policing environment: Research implementation issues. *Crime and Delinquency, 43*(3), 279–297.

Kelling, G. L. (1988). Police and communities: The quiet revolution. NIJ, *Perspectives on Policing,* June (1).

Kennedy, D. M. (1993). The strategic management of police resources. NIJ, *Perspectives on Policing,* January (14).

Kratcoski, P. C. and Dukes, D. (Eds.) (1995). *Issues in community policing.* Cincinnati, OH: Anderson Publishing.

Lurigio, A. J. and Rosenbaum, D. P. (1997). Community policing: Major issues and unanswered questions. In M. L. Dantzker (Ed.), *Contemporary policing: Personnel, issues, and trends,* pp. 195–216. Woburn, MA: Butterworth-Heinemann.

Memory, J. M. (1999). Some impressions from a qualitative study of implementation of community policing in North Carolina. In M. L. Dantzker (Ed.), *Readings for research methods in criminology and criminal justice,* pp. 1–14. Woburn, MA: Butterworth-Heinemann.

Miller, L. S. and Hess, K. M. (1994). *Community policing: Theory and practice.* St. Paul, MN: West Publishing Company.

Moore, M. H., Trojanowicz, R. C., and Kelling, G. L. (1988). Crime and policing. NIJ, *Perspectives on Policing,* June (2), 56–81.

Oliver, W. M. (1998a). Moving beyond "Police-community relations" and "The police and society": Community-oriented policing as an academic course. *Journal of Criminal Justice Education,* 9(2), 303–317.

——(1998b). *Community-oriented policing: A systematic approach to policing.* Upper Saddle River, NJ: Prentice-Hall Publishing Company.

Pace, D. F. (1993). *Community relations: Concepts.* Placerville, CA: Copperhouse Publishing.

Palmiotto, M. J. and Donahue, M. E. (1995). Evaluating community policing: Problems and prospects. *Police Studies, 18* (2), 33–53.

Peak, K. J. and Glensor, R. W. (1999). *Community policing and problem solving: Strategies and practices,* 2nd ed. Upper Saddle Rive, NJ: Prentice-Hall Publishing Company.

Rosenbaum, D. P. (Ed.) (1994). *The challenge of community policing: Testing the promises.* Thousand Oaks, CA: Sage Publishing Company.

Rosenbaum, D. P. (1998). The changing role of the police: Assessing the current transition to community policing. In J. P. Brodeur (Ed.), *How to recognize good policing: Problems and issues,* pp. 3–29. Thousand Oaks, CA: Sage Publishing Company.

Skogan, W. G. (1998). Community participation and community policing. In J. P. Brodeur (Ed.), *How to recognize good policing: Problems and issues,* pp. 88–106. Thousand Oaks, CA: Sage Publishing Company.

Skogan, W. G. and Hartnett, S. M. (1997). *Community Policing, Chicago Style.* New York: Oxford University Press.

Sparrow, M. K. (1988). Implementing community policing. NIJ, *Perspectives on Policing,* November (9).

———, Moore, M. and Kennedy, D. M. (1990). *Beyond 911: A new era for Policing.* NY: Basic Books.

Strecher, V. G. (1997). *Planning community policing: Goal specific cases and exercises.* Prospect Heights, IL: Waveland Press.

Toch, H. and Grant, J. D. (1991). *Police as problem solvers.* NY: Plenum Press.

Trojanowicz, R. and Bucqueroux, B. (1994). *Community Policing: How to get started.* Cincinnati, OH: Anderson Publishing Company.

———, Kappeler, V. E., Gaines, L. K., and Bucqueroux, B. (1998). *Community policing: A contemporary perspective,* 2nd ed. Cincinnati, OH: Anderson Publishing Company.

Vardalis, J. (1992). Prospects of community policing and converting police behavior. *Journal of Police and Criminal Psychology, 8*(2), 37–40.

Watson, E. M., Stone, A. R., and DeLuca, S. M. (1998). *Strategies for community policing.* Upper Saddle River, NJ: Prentice-Hall Publishing Company.

Wycoff, M. A (1995). *Community Policing Strategies.* NIJ Research Preview. Washington, D.C.: U.S. Department of Justice.

Name Index

Subject Index

❖